New Testament Greek

An Introduction

This book provides a general introduction to the grammar and syntax of Hellenistic, or New Testament, Greek. With 24 chapters, it is suitable for a two-semester course. Each lesson is structured around equipping students to read passages drawn directly from the Greek New Testament. In addition to the traditional Erasmian system, students are offered the option of using a historical Greek system of pronunciation similar to that used in early Christian preaching and prayer. The book provides extensive reference tools, including paradigms for memorization, grammatical appendices, and illustrations. The text is accompanied by a Web site that offers a workbook of passages for translation. Each chapter of the grammar concludes with a vocabulary list of Greek terms that appear in that lesson's assigned passage for translation, found in the online workbook. Audio recordings of all vocabulary words and translation passages, using the historical Greek system of pronunciation, are provided online.

Features

- Provides the instructor and students the choice of using the historical Greek pronunciation system or the traditional Erasmian system. Audio recordings of all vocabulary and passages for translation are supplied online.
- Students will read continuous sections of Greek New Testament (John 1–6, Matt 9:9–13) rather than artificial classroom sentences, and the online workbook includes additional translation passages as well as syntactical and parsing questions.
- Includes an exhaustive summary of all grammatical paradigms in the appendices.

B. H. McLean is currently Professor of New Testament Language and Literature at Knox College, University of Toronto. He is the author of *An Introduction to the Study of Greek Epigraphy of the Hellenistic and Roman Periods from Alexander the Great down to the Reign of Constantine (323 BCE–337 CE)* (2002) and *Greek and Latin Inscriptions in the Konya Archaeological Museum* (2002). He has taught introductory New Testament Greek for more than twenty years in four institutions, using a variety of textbooks, and serves as the Greek examiner for biblical doctoral candidates at the Toronto School of Theology.

New Testament Greek

An Introduction

B. H. McLean

University of Toronto

CAMBRIDGE UNIVERSITY PRESS
Cambridge, New York, Melbourne, Madrid, Cape Town,
Singapore, São Paulo, Delhi, Tokyo, Mexico City

Cambridge University Press
32 Avenue of the Americas, New York, NY 10013-2473, USA

www.cambridge.org
Information on this title: www.cambridge.org/9780521177023

First published 2011

Printed in the United States of America

A catalog record for this publication is available from the British Library.

Library of Congress Cataloging in Publication data

McLean, Bradley H. (Bradley Hudson), 1957–
New Testament Greek / B.H. McLean.
p. cm.
Includes bibliographical references and index.
ISBN 978-1-107-00352-1 (hardback) – ISBN 978-0-521-17702-3 (paperback)
1. Greek language – Textbooks for foreign speakers – English. 2. Greek language – Grammar.
I. Bible. N.T. Greek. II. Title.
PA258.M345 2011
487′.4–dc23 2011028797

ISBN 978-1-107-00352-1 Hardback
ISBN 978-0-521-17702-3 Paperback

Additional resources for this publication at www.cambridge.org/9781107003521

Contents

Abbreviations

√	root (of verb or noun)
⊕	paradigm for memorization
acc.	accusative case
act.	active voice
adj.	adjective, adjectival
adv.	adverb
anarthrous	without an article
aor.	aorist tense
art.	article
art. infin.	articular infinitive
attrib.	attributive
BDAG	F. Wm. Danker, W. Bauer, W. F. Arndt, F. W. Gingrich. *A Greek-English Lexicon of the New Testament*, 3rd edition. Chicago: University of Chicago Press, 2000.
BDF	F. Blass, A. Debrunner, R. W. Funk. *Greek Grammar of the New Testament and Other Early Christian Literature*. Chicago: University of Chicago Press, 1961.
ca.	about (fr. Latin "circa")
cf.	compare (fr. Latin "confer")
cognate	of the same derivation or root
cohort.	cohortative subjunctive
colloq.	colloquial
comp.	comparative
cond.	conditional
conj.	conjunction
dat.	dative case
decl.	declension
dep.	deponent

esp.	especially
fig.	figuratively
fm.	feminine gender
fr.	from
freq.	frequently
fut.	future tense
gen.	genitive case
gen. absol.	genitive absolute
GNT	Greek New Testament
hapax legomenon	a word that is only attested once in a particular corpus[1]
HGr	Hellenistic Greek
IBM	*The Collection of Ancient Greek Inscriptions in the British Museum*. 4 vols. Oxford 1874–1916.
i.e.	that is (Latin, "id est")
IEph	*Die Inschriften von Ephesos*. 8 vols. 1979–.
IJudDonateurs	*Donateurs et fondateurs dans les synagogues juives. Répertoire des dédicaces grecques relatives à la construction et à la réfection des synagogues*. Ed. B. Lifshitz. Paris 1967.
IKonya	B. H. McLean. *Greek and Latin Inscriptions in the Konya Archaeological Museum*, Regional Epigraphic Catalogues of Asia Minor IV. British Institute of Archaeology at Ankara Monograph 39. BAR International Series, 2002.
impers.	impersonal, no expressed subject, only an impersonal "it (is)/there (are)"
impf.	imperfect tense
impv.	imperative mood
ind.	indicative mood
indecl.	indeclinable
indef.	indefinite, referring to no specific person or thing
infin.	infinitive
instr.	instrumental, that is, of the means or instrument used by an agent
intrans.	intransitive, that is, verb does not take a direct object

[1] E.g., attested once in GNT, or attested once in early Christian literature, or attested once in all ancient Greek literature.

irreg.	irregular
lit.	literally
Louw/Nida	J. P. Louw and E. A. Nida. *Greek-English Lexicon of the New Testament: Based on Semantic Domains*, 2 vols. 1988.
LXX	Septuagint, the Greek translation of the Hebrew Bible
m.	masculine gender
MGr	Modern Greek
mid.	middle voice
MM	George Milligan, *The Vocabulary of the Greek Testament: Illustrated from Papyri and Other Non-Literary Sources*, 1930.
neg.	negative
New Docs	G. H. R. Horsley and S. R. Llewelyn. *New Documents Illustrating Early Christianity*, Vols. 1–9. 1976–2002.
nom.	nominative case
nt.	neuter gender
obj.	object
opt.	optative mood
pass.	passive voice
passim	very frequently attested
pf.	perfect tense
pl.	plural
pleon.	pleonastic, that is, the use of more words than are necessary to convey an idea
plpf.	pluperfect tense
prep.	preposition
pres.	present tense
prpt.	principal part(s)
ptc.	participle
refl.	reflexive
rel.	relative
sby	somebody
sc.	implied but not written (fr. Latin "scilicet")
sg.	singular
Smyth	Herbert Weir Smyth. *Greek Grammar*. Revised by Gordon M. Messing. Cambridge, MA: Harvard University Press, 1959.

sthg	something
subj.	subjunctive mood
superl.	superlative
s.v.	*sub verbo*, under the word
Tanakh	Hebrew acronym for the three sections of the Hebrew Bible, or "Old Testament": It contains the Torah (Pentateuch), *Nevi'im* (Prophets), and *Ketuvim* (Writings).
trans.	transitive verb
UBS	*Greek New Testament*. United Bible Society. 4th revised edition. Ed. B. Aland, K. Aland, J. Karavidopoulos, C. M. Martini, B. M. Metzger. Stuttgart: Deutsche Bibelgesellschaft, 1993.
v./vv.	verse(s)
viz.	*videlicet*, namely
w.	with

Introduction

The great philosophers Plato and Aristotle and the Greek dramatists of Classical Athens wrote in what is now known as Attic Greek (or Classical Greek), which is one of the four major dialects of the antique Greek-speaking world, the others being Ionic, Doric, and Aeolic.[1] However, in the centuries following the Classical period, Ionic Greek came to have a strong influence on the Attic dialect, transforming it into what we now know as Hellenistic Greek.

Hellenistic Greek spread throughout the eastern Mediterranean in the wake of Alexander the Great's conquest of the Persian Empire. The wave of Greek colonization that followed brought with it the Hellenistic Greek language, which quickly became the common language of the region. Hellenistic Greek continued in use throughout the Roman provinces of the eastern Mediterranean during the Roman period. Owing to its widespread usage, Hellenistic Greek was known, even in ancient times, as the *koine* language or dialect (ἡ κοινὴ διάλεκτος), meaning the "common" language of the people.[2] This explains why the Hebrew Bible was translated into Hellenistic Greek (the so-called "Septuagint") in the third and second centuries BC, and why the New Testament was also written in Hellenistic Greek, rather in than another language such as Aramaic or Syriac.[3] In the centuries that followed,

---

1 These dialects correspond to ethnic divisions. Ionic was spoken by the Ionians, Aeolic by the Aeolians, and Doric by the Dorians. Geographically, Ionic was spoken in Ionia and in most of the islands of the Aegean. Aeolic was spoken in Lesbos and Aeolia. Doric was spoken in the Peloponnesus (except Arcadia and Elis) and on the islands of Crete, Melos, Thera, Rhodes, and in parts of Sicily and southern Italy.

2 Some of the best-known Hellenistic authors are Polybius, Diodorus, Plutarch, Arrian, Cassius Dio, Dionysius of Halicarnassus, Lucian, Strabo, Philo, and Josephus.

3 The Greek translation of the Old Testament or Hebrew Bible is known as the *Septuagint* (LXX). It was translated by the Jewish community in Alexandria, Egypt. In many significant ways, the Greek of the Septuagint is different from typical Hellenistic Greek. This is because its translators tried to preserve the formal properties of the underlying Hebrew text. They were more concerned with preserving a degree of transparency with respect to the Hebrew sources than they were in producing an acceptable literary,

Figure: Ancient Greek inscription (Ephesus).

the Septuagint became the de facto liturgical text of countless synagogues and early churches. Indeed, as the basis for early Christian liturgy, devotion, and theology, the Septuagint emerged as the most significant body of literature in late antiquity.

Given the fact that the New Testament is written in Hellenistic Greek, it follows that those who desire a deeper understanding of its message must strive to attain a thorough knowledge of this language. Learning Greek requires patience, perseverance, and the willingness to struggle. But those who are committed to understanding the Christian gospel should not view this task as an imposition, but as a blessing, for with it comes a deeper knowledge of Scriptures. There can be no doubt that *the ability to read and interpret the New Testament in its original language is a central component of the Reformed tradition.*

Indeed, all theologians since the Renaissance, including Erasmus, Calvin, and Luther, emphasized the importance of studying the Bible in its original languages.[4] For example, Desiderius Erasmus upheld the knowledge of Greek as an essential component of a sound theological education. He once stated that "While mere knowledge of [Greek] grammar does not make a theologian; still less does ignorance of it."[5]

Similarly, in our own case, while mastering Hellenistic Greek may not be a realistic goal for every student of theology, total unfamiliarity with the original language of the New Testament is indefensible for theologians and seminarians. After all, there is probably no rabbi who cannot read the Tanakh in the original Hebrew, or imam who cannot read the Qur'an in the original Arabic language. But Christians should not approach the study of Hellenistic Greek as if it were a trial or obstacle to overcome. Those who really commit themselves to the regular lifelong study of the Greek New Testament will come to know the true joy of being led through, and beyond, its words to a lived, faithful, transformative relationship with the living God. Indeed, we must not forget that patience in the study of sacred Greek Scriptures nurtures patience in the grace of God!

I.1. PRONOUNCING HELLENISTIC GREEK

You may be surprised to learn that many introductions to Hellenistic Greek employ a system of pronunciation developed *by a Dutchman* named Erasmus, who lived

Greek composition. This practice suggests that the Septuagint functioned more as a kind of "inter-text" than as a translation. It probably supplemented the reading and study of the Hebrew Bible rather than functioning independently (cf. see Cameron Boyd-Taylor, "The Evidentiary Value of Septuagintal Usage," *Bulletin of the International Organization for Septuagint and Cognate Studies*, 34 [2001], 72).

4 The term "Renaissance" describes the period of European history from the early fourteenth to the late sixteenth century. The Renaissance preceded the Reformation by about a century and a half. During the fifteenth century, students from many European nations traveled to Italy to study Greek and Latin literature as well as philosophy, eventually spreading the Italian Renaissance north into Western Europe. In Northern Europe, these changes radically affected religious life.

5 Marjorie O'Rourke Boyle, *Erasmus on Language and Method in Theology* (Toronto/Buffalo: University of Toronto Press, 1977), 22, n. 69; cf. 36, n. 26.

Desiderius Erasmus (1466/69–1536).

from 1466/69 to 1536 AD, during the period now known as the Renaissance. Thus, Erasmus was literally, as well as figuratively, a "Renaissance" man. He was among those who pioneered a movement to read the Bible in its original languages. To this end, he collated the ancient manuscripts available at the time to produce the first Greek New Testament in 1516. It was this Greek text – republished later by Robert Stephanus in 1550 – that was used as the basis of the English translation known as the Authorized Version, or King James Version, of 1611. Thus, we have every reason to hold Erasmus in the highest esteem.

The system of pronunciation developed by Erasmus is known as the Erasmian pronunciation system. It gives the same values to Greek letters as their corresponding Latin equivalents. It is also based on the non-linguistic principle that each letter should be pronounced differently.[6]

As might be expected from its origins, this system of pronunciation is entirely artificial. It is merely a "classroom" pronunciation, which has *never been used by Greeks in any period of their history*. We now know, on the basis of thousands of papyri and inscriptions that have been discovered since the time of Erasmus, that this Latinized pronunciation contradicts how Greek was actually spoken.

Even in Erasmus' own time, other pronunciation systems were also in use. For example, the German scholar Johann Reuchlin (1455–1522) introduced a Byzantine pronunciation in Western Europe. This pronunciation system is very similar to the pronunciation system used in this grammar. The ensuing debate over the relative merits of the Erasmian and Byzantine systems became so heated at Cambridge University that, in 1542, the Erasmian pronunciation was actually *forbidden* from use, under penalty of removal from one's degree program (in the

6 Actually, this system is not consistent in following this rule: Both η and ει, and ευ and ηυ, are assigned the same phonic value.

case of university students) and physical "chastisement" (in the case of primary education). Nonetheless, by the twentieth century, it was the Erasmian pronunciation that won the day in America and Europe.

In retrospect, it is indeed surprising that a pronunciation system invented by a Dutchman living 500 years ago in Northern Europe, with no real contact with Greek culture, should still be in use in the modern university of the twenty-first century. Nevertheless, in our own era, many New Testament scholars, most notably Chrys C. Caragounis, are now advocating a return to what is termed the *historical Greek pronunciation system*, just as many scholars of biblical Hebrew have adopted a modern Hebrew system of pronunciation.[7] This makes good sense because the historical Greek pronunciation system is very close to the pronunciation employed by Paul and the first apostles.[8]

There are a number of advantages associated with this historical Greek pronunciation system:

1. In contrast to the Erasmian system, the historical Greek pronunciation system is a *real*, euphonic system that is very close to the pronunciation system employed by the first Greek-speaking Christians. It is also known as the modern Greek pronunciation system. Students who adopt this pronunciation system will experience the joy of hearing the sound of the living language of early Christianity. This pronunciation system will allow you to develop a more holistic experience of the sound of early Christian preaching and prayer.

   On the other hand with the Erasmian pronunciation system, one gives up the possibility of learning to speak and hear the Greek as a living language. Indeed, if you were to attempt to speak to any Greek person using an Erasmian pronunciation, that person would be bewildered and perplexed by the strange sounds coming out of your mouth. In contrast, the historical Greek pronunciation system would allow you to be understood.
2. Many textual variants in the text of the Greek New Testament resulted from misunderstanding when the manuscripts were produced by *oral* dictation in scriptoria. An understanding of the original pronunciation aids the New Testament interpreter in explaining such errors in comprehension.
3. Perhaps the best reason to adopt the historical Greek pronunciation system concerns the expectations that we bring to the text. The use of the Erasmian

---

7 Chrys C. Caragounis, *The Development of Greek and the New Testament: Morphology, Syntax, Phonology, and Textual Transmission*, WUNT 167, Corrected edition (Ada, Michigan; Baker Academic, 2007), 337–96.

8 Chrys C. Caragounis, "The Error of Erasmus and Un-Greek Pronunciations of Greek," *Filologia Neotestamentaria* 8 (1995), 151–85; cf. A. T. Robertson wrote that "We may be sure of one thing, the pronunciation of the vernacular κοινή was not exactly like the ancient literary Attic [i.e., Classical Greek] nor precisely like the modern Greek vernacular, but veering more toward the latter" (*A Grammar of the Greek New Testament in the Light of Historical Research* [Nashville, Tennessee: Broadman Press, 1934], 239).

system encourages one to think of the Greek New Testament as a secret code, whose arcane symbols, once deciphered, will yield God's secret mysteries. The Greek New Testament is not some kind of mysterious secret code that needs to be solved. The use of the historical Greek pronunciation system keeps us always mindful that, in reading the twenty-seven texts of the Greek New Testament, we are reading a real language, once used by real people in real contexts, with all the ambiguities and idiosyncrasies that this implies. Exegesis, when understood in these terms, does not become a quest for hidden treasure, but an open-ended dialogue with the texts themselves.

For those who would argue that the historical Greek pronunciation system does not make absolute phonetic distinctions, one should bear in mind that no language limits itself to such rigid consistency. Moreover, the purported benefits of the Erasmian system of pronunciation shrink when one realizes that there is no consensus, even among those scholars who employ it. There are actually several Erasmian pronunciations according to whether one learns *koine* Greek in the United States, Germany, or Britain.

Learning the historical Greek pronunciation system is not very difficult because it is *entirely regular*. In contrast to English, where the pronunciation of words like "enough," "though," and "through" cause difficulties to non-native speakers, the historical Greek pronunciation system is consistent. This feature allows one to master it easily with a little patience and practice. On the basis of its many advantages, this textbook will employ this system, though the Erasmian system will also be explained for those who wish to use it instead.[9]

I.2. THE USE AND ABUSE OF MEMORY

The study of Hellenistic Greek, like the study of any language, requires time and practice. By its very nature, this task also requires much memorization. If you have not previously learned another language, the task of memorizing significant amounts of information may be an unfamiliar challenge to you. To meet this challenge, it is important that you understand how your memory works.

According to nutritionists, it is better to eat many small meals than to gorge oneself on a huge meal near the end of the day. This principle is equally true for learning Greek. Many short study sessions are preferable to infrequent Greek "gorging" sessions. In other words, frequent study sessions will result in better memory retention than will long, uninterrupted study sessions. Therefore, try to avoid the demoralizing task of attempting to play catch-up after having ignored your Greek

---

[9] See Section 1.9.

studies for several days. This type of intensive, uninterrupted study usually results in *cognitive overload*. It occurs when your memory cannot process information in the quantities or speed it is presented.

Before entering your long-term memory, your *working memory* must first process new material. While your working memory is busy, it cannot learn new material. Because your working memory can handle only a fixed amount of information at any one time (e.g., six to eight new words), a wise strategy is to practice for relatively *short* periods of time with *repeated* study sessions. In other words, *"little and often" is the rule.*

Also bear in mind that there are two types of memory practice: maintenance rehearsal and elaborative rehearsal. Maintenance rehearsal, or what might be called rote memorization, involves repetition and memorization. Such maintenance practice requires a great deal of energy and a high number of repetitions before a learner can perform the skill or use the knowledge with confidence. Though maintenance rehearsal serves to keep information active in the working memory, it also clutters the short-term memory. Consequently, it is not very efficient.

Elaborative rehearsal causes learners to *interact* with the content. This type of practice connects the new content with what learners already know, or it applies practice to solving real problems, such as translating the Greek New Testament. You will learn Greek more quickly and easily if you attempt to deal with the material in multiple perspectives, as well as trying to memorize facts by rote. To help students meaningfully *interact* with Hellenistic Greek, this grammar textbook is supplemented by a workbook (available online). The Workbook will give you the opportunity to translate real passages from the Greek New Testament, thereby applying your growing knowledge of Hellenistic Greek to real problem solving. The vocabulary lists at the end of each lesson will provide the words required for the translation of each new set of biblical texts.

1.

Alphabet and Pronunciation

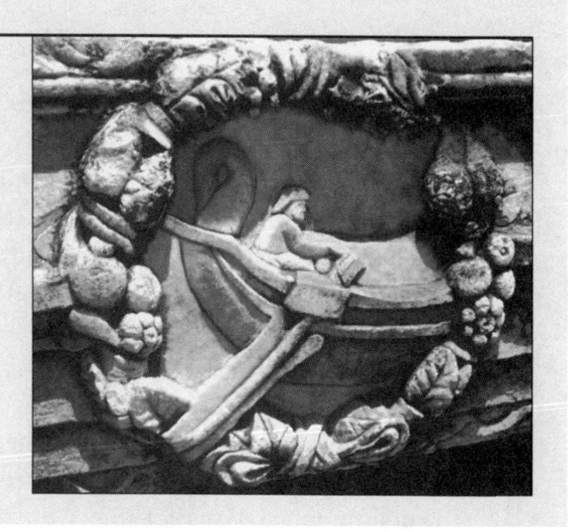

Let us begin our Greek odyssey by becoming acquainted with some of the features of ancient manuscripts of the New Testament. Many of the features that one associates with a printed Greek edition of the New Testament were absent in the oldest manuscripts. For example, a typical New Testament manuscript recording John 1:3–4 would look something like this:

ΠΑΝΤΑΔΙΑΥΤΟΥΕΓΕΝΕ
ΤΟΚΑΙΧΩΡΙϹΑΥΤΟΥΕΓΕ
ΝΕΤΟΟΥΔΕΕΝΟΓΕΓΟΝΕ
ΝΕΝΑΥΤΩΖΩΗΗΝΚΑΙΗ
ΖΩΗΗΝΤΟΦΩϹΤΩΝΑΝ
ΘΡΩΠΩΝ

Among the differences between modern printed editions of the Greek New Testament and ancient New Testament manuscripts are the following:

1. The original manuscripts were written only in rounded capital letters (known as *uncials*), whereas modern printed editions use mostly lowercase letters.[1]

[1] Greek paleography divides letters into two primary classes: large and small. Small letters are also known as *cursives* or *minuscules*. The class of large letters is subdivided into *capitals*, which are used in Greek inscriptions, and uncials, which are adaptations of capitals used in manuscripts. Whereas capital letters are characterized by a preference for straight strokes meeting at angles, uncials make more use of curved strokes.

Figure: Relief of man holding the tiller of a small boat (ancient Corinth).

2. The original manuscripts abbreviated sacred names (so-called *nomina sacra*) for "God," "Jesus," and others.[2]
3. In printed editions of the New Testament, editors also add a variety of other marks that were *not* used in the original manuscripts. These editorial marks include the following: breathing marks, accents, iota subscripts, diaeresis marks, apostrophes, letter spacing, and most punctuation. These marks will be discussed in Chapter 2.

These features were introduced by editors in later centuries to facilitate the reading and comprehension of these ancient texts. If you are wondering about the value of such editorial work, consider the following text. Would you rather read *this* version of Galatians 1:1–5?

ΠΑΥΛΟϹ ΑΠΟϹΤΟΛΟϹ ΟΥΚ ΑΠ ΑΝΘΡΩΠΩΝ ΟΥΔΕ
ΔΙ ΑΝΘΡΩΠΟΥ ΑΛΛΑ ΔΙΑ Ι̅Η̅Υ̅ Χ̅Ρ̅Υ̅ ΚΑΙ Θ̅Υ̅ ΠΑΤΡΟϹ
ΤΟΥ ΕΓΕΙΡΑΝΤΟϹ ΑΥΤΟΝ ΕΚ ΝΕΚΡΩΝ ΚΑΙ ΟΙ ϹΥΝ ΕΜΟΙ
ΠΑΝΤΕϹ ΑΔΕΛΦΟΙ ΤΑΙϹ ΕΚΚΛΗϹΙΑϹ ΤΗϹ ΓΑΛΑ
ΤΙΑϹ ΧΑΡΙϹ ΥΜΕΙΝ ΚΑΙ ΕΙΡΗΝΗ ΑΠΟ Θ̅Υ̅ ΠΑΤΡΟϹ
ΚΑΙ Κ̅Υ̅ ΗΜΩΝ Ι̅Η̅Υ̅ Χ̅Ρ̅Υ̅ ΤΟΥ ΔΟΝΤΟϹ ΑΥΤΟΝ ΠΕΡΙ
ΑΜΑΡΤΙΩΝ ΗΜΩΝ ΟΠΩϹ ΕΞΕΛΗΤΑΙ ΗΜΑϹ ΕΚ ΤΟΥ
ΑΙΩΝΟϹ ΤΟΥ ΕΝΕϹΤΩΤΟϹ ΠΟΝΗΡΟΥ ΚΑΤΑ ΤΟ ΘΕΛΗΜΑ
ΤΟΥ Θ̅Υ̅ ΚΑΙ Π̅Ρ̅Ϲ̅ ΗΜΩΝ Ω Η ΔΟΞΑ ΕΙϹ ΤΟΥϹ ΑΙΩΝΑϹ
ΤΩΝ ΑΙΩΝΩΝ ΑΜΗΝ

Or would you rather read *this* edited version?

1:1 Παῦλος ἀπόστολος οὐκ ἀπ' ἀνθρώπων οὐδὲ δι' ἀνθρώπου ἀλλὰ
διὰ Ἰησοῦ Χριστοῦ καὶ θεοῦ πατρὸς τοῦ ἐγείραντος αὐτὸν ἐκ
νεκρῶν, **2** καὶ οἱ σὺν ἐμοὶ πάντες ἀδελφοὶ ταῖς ἐκκλησίαις τῆς
Γαλατίας, **3** χάρις ὑμῖν καὶ εἰρήνη ἀπὸ θεοῦ πατρὸς ἡμῶν καὶ
κυρίου Ἰησοῦ Χριστοῦ **4** τοῦ δόντος ἑαυτὸν ὑπὲρ τῶν ἁμαρτιῶν
ἡμῶν, ὅπως ἐξέληται ἡμᾶς ἐκ τοῦ αἰῶνος τοῦ ἐνεστῶτος πονηροῦ
κατὰ τὸ θέλημα τοῦ θεοῦ καὶ πατρὸς ἡμῶν, **5** ᾧ ἡ δόξα εἰς τοὺς
αἰῶνας τῶν αἰώνων, ἀμήν.

If you are not sure, you might want to return to this question in a couple of weeks. In any case, though the editing of ancient New Testament texts is necessary, my point is

[2] E.g., **θϲ** for θεός (God), **ιϲ** for Ἰησοῦς (Jesus), **κϲ** for κύριος (Lord), **χϲ** for Χριστός (Christ).

this: This editing does constitute a kind of *interpretation* of the text. It actually *adds* information to the text that is not explicitly in the text itself. Even though these editorial additions are helpful and necessary, they are subject to being questioned and changed.

1.1 THE GREEK ALPHABET AND PRONUNCIATION

Whereas the English alphabet consists of twenty-six letters, the Greek alphabet has only twenty-four characters. Many of these letters are similar to the English (i.e., Latin) characters that you already know. However, in many cases their pronunciation is different from their corresponding Latin letters. Nonetheless, Greek is a regular phonetic language, which is to say that words are spelled as they are pronounced.

Given that it is the practice of modern editions of the Greek New Testament to employ mostly lowercase letters, it is suggested that you begin by learning the lowercase letters. The column labeled "phonic value" in the following table provides the historical Greek pronunciation for each letter. The Erasmian pronunciation system is provided in the appendix to this lesson for those who prefer to use it (Section 1.9).

Upper case	*Lower case*	*Letter name*	*Pronunciation guide*	*Phonic value*
Α	α	**al**fa	f*a*ther	[a]
Β	β	**vi**ta	*v*at	[v]
Γ	γ	**gha**ma	*y*et (when followed by *e* and *i*-sounds), before other vowels, as "go," but deeper from the throat: "gho"	[y] or [g]
Δ	δ	**dhel**ta	*the*	[dh]
Ε	ε	**e**psilon	b*e*t	[e]
Ζ	ζ	**zi**ta	*z*oo	[z]
Η	η	**i**ta	between "d*i*d" and "s*ee*"	[i]
Θ	θ	**thi**ta	*th*ink	[th]
Ι	ι	**io**ta	between "d*i*d" and "s*ee*"	[i]
Κ	κ	**kap**pa	*k*eep	[k]
Λ	λ	**lam**dha	*l*etter	[l]
Μ	μ	**mi**	*m*oon	[m]

Upper case	*Lower case*	*Letter name*	*Pronunciation guide*	*Phonic value*
Ν	ν	**ni**	*n*oon	[n]
Ξ	ξ	**ksi**	o*x*	[ks]
Ο	ο	**o**mikron	d*o*g	[o]
Π	π	**pi**	*p*ut	[p]
Ρ	ρ	**rho**	r (trilled)[3]	[r / rh][4]
Σ	σ/ ς[5]	**sig**ma	ro*s*e	[s][6]
Τ	τ	**taf**	*t*op	[t]
Υ	υ	**i**psilon	between "d*i*d" and "s*ee*"	[i]
Φ	φ	**fi**	*f*ind	[f]
Χ	χ	**khi**	"lo*ch*,"[7] but softer as in German, "I*ch*", before [i] sounding vowels	[kh]
Ψ	ψ	**psi**	hi*ps*	[ps]
Ω	ω	**o**mega	d*o*g	[o]

1.2 PRONOUNCING VOWELS

Letter	*Phonic value*	*Example*	*Pronunciation*
α	[a]	ἀπό	(a-**po**)
ε	[e]	ἐλπίς	(el-**pis**)
ι	[i]	ἴσος	(**i**-sos)
ο	[o]	ὄνομα	(**o**-no-ma)
η	[i]	μή	(mi)
υ	[i]	κύριος	(**ki**-ri-os)
ω	[o]	φῶς	(fos)

Notice that ι, η, and υ are all pronounced the same way, [i] (between "d*i*d" and "s*ee*"). During the Hellenistic period, there was a loss of qualitative distinction between these vowels. This phenomenon is termed *itacism*.

---

3 Like a trilled French *r*.

4 Transliterated *rh* when the first letter of a word.

5 Initial or internal sigma is written as σ. This sigma is known as *medial sigma*. But as the last letter of a word, sigma is formed like ς. This sigma is known as *final sigma*.

6 But like *z* as in "zoo" before voiced consonants (β, γ, δ, μ, λ, μ ν, ρ), e.g., κόσμος, προσδῶ, σγουρός, σβέννυμι.

7 Rough guttural or aspirated sound: *ch* as in Scottish "lo*ch*" or German "Bu*ch*."

1.3 PRONOUNCING DOUBLE VOWELS

These two-letter combinations are known as *double vowels*. They are pronounced as follows:

Double vowel	*Pronunciation guide*	*Phonic value*
αι	bet	[e]
ει, οι, υι	between "d*i*d" and "s*ee*"	[i]

As a result of itacism, the sound of the double vowels ει, οι, and υι all converged with η, υ, and ι on the sound [i], and αι converged with ε on the sound [e]. Thus, there was a corresponding loss of qualitative distinction between these vowel groups.

Double vowel	*Pronunciation guide*	*Phonic value*
ου	look	[ou]
αυ	*av* before vowels and β, δ, γ, λ, μ, ν, ρ, ζ	[av]
	but *af* before all other consonants	[af]
ευ	*ev* before vowels and β, δ, γ, λ, μ, ν, ρ, ζ	[ev]
	but *ef* before all other consonants	[ef]
ηυ	*iv* before vowels and β, δ, γ, λ, μ, ν, ρ, ζ	[iv]
	but *if* before all other consonants	[if]

If all of this seems a little confusing at this point, do not worry about it. These rules will become familiar to you with practice over time.

1.4 THE PRONUNCIATION OF STOPS AND FRICATIVES

In some Greek grammars, the consonants β, δ, γ, π, τ, κ are called *stops* because, in the earlier Classical period (fifth–fourth centuries BC), these sounds were produced by the closing of the vocal (orinasal) passage so as to *stop* the breath. The stops of Attic Greek can be divided into two orders as follows:

1. *voiced* (β, δ, γ)
2. *voiceless* or *smooth* (π, τ, κ)

To say that β, δ, and γ were *voiced* stops in Attic Greek means that one's vocal chords are employed to pronounce them. For example, try resting two fingers on your vocal chords and say the English sounds "b," "d," and "g." You can actually feel your vocal chords vibrate. In contrast, π, τ, κ are voiceless (i.e., your vocal chords are not used).

However, in the Hellenistic period, β, δ, and γ shifted from being voiced stops to voiced *fricatives*. In other words, rather than stopping one's breath by closing the orinasal passage, one simply narrows the orinasal passage.

φ, θ, χ as [f], [θ], and [kh]

In Attic Greek, the letters φ, θ, and χ were stops, not fricatives (contrary to the Erasmian pronunciation!). In other words, they were pronounced like aspirated *p* [p^h], *t* [t^h], and *k* [k^h], not like *f*, *th*, and *ch* (as in "Ba*ch*"). However, these letters gradually lost their plosive aspiration and became fricatives:

φ	[p^h]	→ [f]	*f*un: thus, in the first century AD, φ became the transliteration equivalent of Latin *f*
θ	[t^h]	→ [th]	*th*ink
χ	[k^h]	→ [kh]	Scottish "lo*ch*"

The pronunciation of stops and fricatives in Hellenistic Greek can be summarized as follows:

1.4.1 Labials: π, β, φ

π like *p* in "*p*age": e.g., πόλις (**po**-lis)
β like *v* in "*v*an": e.g., βιβλίον (vi-**vli**-on)
φ like *f* in "*f*act": e.g., φίλος (**fi**-los)

1.4.2 Dentals: τ, δ, θ

τ like *t* in "*t*op": e.g., τόπος (**to**-pos)
δ like *th* in "*th*e" [dh]: e.g., δοῦλος (**dhou**-los)
θ like *th* in "*th*ink" [th]: e.g., θάνατος (**tha**-na-tos)

1.4.3 Velars: κ, γ, χ

κ like *k* in "*k*een": e.g., κύριος (**ki**-ri-os)
γ like *y* in "*y*et" when followed by *e*- and *i*-sounds (namely, ε, η, ι, υ, αι, ει, οι, υι): e.g., γυνή (yi-**ni**), γενεά (ye-ne-**a**), γῆ (yi), γινώσκω (yi-**no**-sko), ἅγιος (**a**-yi-os), γελῶ (ye-**lo**)
γ like *g* as in "*g*o" (but deeper from the throat: "gho") before other vowels: e.g., γάμος (**ga**-mos),γάλα (**ga**-la), ἐγώ (e-**go**)
χ like *ch* in Scottish "lo*ch*": e.g., χαρά (kha-**ra**), χάρις (**kha**-ris), χρόνος (**khro**-nos)

1.5 PRONOUNCING SPECIAL GROUPS OF VELAR CONSONANTS

When γ is followed by γ, κ, χ, or by ξ, the nasal sound [ng] is produced (cf. the sound of the final consonants in the English word "si*ng*"):

γγ/ γκ	fi*ng*er	[ng-g]	ἄγγελος	(**a**^{ng}-ge-los)
		[ng-g]	ἀγκάλη	(a^{ng}-**ga**-li)
γχ		[ng-kh]	ἐλέγχω	(e-**le**^{ng}-kho)
γξ	ba*nks*	[ng-ks]	ἔλεγξις	(**e**-le^{ng}-ksis)

1.6 PRONOUNCING OTHER CONSONANT CLUSTERS

Similarly when π follows μ, and τ follows ν, in the middle of a word, they become [mb] and [nd] sounds, respectively (i.e., a real English "b" and "d" sound results):

μπ	[mb][8]	πέμπω	(**pem**-bo)
		ἐμπλοκή	(em-blo-**ki**)
ντ	[nd][9]	ἀντί	(an-**di**)

1.7 ON THE TRANSLATION OF GREEK WORDS IN VOCABULARY LISTS

At the end of each lesson, you will find vocabulary lists of Greek words, followed by English *glosses*. This grammar has taken special care with some Greek words that I call *stained-glass* words. These are words that have special prominence in Christian belief and theology but are not employed in everyday English speech. For example, almost all introductions to New Testament Greek will translate Greek words such as λόγος, ἐκκλησία, ἅγιος, δόξα, and χάρις as "word," "church," "holy," "glory," and "grace," respectively.

These translations are not wrong. However, the preferential use of these particular English glosses has several disadvantages. In the act of creating a one-to-one correspondence between these Greek words and specific English theological words, students do not learn the actual range of their meanings, nor do they appreciate their context-specific uses.

Take, for example, the translation of χάρις with the English word "grace," which does not clarify the meaning of the Greek phrase "saved through God's χάρις,"

[8] In MGr, μπ at the beginning of a word is pronounced [b]: e.g., μπανάνα (banana).

[9] In MGr, ντ at the beginning of a word is pronounced [d].

because the English word "grace" is not used this way in everyday colloquial speech. A much better translation is "saved through God's *generosity*," because the word "generosity" *is* frequently used in contemporary English and is readily understandable. The habitual use of English "glosses" such as "grace" leads to a vagueness that limits the possibilities of exegesis and undermines the possibility of understanding the meaning of the text. The lexicographer Frederick Danker laments those who take refuge in such "sanctified vagueness," for "despite the patina of centuries of usage," this practice "may invite liability to the charge of linguistic incest."[10]

In actual fact, there is no one-to-one correspondence between the individual Greek words in a biblical text and English words because most Greek words belong to more than one *semantic domain*.[11] A semantic domain is an associative field of interrelated words that refer to a single conceptual category (e.g., kinship, names of animals, emotions, words having to do with eating, thinking, believing, etc.). By virtue of their belonging to different semantic domains, many words can be employed to express two or more *different*, and even *unrelated*, meanings. For example, the English word "foot" has a different meaning in the sentence "one of his shoes felt too tight on his *foot*" than it does in the sentence "the house is at the *foot* of the mountain." Similarly, the Greek term τράπεζα, which is often "translated" to the English word "table," has three different meanings corresponding to three different semantic domains.[12] The term τράπεζα occurs in the New Testament in contexts such as:

1. "He overturned their *tables*" (John 2:15)
2. "He served them a *meal*" (Acts 16:34)
3. "You put your money in the *bank*" (Luke 19:23)

Thus, the word τράπεζα belongs to three different semantic domains: 1) when it is employed to mean "table" (John 2:15), it belongs to the associative field of words denoting furniture and household objects; 2) when it is employed to mean "meal," it belongs to the associative field of words involving eating; 3) when it is employed to mean "bank," it belongs to the associative field of words denoting institutions for the safeguarding of money. Thus, there is no one-to-one correspondence between the Greek word τράπεζα and any one English word: In other words, τράπεζα does not mean "table." This single Greek word can be used in different literary contexts to express *different*, and sometimes *totally unrelated*, meanings by virtue of the fact that it belongs to multiple semantic domains.[13] Therefore, one's starting point for

[10] Frederick Danker, "Lexical Evolution & Linguistic Hazard," Paper presented at the meeting of the Semantic of Biblical Language, Boston, MA, November 21, 1999, 1–34, esp. 27–8.

[11] J. P. Louw, *Semantics of New Testament Greek* (Atlanta, GA: Scholars, 1982), 39–60; James Barr, *Semantics of Biblical Language* (Oxford: Oxford University Press, 1961), 206–46.

[12] Louw, *Semantics of New Testament Greek*, 36–7.

[13] In the words of Louw and Nida, "In general, the different meanings of a single word are relatively far apart in semantic space . . . that is to say they differ appreciably in certain distinctive features and often

understanding the *meaning* of a text should not be isolated Greek words but the specific literary context. In actual fact, the semantic range of a given Greek word never perfectly overlaps with the range of possible meanings of its corresponding English gloss. Therefore, when translating the Greek New Testament, one should not mechanically substitute the same English word for a given Greek word, every time it appears in a text.

There is also a second disadvantage of using English glosses for Greek words: If you translate New Testament texts in this manner, your translations will be virtually identical to the English translations already available to you. This raises the question, why bother to learn Greek at all?

Given the importance of literary context in the determination of the meaning of Greek words, the practice of presenting students with lists of Greek words followed by, what appear to be, the equivalent English words, can be quite misleading. Nonetheless, this is a necessary practice to help students advance quickly in learning vocabulary. However, you should *not* think of the English glosses, which appear in the vocabulary lists of this book, as English equivalents of the Greek words that follow.

These English glosses are only intended to give you some idea of the *range* of possible meanings that a given Greek word can have. After you have completed this course, you should consult a scholarly Greek lexicon to acquire a more nuanced appreciation of Greek vocabulary. A good academic lexicon, such as Frederick Danker's *A Greek-English Lexicon of the New Testament* (2000), will guide you in the selection of more illuminating translations. Louw and Nida's *Greek-English Lexicon of the New Testament Based on Semantic Domains* is also an excellent lexical resource.[14]

If you take the time to reflect on the specific literary context and the semantic domains of Greek words, *your* English translations of the New Testament will be superior to the ones you already read. To achieve this goal, however, you must avoid the practice of mechanically substituting the same English word every time you encounter a particular Greek term. Instead, you should give due consideration

---

belong to quite different major semantic domains" (*Greek-English Lexicon of the New Testament: Based on Semantic Domains*, 2 vols. [New York: United Bible Societies, 1988], x). This phenomenon should not be confused with the common occurrence of a lexeme, with an unmarked meaning, having multiple contextual meanings. The distinction being made here is between the *multiple semantic domains* of a single lexeme, not the distinction between the unmarked and contextual meaning of a word.

[14] Frederick W. Danker, Walter Bauer, William Arndt, F. W. Gingrich, *A Greek-English Lexicon of the New Testament and Other Early Christian Literature*, 3rd revised edition (Chicago/London: University of Chicago Press, 2000) (BDAG); J. P. Louw and E. A. Nida, *Greek-English Lexicon of the New Testament: Based on Semantic Domains*, 2 vols. (New York: United Bible Societies, 1988) (= Louw/Nida). George Milligan's *The Vocabulary of the Greek Testament: Illustrated from Papyri and Other Non-Literary Sources* (Grand Rapids: Wm. B. Eerdmans Publ. Co., 1930) (= MM) has been somewhat superceded by the series, *New Documents Illustrating Early Christianity* (vols. 1–9; 1976–2002), by G. H. R. Horsley and S. R. Llewelyn (= *New Docs*), which is an annual review of the Greek inscriptions and papyri bearing on New Testament interpretation.

both to the specific linguistic context of the term and to the clarity of expression in contemporary everyday English.

1.8 VOCABULARY TO BE MEMORIZED

As noted earlier, this chapter (and indeed every chapter) ends with a list of vocabulary for memorization. The assigned vocabulary is a mixture of words that occur with very high frequency in the New Testament and important words that occur in the first six chapters of the Gospel of John. (Beginning with Chapter 6, you will be reading through the first six chapters of John's Gospel, followed by the Matthean version of the Lord's Prayer.) This lesson's vocabulary assignment should be quite easy. It consists of words that have English cognates (i.e., English words that have been formed on the basis of Greek words).

One strategy for learning Greek words is to construct flashcards from recipe cards. Simply write the Greek lexeme (word) on one side of the card and write one or more English glosses on the opposite side. Over time, you can put aside the cards you know well and concentrate your efforts on those Greek words that you are having more difficulty memorizing. Note: the Greek words below have special marks above (and/or before) some of the letters. These marks will be explained in Chapter 2.

1. ἄγγελος (**a**$^{\mathbf{ng}}$-ge-los), a messenger, sometimes a heavenly messenger (angel)
2. ἀμήν (a-**min**), amen, truly, indeed
3. ἀπόστολος (a-**po**-sto-los), apostle, an emissary, one who is sent to fulfill a task, a messenger
4. Γαλιλαία (ga-li-**le**-a), Galilee
5. θεός (the-**os**), God, a god (of Greek or Roman religion); in GNT, always θεός, never Θεός
6. Ἱεροσόλυμα (i-e-ro-**so**-li-ma), Jerusalem (sometimes Ἰερουσαλήμ)
7. Ἰησοῦς (i-i-**sous**), Jesus
8. Ἰορδάνης (i-or-**dha**-nis), Jordan (river)
9. Ἰουδαία (i-ou-**dhe**-a), Judaea
10. Ἰσραήλ (is-ra-**il**), Israel
11. Ἰωάννης (i-o-**an**-nis), John
12. κόσμος (**kos**-mos), the world (as a place of habitation)
13. Μεσσίας (mes-**si**-as), Messiah, annointed one
14. Παῦλος (**pav**-los), Paul
15. Πέτρος (**pe**-tros), Peter
16. Πιλᾶτος (pi-**la**-tos), Pilate
17. ῥαββί (also ῥαββεί) (rha-**vi**), rabbi, teacher, master, "my lord," as an honorary form of address for teachers of the Torah

1.9 THE ERASMIAN SYSTEM OF PRONUNCIATION

Upper case	*Lower case*	*Letter name*	*Pronunciation guide*	*Phonic value*
Α	α	alfa	h*a*t	[a]
Β	β	beta	*b*at	[b]
Γ	γ	gamma	*g*o but nasal *n* before κ, γ,χ, ξ	[g]
Δ	δ	delta	*d*og	[d]
Ε	ε	epsilon	b*e*t	[e]
Ζ	ζ	zeta	*z*oo	[zd]
Η	η	eta	a as in "l*a*te"	[e]
Θ	θ	theta	*th*ink	[th]
Ι	ι	iota	p*i*azza, prist*i*ne	[i]
Κ	κ	kappa	*k*eep	[k]
Λ	λ	lambda	*l*etter	[l]
Μ	μ	mu	*m*oon	[m]
Ν	ν	nu	*n*oon	[n]
Ξ	ξ	xi	o*x*	[x]
Ο	ο	omicron	d*o*g	[o]
Π	π	pi	*p*ut	[p]
Ρ	ρ	rho	r	[r / rh]
Σ	σ / ς	sigma	*s*ing	[s]
Τ	τ	tau	*t*op	[t]
Υ	υ	upsilon	pr*u*ne	[u]
Φ	φ	phi	*ph*one	[ph]
Χ	χ	chi	lo*ch*	[ch]
Ψ	ψ	psi	hi*ps*	[ps]
Ω	ω	omega	n*o*te	[ô]

ASPIRATION IN THE ERASMIAN SYSTEM

Every Greek word that begins with a vowel carries a so-called *breathing* mark above the vowel.[15] These marks have the appearance of an English single quotation mark. There are two types of breathing marks: a *rough* breathing mark (e.g., ἁ) and a *smooth* breathing mark (e.g., ἀ). According to the Erasmian system of pronunciation, a rough breathing mark adds an "*h*" sound (i.e., aspiration) to the pronunciation. Thus, ὁ would be pronounced "*ho*" according to the Erasmian system. A

[15] The letter *rho* (ρ) also always has a rough breathing mark when it is the first letter of a word.

smooth breathing is really a rough breathing that has been turned down, so to speak. It indicates that the letter is not aspirated. Thus, ὀ would be pronounced simply as "o" (not as "*h*o").

Pronouncing Double Vowels and Vowels with Iota Subscripts According to the Erasmian Pronunciation

Two-letter combinations of a vowel with ι produce a *single* distinct sound. These two-letter combinations are known as double vowels, or diphthongs. They are pronounced as follows in the Erasmian system:

Double vowel	*Pronunciation guide*	*Phonic value*
αι	"ai" as in *ai*sle	[ai]
ει	"a" as in "f*a*te" (American pronunciation) "ai" as in *ai*sle (European pronunciation)	[ei]
οι	"oi" as in *oi*l	[oi]
υι	"uee" as in q*uee*n	[ui]
ου	"oo" as in p*oo*l	[ou]
αυ	"ow" as in "c*ow*"	[au]
ευ	"eu" as in "f*eu*d"	[eu]
ηυ	"eu" as in "f*eu*d"	[eu]
ᾳ	pronounced like α	[a]
ῃ	pronounced like η	[e]
ῳ	pronounced like ω	[ô]

2.

Writing Greek Letters, Accents, Diacritical Marks, and Punctuation

Given the similarities between Greek letters and English letters, it is important to note any important differences between them. In some cases, superficial resemblances can lead to significant errors. Writing Greek letters clearly is also an important aid to memorization. The following guidelines will help you form your letters correctly, especially in those cases in which a given Greek letter bears a strong resemblance to the Latin (English) letters you already know:

1. Not all Greek letters are the same height. Parts of the following letters are written *below* the line: β γ ζ η μ ξ ρ φ χ ψ ς.
2. Greek β should be made with one continuous stroke in contrast to English "b," which is made with two strokes.
3. *Never* dot an ι (iota) and make sure it curls up at the bottom, unlike English "i."
4. Greek κ should be half the height of English "k."
5. Carefully form η to distinguish it from English "n."
6. Carefully form ν to distinguish it from Greek υ and English "v."
7. ξ is written below the bottom line.
8. Carefully form ρ to distinguish it from English "p," which is made with two strokes.
9. Carefully form medial σ to distinguish it from Greek ο.
10. Carefully form Greek τ to distinguish it from English "t," which is taller.
11. Carefully form the Greek letter υ, which is made with *one* stroke, not two. This will help you distinguish it from the English "u," which is made with *two* strokes.

Figure: Statue of Eros riding a dolphin (ancient Neapolis).
Figure: Theater mask (ancient Attaleia).

2.1 THE IOTA SUBSCRIPT

A small ι is sometimes written under the vowels α, η, or ω, especially when they are final. This small ι is known as an *iota subscript* because it is written *below* (i.e., *sub*) the vowel. This iota subscript does not affect pronunciation. Vowels with an iota subscript are pronounced in the same way as the corresponding vowel without an iota subscript.

ᾳ pronounced like α [a]
ῃ pronounced like η [i]
ῳ pronounced like ω [o]

It may surprise you to learn that the iota subscript was never used during the Classical or Hellenistic period. None of the oldest New Testament manuscripts include them. When written at all, it was written *adscript*. In other words, it was written *after* the thematic vowel of verbs (-ηι, -αι, -ωι) and after the stem vowels of nouns. Throughout the Hellenistic period, these double vowels with adscripts were gradually *monophthongized* in popular speech. Consequently, they were written simply as -η, -α, and -ω, without an adscript because there was no longer any qualitative distinction in terms of pronunciation between these vowels and their corresponding simple vowels.

The iota subscript was introduced by Byzantine scholarship in the twelfth century AD. In other words, these are editorial marks. Nonetheless, you should pay attention to them because they will help you distinguish between different grammatical forms of nouns, adjectives, verbs, and participles.

2.2 BREATHING MARKS

Every Greek word (in an edited Greek text) that begins with a vowel carries a so-called *breathing* mark above the vowel.[1] These marks have the appearance of an English single quotation mark. There are two types of breathing marks:

- ῾ *rough* breathing mark (e.g., ἁ)
- ᾿ *smooth* breathing mark (e.g., ἀ)

The rough breathing mark was used to indicate *aspiration* in Attic (Athenian) Greek, that is, an [h] sound at the beginning of words. In point of fact, even though Attic Greek did have aspiration at the beginning of certain words, it never used rough breathing marks. Moreover, such aspiration was used only for a relatively brief period, and then only erratically. The other main dialects of Greek, namely

[1] The consonant *rho* (ρ) also always has a rough breathing mark when it is the first letter of a word.

Ionic, Doric, and Aeolic, never employed aspiration. In fact, all *aspiration in Greek died out prior to the first century AD.*[2] Therefore, there is no good reason to continue using these breathing marks in modern editions of the Greek New Testament.

Nevertheless, editors of the New Testament have continued to add rough breathing marks when they edit New Testament texts, in conformity to what is perceived to be Attic usage. From a historical perspective, it is clear that the *addition* of breathing marks to the Greek New Testament does is artificial. For this reason, the historical Greek pronunciation system *ignores* these artificial rough breathing marks. Likewise, you should ignore these rough breathing marks when pronouncing Hellenistic Greek words. (However, breathing marks can be helpful in distinguishing between similar words.)

2.3 GREEK ACCENTS

Accents (τόνοι) were not used in the oldest manuscripts of the Greek New Testament, nor in Hellenistic Greek inscriptions. The earliest example we have of the use of accents in a New Testament manuscript dates to the fifth century AD.[3] Accents were developed as editorial marks to help preserve important features of Attic Greek, which were in danger of being forgotten. Three different accents were used in editing the Greek New Testament:

´ acute (ά)
` grave (ὰ)
˜ circumflex (ᾶ)

In the late Classical and Hellenistic periods, Greek words had stressed syllables.[4] All three accents were employed to indicate the *stressed* syllable of a word. In other words, they all have the same effect on pronunciation.

---

2 This ancient aspiration only leaves its mark in the language in some forms of elision. But according to the artificial Erasmian system of pronunciation, a rough breathing mark adds an "*h*" sound (i.e., aspiration) to the pronunciation. Thus, ὁ would be pronounced "*ho*" according to the Erasmian system. A smooth breathing is really a rough breathing that has been "turned off," so to speak. Thus, ὀ would be pronounced simply as "o" (not as "*ho*"), that is, without aspiration. These breathing marks were *never* written in the oldest New Testament manuscripts.

3 This mansucript is known as Bezae Cantabrigiensis. Even though the full accentual system was not completed until medieval times, it should be noted that the *acute* and *grave* accents are already mentioned by Plato (*Kratylos* 399) and the *circumflex* by Ephoros and Heraclides (fourth century BC).

4 Centuries before the development of Attic Greek, Greek words had *tonic* or musical accent. Like modern Chinese, some words were spoken with a rising tone (e.g., "Really?"), some with a falling tone (Really!), and others with a rising-then-falling tone. The addition of the acute, grave, and circumflex helped scholars remember these three changing tones. This explains why Greek editors originally developed three different accent signs. However, over time, this *pitch* accent changed into a *stress* accent.

2.3.1 When the last syllable of a Greek word is accented with an acute accent, it changes to a *grave* accent, except when followed by punctuation (e.g., by a comma or semicolon [cf. Section 2.6]).[5]

2.3.2 Double vowels always receive their accent on the second letter, for example, καί not κάι.

2.3.3 Words beginning with a vowel will have *both* an accent and a breathing mark on the first syllable. These accents are combined with breathing marks as follows

ἄ ἅ ἂ ἃ ἆ ἇ

2.4 BASIC INFORMATION ABOUT USING GREEK ACCENTS

The rules for the placement and movement of accents are somewhat complicated but are well worth knowing. At this point, only the following basic facts need to be noted:

2.4.1 When pronouncing a Greek word, place the stress on the accented syllable.

2.4.2 Some Greek words are spelled identically but have different accents, or even different accented syllables. You should pay close attention to the accents on these particular words in order to distinguish one word from another.

2.4.3 A Greek word can only be accented on one of its last three syllables. A Greek word can carry only *one* accent (except when followed by an enclitic [see Section 5.6], in which case it will sometimes carry a second accent).

2.4.4 Definitions

- The *ultima* is the final syllable of a word.
- The *penult* is the second-to-last syllable of a word.
- The *antepenult* is the third-to-last syllable of a word.

There are as many syllables in a Greek word as there are separate vowels or double vowels. As an example, the word ἄνθρωπος (**an**-thro-pos) has three vowels and, therefore, three syllables:

3 2 1
ἄν-θρω-πος

1 – ultima
2 – penult
3 – antepenult[6]

---

[5] Or when followed by an *enclitic*, which prefers to throw off its accent onto the preceding word (see Section 5.6).

[6] A syllable is considered to be short if it contains a short vowel (e.g., ε and ο) or no consonant at all. If the short vowel is followed by two or more consonants pronounced together, the syllable is usually considered *short*. A syllable is also considered long when its vowel (long or short) or double vowel is followed by two consonants separately pronounced, or by a double consonant.

2.4.5 The vowels η and ω are always considered *long*. The vowels α, ι, and υ can be long or short. A syllable is considered long if it contains a long vowel or a double vowel (the exceptions being αι and οι, which are considered short when found at the very end of a word with no letters following).[7] Vowels formed with an *iota* subscript (ῳ ῃ ᾳ) are always long.

2.4.6 General Accentuation Rules

An acute accent may stand on any one of the last three syllables of a word, but a circumflex can only stand on the penult or ultima. A grave accent can only stand on the ultima.

2.4.7 Antepenult Accented

The antepenult can be accented only if the ultima is short (e.g., κύριος, ἄνθρωπος, πνεύματος, ἀποκρίνομαι). Since a circumflex can never be put on an antepenult, the antepenult, when accented, can only be accented with an acute.

2.4.8 Penult Accented

a) When the penult is long and the ultima is short, the accent on the penult must be a circumflex (e.g., οὗτος, τοῦτο, εἶπον, εἶδον, οἶδα).
b) When the penult is long and the ultima is long, the accent on the penult must be acute (e.g., ἀκούω, πιστεύω, οὕτως, ἀλλήλων, σῴζω, εἰρήνη).
c) When the penult is short, the accent on the penult must be acute (e.g., λόγος).

2.4.9 Ultima Accented

a) Short Ultima: The accent *must* be acute (e.g., αὐτός, οὐρανός, ἀδελφός, υἱός, χριστός, καλόν). But, as noted earlier, it must change to a grave accent when followed by another word, without intervening punctuation.
b) Long Ultima: The accent is usually acute (e.g., γηνή, ἀνήρ, καθώς, χείρ), but can be a circumflex (e.g., ἑαυτοῦ, γῆ, ἡμεῖς).

2.4.10 Grave Accent

A grave accent can only stand on the ultima. It is actually a turned-down acute accent. An acute accent is changed to a grave accent when a word follows without

[7] E.g., final -αι and -οι are short, but final -αις and -οις are long. The exception to this rule is the optative mood (cf. Section 22.8).

ation (except when the following word is an enclitic). It contin- ssed syllable.

THE DIAERESIS

The diaeresis mark (¨) looks like a German *umlaut*. It often appears in words of foreign derivation (e.g., Hebrew and Latin loan words), though it is also used for some Greek words (Ἀχαΐα).[8] It is actually an editorial mark used to indicate that the two vowels, which could be construed as a double vowel, are actually two *separately pronounced* vowels. The diaeresis always appears over the *second* of the two vowels (e.g., ἀΐδιος). Can you guess what the following words mean?

Βηθσαϊδά (Bith-sa-i-**dha**)
Ἀχαΐα (A-kha-**i**-a)
Ἠσαΐας (I-sa-**i**-as)
Μωϋσῆς (Mo-i-**sis**)
Γάϊος (**Ga**-i-os)

2.6 PUNCTUATION MARKS

Greek employs the following punctionation marks:

Comma	,	(as in English)
Period	.	(as in English)
Semicolon	·	(raised dot above the line)
Question mark	;	(do not confuse with English semicolon)

2.7 THE APOSTROPHE

An apostrophe is sometimes encountered at the end of Greek words. It is an editorial mark used to indicate that a final vowel has been deleted before the word following it, which begins with a vowel. This process is known as *elision*. An apostrophe marks the place where the vowel was elided (e.g., ἀλλ' ἐγώ for ἀλλὰ ἐγώ).

If the vowel that begins the following word is aspirated (with a rough breathing mark), then the consonant *preceding* the elision mark may change to its corresponding fricative consonant.[9] (Even though Attic aspiration had died out long before the

---

[8] E.g., πρωΐαν, προϋποτίθημι, ἀϋπνία, ἄϋλος, διϋλίζω, προϊκνοῦμαι, προϊόν, προΐστημι.

[9] Whereas in Attic Greek, final π, τ, and κ change to their aspirated forms φ, θ, χ before the word that etymologically begins with a rough breathing [h] (e.g., μετ' → μεθ', ἐπ' → ἐφ', κατ' → καθ', ἀπ' → ἀφ',

first century AD, it has left its mark in the language in this feature of elision.) For example:

μετά → μεθ' ἡμῶν (me-thi-**mon**) instead of μετ' ἡμῶν
ἐπί → ἐφ' ὑμᾶς (e-fi-**mas**) instead of ἐπ' ὑμᾶς

To sum up, the editors of printed editions of the New Testament have added a variety of other marks that are *not* used in the oldest manuscripts, namely:

- breathing marks: ὅ, ὂ
- accents: ό, ὸ, ῦ
- iota subscript: ῃ, ῳ, ᾳ
- diaeresis (¨) and apostrophe (')
- letter spacing
- most punctuation
- capitalization
- verse, paragraph, and chapter divisions

2.8 VOCABULARY TO BE MEMORIZED

Note: the prepositions listed in the vocabulary below include the abbreviations "acc.," "gen." and "dat." These abbreviations will be explained in Section 5.10.

1. ἀκούω (a-**kou**-o), I hear, listen to
2. ἀνά (a-**na**), each, each one, apiece (+ acc.) (cf. Section 5.10)
3. ἄρτι (**ar**-ti), now, just now
4. καί (ke), and; also, even (adv.); καί…καί…, both…and…(when linking nouns)
5. δέ (dhe), δ' (before word beginning with a vowel), but, and (post-positive);[10] δέ often implies some sort of weak contrast. It can also be used with explanatory force meaning "indeed," "and moreover"
6. ἀλλά (al-**la**), but (much stronger than δέ); ἀλλά is abbreviated to ἀλλ' before a word beginning with a vowel
7. κατά (ka-**ta**), κατ', καθ',[11] (1) (w. acc.) according to; (2) (w. gen.) against, down from (cf. Section 5.10)
8. ἐγγύς (e^{ng}-**gis**), (w. gen.) near, close to (cf. Section 5.10)
9. ἕξ (eks), six (6) (cf. "hexagon")

οὐκ → οὐχ, ὑπ' → ὑφ'), this change does not always occur in the Hellenistic Greek because of its psilotic nature (i.e., its lack of an "h" sound).

[10] This is a *post-positive* word; i.e., this word never comes first in a Greek sentence, but you should translate it as the first word.

[11] κατ' when followed by a word beginning with a vowel; καθ' when followed by a word beginning with a vowel carrying a rough breathing mark.

10. ἤ(i), or, than
11. λύω (**li**-o), I loose, untie, set free; destroy, do away with, abolish
12. λόγος (**lo**-gos), a statement, a message, a saying, reply, story, speech, reasoning[12]
13. μετά (me-**ta**), μετ', μεθ',[13] (1) (w. gen.) with, among; (2) (w. acc.) after (temporal), behind (spatial) (cf. Sections 5.9–10)
14. οὖν (oun), then (temporal), therefore (in a discourse or making an argument)
15. οὔτε (ou-**te**) (always post-positive), not, nor; οὔτε...οὔτε..., neither... nor...(combination of οὐ + τέ)
16. πιστεύω (pi-**stev**-o), I believe (in), I entrust myself to, I have confidence in (usually followed by dat. or with εἰς + acc.)
17. προφήτης (pro-**fi**-tis), prophet
18. συναγωγή (si-na-go-**yi**), usually a "Jewish synagogue" (place of assembly), but can also designate a meeting for synagogal worship
19. τέ (te), and; τέ...δέ..., both...and...(usually follows the word it modifies); τέ is an enclitic (see Section 5.6)[14]
20. χριστός (khri-**stos**), anointed one, messiah, Messiah, Christ; the term χριστός is the Greek equivalent of the Hebrew term meaning Messiah. (Needless to say, it is common practice to "translate" the term Χριστός as "Christ." But this is not really a translation. It is a transliteration. In fact, the rendering of the term Χριστός as "Christ" really leaves the term *untranslated*. The term Χριστός, being the Greek equivalent of the Hebrew word "Mashiach," can also be translated as "Messiah," cf. μεσσίας.)

---

[12] In very rare cases, this word is translated as "divine Wisdom" or "Word," meaning the personified expression of God (e.g., John 1:1). This is a highly specialized philosophical meaning, which we shall discuss in the Workbook (cf. John 1:1).

[13] μετ' when followed by a word beginning with a vowel; μεθ' when followed by a word beginning with a vowel carrying a rough breathing mark.

[14] An *enclitic* is a word that is read so closely with the preceding word that it "leans on" the preceding word and therefore has no accent of its own (cf. 5.6).

3.

Present and Future Active Indicative, Present Active Indicative of the Verb "to be," and Particles

A *verb* is a word that expresses an action or a state of being. Speakers of English tend to think about verbs primarily in terms of their tense (e.g., past, present, future). In Greek, verbs also have other important characteristics, namely, *aspect* and *voice*.

3.1 VERBAL ASPECT

The term "aspect" refers to the *kind* of action that is depicted by a verb. The meaning of a verb is not related only or exclusively to temporal categories but also to the kind of action, or the way that an event occurs. There are three verbal aspects in Greek. Each of these aspects is linked to specific tenses. In other words, the morphology of the verb will you (some extent) specify the aspect of a given verb.[1] In the indicative mood, Greek verbs express both time and tense as well as aspect.[2]

The three verbal aspects are as follows:

1. *Aoristic aspect*
   The aoristic aspect is associated with the simple past (aorist) tense. It expresses the simple (or summary) occurrence of a verbal action. The aoristic aspect is sometimes also associated with the present and future tenses.

[1] In recent years, the function of aspect in Hellenistic Greek has become the most contested feature of the language. Some scholars have privileged aspect over tense, especially Stanley E. Porter, *Verbal Aspect in the Greek of the New Testament, with Reference to Tense and Mood* (New York: Peter Lang, 1989); cf. Buist Fanning, *Verbal Aspect in New Testament Greek* (New York: Oxford University Press, 1990).

[2] See Section 3.3 for an explanation of the indicative move. We shall return to this subject in Chapters 9 and 16.

Figure: Statue of a man (ancient Iconium).

2. *Imperfective aspect*
   The imperfective aspect is associated with the imperfect tense. It expresses a progressive kind of action (e.g., continuous or repetitive). This aspect is usually associated with the present and future tenses as well.
3. *Perfective aspect*
   The perfective aspect is associated with the perfect and pluperfect tenses. It expresses a completed action with ongoing results. It may also express states of being.

The imperfective aspect requires our attention in this lesson because the present and future tenses often have an imperfective aspect. The imperfective aspect normally conceives of the verbal action as being in progress or as unfolding without reference to its completion. This may consist of a single activity that is in progress or that is continuous (e.g., "he is walking"), or a series of repetitions of an action (e.g., "he repeatedly asked") (see Chapter 12 for other uses).

3.2 FORMATION OF VERBS

All verbs consist of a *stem*. This stem identifies the word in terms of its lexical meaning. It also provides the basic building block for creating other forms of the verb in the same tense. To determine the stem of a verb, simply remove the verbal ending (either -ω, or -ομαι) from its lexical form (i.e., the form given in the vocabulary lists). For example, the stem of λύω is λυ-.

The segment following the stem is the verbal ending, or suffix. This verbal ending consists of two parts: a connecting vowel and a personal ending. By means of these verbal endings, Greek verbs can express the following information.

1. Person
   1. first person
   2. second person
   3. third person
2. Number
   1. singular
   2. plural
3. Tense
   1. present
   2. future
   3. imperfect
   4. first aorist/second aorist
   5. perfect

    6. pluperfect
    7. future perfect[3]
4. Voice (see Section 3.4)
    1. active
    2. middle
    3. passive
5. Mood
    1. indicative
    2. subjunctive
    3. imperative
    4. optative (cf. Section 22.8)

Note: The infinitive and participle are not moods. However, for the purposes of parsing, we will treat them as if they were moods.

3.3 PARSING VERBS

In the workbook exercises you will be asked to *parse* verbs. To "parse" a verb means to specify the following information:

1. Person
2. Number
3. Tense
4. Voice
5. Mood
6. Lexical form (i.e., the *dictionary* form)
7. Short gloss or definition of the lexical form (translating the conjugated form is often impossible without knowing the specific context)

In Chapters 1–17, all the verbs you will study will be in the *indicative* mood. This is the most usual mood of everyday discourse and narrative. It is the mood of direct statements, assertions, direct questions, and narrative.

You may have observed that verbal *aspect* is not listed among the information required for parsing. This is because aspect is *morphologically* tied to verbal tense. Therefore, when you specify the tense, the aspect is also specified, though context must also be taken into consideration.

[3] In the Greek New Testament, the future perfect is mostly formed with a periphrastic construction (see Chapter 19.8).

3.4 VOICE

The term "voice" describes how the subject of a verb is related to the action of the verb. There are three voices:

1. Active voice
2. Middle voice
3. Passive voice

We will discuss the active voice in this lesson and return to the middle and passive voices in Chapter 11. In the case of the active voice, the subject is performing the action of the verb (e.g., "she buys the book").

3.5 PRIMARY AND SECONDARY VERBAL ENDINGS

The verb tenses can be divided into two categories:

1. Primary tenses
2. Secondary tenses

The distinction between primary and secondary tenses concerns the time of action (in the indicative mood).

1. The primary tenses are oriented to the present and future (namely the present, future, and perfect tenses).
2. The secondary tenses are oriented to the past (imperfect, aorist, and pluperfect tenses).

A basic familiarity with the primary and secondary endings will help you recognize common features between the verbal endings of the various tenses. In theory, one should only need to memorize two sets of verbal endings: the primary and the secondary endings. Unfortunately, the facts of the matter are more complicated than this because these primitive verbal endings evolved and changed over time in the various tenses. The primary active verbal endings are as follows:

Primary Active Endings

	Singular	*Plural*
1	-μι	-μεν
2	-σι	-τε
3	-τι	-ντι

3.6 PRESENT ACTIVE INDICATIVE TENSE

In the present tense, the primary endings are added to the verbal stem by means of a thematic connecting vowel, either ε or ο. To make rapid progress in your Greek reading, it is suggested that you learn the endings as they occur in the present tense paradigm (see chart below) because verbal endings are easier to memorize if you learn them as they are formed on an actual verb stem.

In the teaching of Greek, it is customary to use the verb λύω ("I loose, I untie, I destroy") as the example verb because it is *regular* in all of its tenses. In each case, a connecting vowel, either ε or ο, has been used to join the verbal ending to the verbal stem (i.e., present verbal stem + connecting vowel ε/ο + primary active ending):

Present Active Indicative of λύω

⊕	*Sg.*		*Pl.*	
1	λύ-ω (**li**-o)	[I untie]	λύ-ομεν (**li**-o-men)	[we untie]
2	λύ-εις (**li**-is)	[you untie]	λύ-ετε (**li**-e-te)	[you (pl.) untie]
3	λύ-ει (**li**-i)	[he/she/it unties]	λύ-ουσι(ν) (**li**-ou-si[n])	[they untie]

The ⊕ symbol beside this paradigm and other paradigms in this book means that you must memorize it.

If you compare these endings with the primary endings listed above, you will note some differences:

- λύω: the ο connecting vowel has lengthened, and the primary ending, μι, has dropped off (-ο + μι > -ω). In other words, there is no suffix.
- λύεις: the primary ending, -σι, has been added to the stem with the connecting vowel, ε, forming -εσι. But when σ becomes intervocalic (as εσι), it drops out and another σ is added to the end, resulting in the ending, -εις.
- λύει: the primary ending, τι, has become σι, and the now-invocalic σ (as εσι) drops out, leaving -ει.
- λύ-ουσι: the τ of the primary ending, -ντι, has changed to σ, and ν has dropped out before σ. Then the connecting vowel, ο, lengthens in compensation to form ου (-ο + ντι > -ονσι > -οσι > -ουσι).

You do not need to memorize the reasons for these changes. Simply memorize the endings as they actually occur on the stem of λύω.

Note:

1. Any verb whose lexical form ends in -ω can take these endings.
2. Unlike English, Greek does not require an explicit subject. For example, λύω means "I untie," and λύει means "he unties," or "she unties," or "it unties." However, in practice, an explicit subject is often specified in Greek texts.

3. *Movable ν*: the third-person plural ending often has ν added. This so-called "movable ν" is added for euphony (i.e., the formation of a pleasing sound to the ear). It does not affect the meaning of the verb. The movable ν often occurs when the following word begins with a vowel, or at the end of a sentence. However, there are many exceptions to this rule in the GNT.
4. *Verbal Agreement*: as you would expect, a singular subject is normally followed by a singular verb, and a plural subject is normally followed by a plural verb. However, there is one important exception: *Neuter* plural subjects are normally followed by *singular* verbs.[4]

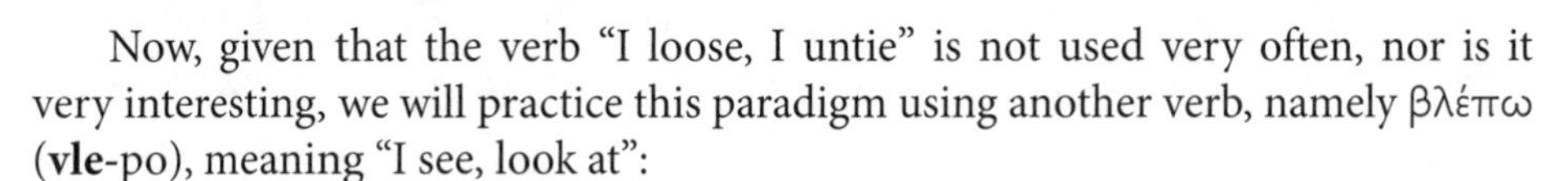

Now, given that the verb "I loose, I untie" is not used very often, nor is it very interesting, we will practice this paradigm using another verb, namely βλέπω (**vle**-po), meaning "I see, look at":

Present Active Indicative of βλέπω

	Sg.			*Pl.*		
1	βλέπω	(**vle**-po)	[I see]	βλέπομεν	(**vle**-po-men)	[we see]
2	βλέπεις	(**vle**-pis)	[you see]	βλέπετε	(**vle**-pe-te)	[you (pl.) see]
3	βλέπει	(**vle**-pi)	[he/she/it sees]	βλέπουσι(ν)	(**vle**-pou-si[n])	[they see]

As noted above, the present tense often has an imperfective aspect, expressing a progressive kind of action (e.g., "I am seeing"), although this is not true in every case. But the present tense sometimes simply carries an aoristic aspect and expresses a simple (or summary) occurrence of a verbal action ("I see").

3.7 ACCENTING VERBS IN THE INDICATIVE MOOD

The accent on verbs is *recessive*.[5] This means that the accent is placed as far away from the end of the last syllable (ultima) as the general rules permit (i.e., the accent shifts to the left, cf. Section 2.4). As you know, Greek words can only be accented on the last three syllables. Therefore, the fourth-to-last syllable of a verb will never be accented.

Thus, the antepenult of βλέπομεν, βλέπετε, βλέπουσιν and λύομεν, λύετε, λύουσιν are all accented because the last syllable of each is short. Since a circumflex can only occur on the penult when the penult contains a long vowel and the ultima is short, the accent on the penult is normally an acute (e.g., βλέπει). The verb εἰμί ("I am") has its own particular accent rules because it is an *enclitic* (see Section 3.10.1).

---

[4] This is known as the rule of *Attic construction* (BDF, Chapter 133). This rule applies to subjects that do not refer to human beings. For example, this rule would not apply to the neuter plural noun ἔθνη ("Gentiles"). It sometimes does not apply to the nouns τένκα ("children") and δαιμόνια ("demons").

[5] Infinitives and participles are excluded from this rule.

3.8 THE "HISTORIC" PRESENT

When reading the canonical Gospels, one often encounters the present tense in contexts where one would expect the past tense.[6] For example, a passage may say "Jesus says" (Ἰησοῦς λέγει) where the context would imply "Jesus said" (Ἰησοῦς εἶπεν). This use of the present tense is known as the "historic" present. It is used by authors to give a narrative greater vividness. Verbs in the historic present tense should be translated as *past tense* verbs (e.g., "Jesus said"). Of course, this phenomenon also occurs in English.

One convenient way of signaling to your instructor that you recognize this usage is to translate such verbs as past tense verbs, followed by "(h.p.)," meaning "historic present."

3.9 THE FUTURE ACTIVE INDICATIVE TENSE

The most common use of the future tense is to express simple future action ("he will go") or future progressive action ("he will be going"). As in English, the future tense can also be used to express a command or prohibition: for example, "*You will* love your neighbor as yourself" (Jas 2:8).[7]

3.9.1 Forming the Future Tense

The consonant, σ, functions as the *tense formative* of the future tense. In other words, the addition of a σ to the stem tells you that the verb may be in the future tense.

The future tense is very easy to form: Simply add the tense formative -σ to the verbal stem, followed by a connecting vowel (ε/ο), and the present active tense endings (i.e., future stem + σ + ε/ο + primary/present active endings [Section 3.6]):

Future Active Indicative of λύω

⊕	*Sg.*		*Pl.*	
1	λύσω (**li**-so)	[I will untie]	λύσομεν (**li**-so-men)	[we will untie]
2	λύσεις (**li**-sis)	[you will untie]	λύσετε (**li**-se-te)	[you (pl.) will untie]
3	λύσει (**li**-si)	[he/she/it will untie]	λύσουσι(ν) (**li**-sou-si[n])	[they will untie]

You will notice that λύσουσι(ν) is accented on the antepenult. This tells you that the ι in the verbal ending must be short.

---

[6] E.g., Matt 3:1; John 1:29.

[7] Ἀγαπήσεις τὸν πλησίον σου ὡς σεαυτόν .

3.10 PRESENT ACTIVE INDICATIVE TENSE OF εἰμί ("I AM")

Greek actually has two ways of forming verbs. These two families of verbs are named after their first-person singular endings, namely:

Thematic verbs (or ω-verbs) such as λύω (I untie)
Athematic verbs (or μι-verbs) such as εἰμί (I am)

Historically speaking, athematic verbs are older verbal forms than ω-verbs. Indeed, many μι-verbs were gradually replaced by ω-verbs during the Hellenistic period. As you can see, in the following example of εἰμί, there are many similarities between athematic verb endings and the thematic verb endings listed above.

Present Active Indicative of εἰμί

⊕	*Sg.*			*Pl.*		
1	εἰμί	(i-**mi**)	[I am]	ἐσμέν	(es-**men**)	[we are]
2	εἶ	(i)	[you are]	ἐστέ	(e-**ste**)	[you (pl.) are]
3	ἐστί(ν)	(e-**sti[n]**)	[he/she/it is]	εἰσί(ν)[8]	(i-**si[n]**)	[they are]

3.10.1 εἰμί as an Enclitic

When you encounter present indicative disyllabic forms of εἰμί in the GNT, they will often lack an accent. This is because two-syllable forms of εἰμί are enclitic. The word "enclitic" is derived from the Greek word, ἐκλίνειν, meaning "to lean upon." An enclitic is a word that is read so closely with the *preceding* word that it is said to "lean upon" it and, therefore, appears to have no accent of its own.[9] Enclitics can be said to "throw" their accents onto the previous word. Thus, the accent of many forms of εἰμι can be found on the last syllable of the previous word. For this reason, enclitic forms of εἰμι should be pronounced as if they were part of, or joined to, the previous word.

1. If the previous word has an accented antepenult, or a circumflex on the penult, then the accent on ἐιμί will shift to the ultima of the preceding word and will remain acute: for example, πρόσκαιροί ἐστιν (Mark 4:17), οὗτοί εἰσιν (Mark 1:16).

---

[8] Actually only occurs as εἰσιν in GNT, with or without an accent.

[9] Except when standing at the beginning of a sentence. Other examples of enclitics include με, μου, μοι, σε, σου, σοι, τις, που, ποτε, πως, γε, τε, and all present indicative forms of εἰμι and φημι (except second-person singular), and the indefinite pronoun τις, τι (see Chapter 15).

2. But, if the preceding word has an *acute* accent on the penult, then the disyllabic form of εἰμί will retain its accent: for example, ἄλλοι εἰσίν (Mark 4:18), ἐν οἴκῳ ἐστίν (Mark 2:1).
3. When forms of εἰμι are accented, in circumstances that allow them to shift their accent to the preceding word (an editorial decision), it indicates emphasis. However, εἰμι is also accented under the following conditions: 1) when it stands at the beginning of a sentence or clause; 2) when it is preceded by οὐκ, μή, ὡς, εἰ, καί, ἀλλά (or ἀλλ'), τοῦτο (τοῦτ '); 3) when it signifies existence or possibility.

3.10.2 Impersonal Use of εἰμί

The third-person forms of εἰμί are sometimes used impersonally, without an implied subject:

ἐστί(ν) – "there is"
εἰσί(ν) – "there are"

3.11 FUTURE OF VERBS ENDING IN LABIALS, VELARS, AND DENTALS

Nine of the Greek consonants are interrelated as follows:

1. *Labial* consonants, π, β, φ, are formed by the lips.
2. *Velar* consonants, κ, γ, χ, are formed at the back of the palate.
3. *Dental* consonants, τ, δ, θ, are formed by placing the tongue behind the teeth.

As previously noted, these consonants can be subdivided according to whether they are:

1. Unvoiced stops
2. Voiced fricatives
3. Unvoiced fricatives

Voiced means that you use your vocal chords to pronounce the sound.[10] In contrast, unvoiced means that vocal chords are not used.[11] This classification can be summarized as follows:

[10] Try resting two fingers on your vocal chords and say the English sounds "b," "d," and "g." You can feel your vocal chords vibrate.
[11] Now put your two fingers on your vocal chords again and say the English sounds "p," "t," and "k." You cannot feel your vocal chords vibrate.

	unvoiced stops	*voiced fricatives*	*unvoiced fricatives*
labial	π	β	φ
velar	κ	γ[12]	χ
dental	τ	δ	θ

When a verbal stem ends in a final labial consonant (π, β, φ) and is followed by σ (future tense formative), the labial consonant combines with the σ to form the consonantal blend ψ. For example:

βλεπ + σω → βλέψω (**vle**-pso) "I will see"
γραφ + σω → γράψω (**gra**-pso) "I will write"

When a verbal stem ends in a final velar consonant (κ, γ, χ, as well as ζ) and is followed by σ (future tense formative), the velar consonant combines with the σ to form the consonantal blend ξ. For example:

ἀγ + σω → ἄξω (**a**-kso) "I will lead"

When a verbal stem ends in a final dental consonant (τ, δ, θ) and is followed by σ (future tense formative), the dental is deleted leaving only σ. For example:

βαπτιδ + σω → βαπτίσω (vap-**ti**-so) "I will baptize"[13]

This can be summarized as follows:

π, β, φ + σ = ψ
κ, γ, χ + σ = ξ
τ, δ, θ, ζ + σ = σ

Future Active Indicative of βλέπω

	Sg.			*Pl.*		
1	βλέψω	(**vle**-pso)	[I will see]	βλέψομεν	(**vle**-pso-men)	[we will see]
2	βλέψεις	(**vle**-psis)	[you will see]	βλέψετε	(**vle**-pse-te)	[you (pl.) will see]
3	βλέψει	(**vle**-psi)	[he/she/it will see]	βλέψουσι(ν)	(**vle**-psou-si[n])	[they will see]

[12] γ as hard [g] is actually a voiced stop.
[13] The verb βαπτίζω requires an explanation. The real present stem of this verb ends in a δ (√ βαπτιδ-), not ζ.

3.12 PRESENT AND FUTURE OF ἔχω ("I HAVE")

The verb ἔχω (**e**-kho) means "I have." Thus, the present active paradigm of ἔχω with a direct object such as βιβλίον (scroll) is as follows:

	Sg.		
1	ἔχω βιβλίον	(**e**-kho vi-**vli**-on)	[I have a scroll]
2	ἔχεις βιβλίον	(**e**-khis vi-**vli**-on)	[you have a scroll]
3	ἔχει βιβλίον	(**e**-khi vi-**vli**-on)	[he/she/it has a scroll]
	Pl.		
1	ἔχομεν βιβλίον	(**e**-kho-men vi-**vli**-on)	[we have a scroll]
2	ἔχετε βιβλίον	(**e**-khe-te vi-**vli**-on)	[you (pl.) have a scroll]
3	ἔχουσι(ν) βιβλίον	(**e**-khou-si[n] vi-**vli**-on)	[they have a scroll]

Some verbs will require special attention because they exhibit irregularities or unexpected forms. One such verb is the future form of ἔχω ("I have"). The root of ἔχω is actually not √ εχ- (as one would expect), but √ σεχ (here, the symbol √ is employed to designate the verbal root of a verb).[14] In the present tense, the initial σ of σέχω has dropped off, leaving ἔχω.

√ σεχ → εχ

The future of ἔχω is formed by adding the tense formative σ to the end of the *original* stem (√ σεχ). Thus, σεχ- + σ becomes σεξ- (according to the rule for velars above). However, Greek does not allow two sibilants ("s" sounds) to occur in a row. Therefore, the first sibilant (σ) drops out and is replaced with a rough breathing (by editors) to compensate for loss of the σ. Thus the future of ἔχω is ἕξω.

σεχ + σ → σεξ → ἑξ-

This information will be relevant to understanding the formation of ἔχω in other tenses as well. If all of this seems too complicated, just remember that the future of ἔχω is ἕξω.

3.13 NEGATIVE PARTICLE

Verbs are negated with οὐ, meaning "not." If the following word begins with a vowel, then οὐ is written as οὐκ (or οὐχ).

[14] The verbal root represents the original stock of a verb, from which all of its inflected forms develop.

1	οὐκ ἔχω βιβλίον	[I do not have a scroll]
2	οὐκ ἔχεις βιβλίον	[you do not have a scroll]
3	οὐκ ἔχει βιβλίον	[he/she/it does not have a scroll]
1	οὐκ ἔχομεν βιβλίον	[we do not have a scroll]
2	οὐκ ἔχετε βιβλίον	[you (pl.) do not have a scroll]
3	οὐκ ἔχουσι(ν) βιβλίον	[they do not have a scroll]

If the vowel that follows has a rough breathing mark, then οὐ is written as οὐχ. Once again, even though aspiration had already died out before the GNT was written, it has left its mark on the language in this small change from οὐκ to οὐχ. Similarly, the future form of ἔχω, which is ἕξω, begins with a rough breathing mark: e.g., οὐχ ἕξει βιβλίον (he/she/it will not have a scroll).

3.14 PARTICLES

Though the term "particle" is difficult to define precisely, its function is to change the relation of the parts of the sentence to one another. It is therefore called a function word. The particles δέ ("but/and"), οὖν ("then/therefore"), γάρ ("for"), and μέντοι ("but") are all *post-positives*. In other words, these words *never* appear first in a Greek sentence or clause. They always appear as the second, third, or even fourth word in a clause. But when you translate these post-positive particles, you *must* translate them *first* in your English translation.

The particles καί ("and") and ἀλλά ("but") are used to coordinate sentences and clauses with each other. Given the fact that Greek exhibits much greater freedom of word order than English, close attention to these particles will help you determine how to break up sentences into smaller, coherent phrases. For example, the particles μέν and δέ are often used to coordinate two contrasting clauses. They can be translated as "on the one hand, . . . on the other hand." However, given that such a translation forms an awkward English sentence, it is preferable to explore other options (e.g., "when/while . . . , he/they . . .).[15]

3.15 VOCABULARY TO BE MEMORIZED

1. βαπτίζω (vap-**ti**-zo), I dip or plunge into water, "I baptize"; fut. βαπτίσω (the real root of βαπτίζω is √ βαπτιδ)[16]

---

[15] μέν can also be used alone (i.e., not correlated with a δέ clause). This usage is termed μέν *solitarium*. For example, μὲν οὖν, "so then" is a resumptive phrase introducing a new episode. ὡς can also be correlated with καί ("as [ὡς] we have said before, so [καί] now I say again" [Gal 1:9]). It is more frequently correlated with οὕτως (e.g., 1 Cor 7:17).

[16] Verbs whose present stem ends in -ιζω and -αζω often have a final dental (or sometimes velar) in the original stem.

2. βλέπω (**vle**-po), I see, look (on or at); fut. βλέψω
3. γάρ (gar), for (post-positive)[17]
4. διά (dhi-**a**): (1) (w. gen.) through, by means of; (2
   account of (cf. Sections 5.9–10)
5. διδάσκαλος (dhi-**dha**-ska-los), teacher (cf. didactic)
6. ἐγείρω (e-**yi**-ro), I rise up, get up, wake up; I raise up (the dead)[18]
7. εἶδεν (**i**- dhen), he saw; εἶδον, I saw, they saw[19]
8. εἰμί (i-**mi**), I am[20]
9. ἐκεῖ (e-**ki**), there, in that place
10. εὑρίσκω (ev-**ri**-sko), I find, discover; fut. εὑρήσω[21]
11. ἔχω (**e**-kho), trans. I have, hold; intrans. I am (comparable to εἰμί); fut. ἕξω
12. κἀγώ (ka-**go**), and I, but I, I also (= καὶ ἐγώ)[22]
13. μέν (men), particle indicating contrast, emphasis, or continuation; μέν is used with δέ to coordinate two contrasting clauses (see Section 3.14); μέν used by itself can mean "indeed"
14. μένω (**me**-no), I remain, stay[23]
15. οὐ, οὐκ, οὐχ (ou, ouk, oukh),[24] not; with an accent it means "no" (οὔ)
16. πέμπω (**pem**-bo), I send, appoint; fut. πέμψω
17. Σίμων (**si**-mon), Simon[25]
18. υἱός (i-**os**), son, descendant
19. φαίνω (**fe**-no), I shine, give light to[26]
20. Φαρισαῖος (fa-ri-**se**-os), Pharisee; usually pl. in GNT
21. φωτίζω (fo-**ti**-zo),[27] I give light to, shine on; fut. φωτίσω
22. χρόνος (**khro**-nos), time (chronological time, calendric time), a period of time.

---

[17] This word never comes first in a sentence, but in translation it should be translated first.

[18] We will study the future form of this verb (cf. Chapter 4).

[19] We will learn the paradigm for this verb later (Chapter 10).

[20] We will study the future form of this verb in Chapter 11.

[21] Some present-tense stems add -σκ or -ισκ to the root to differentiate the present stem from the future stem (e.g., εὑρίσκω, ἀποθνήσκω, γινώσκω). The original root of these verbs often shows up in the future form (e.g., the original root of εὑρίσκ- was √ ευρ-).

[22] This is an example of *crasis*. Crasis is the contraction of a vowel (or double vowel) at the end of a word when the word, which follows, begins with a vowel. A *coronis* (') is placed over the contracted syllable. This phenomenon, which was in wide use in Attic Greek, is much less common in the GNT.

[23] We will study the future form of this verb in Chapter 4.

[24] οὐκ is used before a word beginning with a vowel having a smooth breathing; οὐχ (oukh) is used before a word beginning with a vowel having a rough breathing.

[25] This is a third declension noun (see Chapter 14).

[26] We will study the future form of this verb in Chapter 11.

[27] Verbs whose present stem ends in -ιζω often have a concealed final dental in the stem: e.g., φωτίζω → √ φωτιδ.

tract Verbs, esent and Future Active Indicative, and Future Indicative of Liquid Verbs

4.1 CONTRACT VERBS

There are many verbs whose stems end in a vowel, either -ε, -α, or -ο. These final vowels combine, or *contract*, with the connecting vowels of the personal endings. These so-called "contract" verbs can be grouped into the following three categories:

1. ε-contract verbs
2. α-contract verbs
3. ο-contract verbs

As you review the contraction of vowels in the paradigms below, you will notice that some vowels *dominate* other vowels. This is termed the principle of *phonodynamism*.[1] As a way of beginning to understand contract verbs, review some of the basic guidelines of contraction, as oulined below, and then turn to the example verbs for specifics. In general you will note that:

1. o-sounds tend to prevail over all other vowel sounds, whether preceding or succeeding.
2. when a-sounds and e-sounds meet, the intial sound takes precedence; thus α + ε → α, but ε + α → η.
3. iota (ι), whether written as subscript, or sounded, does not disappear.

---

[1] Antonius J. Jannaris, *Historical Greek Grammar Chiefly of the Attic Dialect as Written and Spoken from Classical Antiquity Down to the Present Time* (Hildesheim: Georg Olms, 1968), 84.

Figure: Marble block portraying the figure of a naked man holding a bird (Iconium, *IKonya* 86).

4.2 ε-CONTRACT VERBS

When the present-tense endings are added to a verb stem of ε-contract verbs, the final ε of the stem contracts with the vowel of the personal ending. The following chart helps explain some of the contractions in the paradigm below:

Connecting vowel added

Verbs ends in	ε	ο
ε	ει	ου
ο	ου	ου

For example, the stem of the verb ποιῶ ("I do, I make") actually ends with ε (ποιέ-ω). It is called an epsilon-contract verb. The following paradigm of the present active indicative of this verb results from the contraction of this final ε with the connecting vowel of the endings:

	Sg.		*Pl.*	
1	ποιῶ (pi-**o**)	[-έ + ω]	ποιοῦμεν (pi-**ou**-men)	[-έ + ομεν]
2	ποιεῖς (pi-**is**)	[-έ + εις]	ποιεῖτε (pi-**i**-te)	[-έ + ετε]
3	ποιεῖ (pi-**i**)	[-έ + ει]	ποιοῦσι(ν) (pi-**ou**-si[n])	[-έ + ουσι(ν)]

Observe that the contracted endings are the same as λύω, except in the first person plural and second-person plural. However, you should also note that the accent has moved. It is now positioned *over the contracted vowel* in all forms. Moreover, the accent has changed from an acute to a circumflex. These changes in accentutation will help you identify contract verbs.

4.3 α-CONTRACT VERBS

The rules for the contraction of the final α of α-contract verbs are slightly more complicated. The vocalic contractions are formed according to the following guidelines. We will use ἀγαπῶ ("I love") as an example. The stem of the verb ἀγαπῶ actually ends in α (ἀγαπά-ω). This is why it is called an *alpha-contract* verb. The final α contracts with the connecting vowel of the verbal endings as follows:

	Sg.		*Pl.*	
1	ἀγαπῶ (a-ga-**po**)	[-ά + ω]	ἀγαπῶμεν (a-ga-**po**-men)	[-ά + ομεν]
2	ἀγαπᾷς (a-ga-**pas**)	[-ά + εις]	ἀγαπᾶτε (a-ga-**pa**-te)	[-ά + ετε]
3	ἀγαπᾷ (a-ga-**pa**)	[-ά + ει]	ἀγαπῶσι(ν) (a-ga-**po**-si[n])	[-ά + ουσι(ν)]

Note how the accent has been repositioned over the contracted vowel, as in the case of ποιέω above. The accent has also changed from an acute to a circumflex (e.g., ἀγαπά + ω → ἀγαπῶ, ἀγαπά + εις → ἀγαπᾷς).

4.4 ο-CONTRACT VERBS

In order of frequency, ο-contract verbs are the least common.

1. When -ο contracts with -ει- , the ε is assimilated to the ο and -οι is formed in the second- and third-person singular.
2. When -ο contracts with -ο- , an -ου is formed (see chart in 4.2 above).

For example, the verb stem of πληρῶ ("I fill/fulfill") ends in ο (πληρό-ω). It is called an omicron-contract verb. This final ο contracts with the connecting vowel of the verbal endings as follows:

	Sg.		*Pl.*	
1	πληρῶ (pli-**ro**)	[-ό + ω]	πληροῦμεν (pli-**rou**-men)	[-ό + ομεν]
2	πληροῖς (pli-**ris**)	[-ό + εις]	πληροῦτε (pli-**rou**-te)	[-ό + ετε]
3	πληροῖ (pli-**ri**)	[-ό + ει]	πληροῦσι(ν) (pli-**rou**-si[n])	[-ό + ουσι(ν)]

Throughout this book, the contract verbs will be listed in the assigned vocabulary in their *contracted* forms (e.g., ποιῶ, ἀγαπῶ, and πληρῶ), which are *real* forms that actually occur in the GNT. These forms will be followed by their uncontracted endings (e.g., -έω, -άω, and -όω). You should always memorize these uncontracted endings whenever you learn a new contract verb.

The memorization these uncontracted endings is very useful because the uncontracted ending tells you whether the verb in question is an -έω, -άω, or -όω contract verb. But these *un*contracted forms *never* occur in a real texts in the GNT. In the GNT, they will always appear in their contracted forms (e.g., ποιῶ, ἀγαπῶ, πληρῶ).

4.5 FUTURE TENSE OF CONTRACT VERBS

The future tense of contact verbs is easy to form because there are no vocalic contractions. To form the future tense of these verbs, simply lengthen the final vowel of the verb stem (-ε → η, -α → η, -ο → ω), and then add the σ future tense consonant and the future endings (which are the same as the present-tense endings).

ποιε-	→	ποιη-	+ σ =	ποιήσω (pi-**i**-so) "I will do/make"
ἀγαπα-	→	ἀγαπη-	+ σ =	ἀγαπήσω (a-ga-**pi**-so) "I will love"
πληρο-	→	πληρω-	+ σ =	πληρώσω (pli-**ro**-so) "I will fill/fulfill"

4.6 FORMING THE FUTURE OF VERBS ENDING IN LIQUID CONSONANTS

Some verb stems end in so-called liquid consonants, namely λ, μ, ν, and ρ.[2] Special considerations must be followed when forming the future tense of these liquid verbs, because λ, μ, ν, and ρ *cannot be followed by* σ.[3]

As you now know, σ is the tense consonant of the future tense. How, then, does one form the future tense without using the future tense consonant? When a verb stem ends in either λ, μ, ν, or ρ, the future endings are added directly to the stem *without* the addition of the σ future tense consonant.[4]

The future of these liquid verbs conjugate (i.e., form) as if they were ε-contract verbs. The circumflex accent positioned over the contracted syllable will help you distinguish the future tense form of a liquid verb from its present-tense form. By way of example, consider the future active of the verb μένω ("I remain"):

	Future Active			*Present Active*	
	Sg.				
1	μενῶ [-έ + ω]	(me-**no**)	(I will remain)	μένω	(I remain)
2	μενεῖς [-έ + εις]	(me-**nis**)	(you will remain)	μένεις	(you remain)
3	μενεῖ [-έ + ει]	(me-**ni**)	(he/she/it will remain)	μένει	(he/she/it remains)
	Pl.				
1	μενοῦμεν [-έ + ομεν]	(me-**nou**-men)	(we will remain)	μένομεν	(we remain)
2	μενεῖτε [-έ + ετε]	(me-**ni**-te)	(you [pl.] will remain)	μένετε	(you remain)
3	μενοῦσι(ν) [-έ + ουσι]	(me-**nou**-si[n])	(they will remain)	μένουσι(ν)	(they remain)

To avoid confusion of the present and future forms looking too similar, the *present* stem of these verbs is often modified to distinguish it from its future form. Consequently, in the case of some verbs, the future tense – not the present

[2] Whereas a *stop* consonant blocks airflow and cannot be maintained indefinitely, a liquid consonant has free-flowing air (with some restriction) and can be maintained indefinitely. Technically speaking, μ and ν are nasals, but for the purposes of this topic, we shall consider them to be liquids.

[3] However, this is not a hard- and-fast rule throughout the language. For example, ρ + σ can stand together in third declension nouns, and phonetic changes allow for λσ, ρσ, νσ, and μσ in perfect middle and passive.

[4] To be more precise, the tense formative -εσ is added to the liquid stem. The σ then becomes intervocalic and drops out, and the preceding ε of the tense formative then contracts with the connecting vowel of the ending. Thus, it appears to behave like an ε-contract verb.

tense – will preserve the original verbal root. For example, in the following case, a double consonant is added to form the present stem:

Present		*Future*	
ἀγγέλλω (a^{ng}-**gel**-lo)	(I announce)	← ἀγγελῶ (a^{ng}-ge-**lo**)	(I will announce)
ἀποστέλλω (a-po-**stel**-lo)	(I send)	← ἀποστελῶ (a-po-ste-**lo**)	(I will send)
βάλλω (**val**-lo)	(I throw)	← βαλῶ (va-**lo**)	(I will throw)

Sometimes an *iota* (ι) is added to form the present stem, as in the case of ἐγείρω ("I raise up") and αἴρω ("I take, take up"):

Present			*Future*	
ἐγείρω (e-**yi**-ro)	(I raise)	←	ἐγερῶ (e-ye-**ro**)	(I will raise)
αἴρω (**e**-ro)	(I take up)	←	ἀρῶ (a-**ro**)	(I will take up)

4.7 FUTURES OF IRREGULAR VERBS

While some verbs undergo minor stem changes, other verbs actually change their stem completely. For example, the future of λέγω (**le**-go), meaning "I say," is ἐρῶ (e-**ro**), meaning "I will say." This can be confusing to new students of Greek. It is important that you try to memorize these unexpected verbal stems as you learn them in the assigned vocabulary.

4.8 VOCABULARY TO BE MEMORIZED

1. ἀγαπητός, -ή, -όν (a-ga-pi-t**os, -i, -on**), beloved, dear(est) (adjective, with m., fm., and nt. forms)[5]
2. θέλω (**the**-lo), I will, am willing, wish, want, desire; fut. θελήσω[6]
3. λέγω (**le**-go), I say, speak, tell; fut. ἐρῶ
4. οὐχί (ou-**khi**) is an emphatic form of οὐ meaning "not, not so, no indeed"; it also occurs in questions expecting a positive answer
5. πέραν (**pe**-ran) (with gen.), beyond, across to, on the other side

ε-contract verbs

6. αἰτῶ (-έω) (e-**to**), I ask, request[7]

---

5 ἀγαπητός, -ή, -όν are an abbreviated form of ἀγαπητός, ἀγαπητή, ἀγαπητόν. You will encounter such abbreviated forms of adjectives throughout this text and in lexica.

6 θέλω becomes a contract verb in the future tense.

7 Remember that the uncontracted form never occurs in the GNT. Only the contracted forms are used (e.g., αἰτῶ).

7. καλῶ (-έω) (ka-**lo**), I call, name, invite, summon; fut. καλέσω[8]
8. λαλῶ (-έω) (la-**lo**), I speak, say; fut. λαλήσω (cf. λέγω)
9. ὁμολογῶ (-έω) (o-mo-lo-**go**), I confess, admit, declare; fut. ὁμολογήσω
10. ὅτε (**o**-te), when, while
11. ὅτι (**o**-ti), that, because; also indicates direct and indirect speech
12. φῶς (fos), light[9]
13. χωρίς (kho-**ris**), (with gen.) without, apart from
14. μαρτυρῶ (-έω) (mar-ti-**ro**), I bear witness, testify; fut. μαρτυρήσω
15. μαρτυρία (mar-ti-**ri**-a), testimony, evidence (the cognate noun of μαρτυρῶ)
16. ποιῶ (-έω) (pi-**o**), I do, make; fut. ποιήσω
17. προσκυνῶ (-έω) (pro -ski-**no**), I worship, kneel; fut. προσκυνήσω
18. τηρῶ (-έω) (ti-**ro**), I keep, observe (the Torah); fut. τηρήσω
19. φωνῶ (-έω) (fo-**no**), I call, call to, call out; fut. φωνήσω (cf. φωνή)
20. ὡς (os), as, like, about (with numbers or time), when (with time)

α-contract verbs

21. ἀγαπῶ (-άω) (a-ga-**po**), I love; fut., ἀγαπήσω (cf. ἀγαπητός, -ή, -όν)
22. ζῶ (-άω) (zo),[10] I live, am alive; fut. ζήσω
23. ὁρῶ (-άω) (o-**ro**), I see[11]

ο- Contract Verbs

24. πληρῶ (-όω) (pli-**ro**), I fill, fulfill; fut. πληρώσω
25. φανερῶ (-όω) (fa-ne-**ro**), I make known, show, manifest, reveal; fut. φανερώσω

Box 1. Contract Future Forms of Previously Learned Verbs

- μένω (**me**-no), fut. μενῶ (me-**no**)
- ἐγείρω (e-**yi**-ro), fut. ἐγερῶ (e-ye-**ro**)

---

[8] You will notice that the final ε of καλέω does not lengthen as the rules would dictate. This verb seems to belong to a group of older verbs whose final ε does not lengthen (cf. τελέω).

[9] We will study the declension of this word in Chapter 14.

[10] Note, the root of ζῶ (-άω) is actually $\sqrt{}$ ζη (not $\sqrt{}$ ζα). The present active paradigm of ζῶ is:

	Sg.	*Pl.*
1	ζῶ	ζῶμεν
2	ζῇς	ζῆτε
3	ζῇ	ζῶσι(ν)

[11] For the future form, see Chapter 11.

5.

Second Declension, the Definite Article, and Prepositions

Most English nouns and adjectives do not change their forms when their grammatical function changes, though there are exceptions. For example, the relative pronoun "who" can change to "whom" and "whose," and, of course, many nouns form plurals by the addition of a final "s" or by a stem change (e.g., goose → geese).

In Greek, the situation is a good deal more complicated. Greek is an *inflected* language. This means that the endings of Greek nouns and adjectives *decline,* or are modified, to communicate grammatical information to the reader, such as gender, number, and grammatical function. To be precise, these nominal endings provide the following information:

1. grammatical gender: masculine, feminine, neuter
2. number: singular, plural
3. grammatical function

A *declension* is an orderly system for *inflecting* (i.e., changing) the endings of nouns. Greek nouns form their endings according to three different systems. Each of these systems is termed a "declension." They are classified as follows:

1. *first* declension
2. *second* declension
3. *third* declension

We will study the second declension in this chapter.

Figure: Stele portraying a man walking beside an ox, while a man and woman look on (Dikilitas, NE of Vasada, *IKonya* 150)

5.1 THE FUNCTION OF GREEK INFLECTIONAL FORMS

A declensional ending is termed a case ending. There are five cases in Hellenistic Greek:

1. nominative
2. genitive
3. dative
4. accusative
5. vocative

Historical Note

There were originally eight cases in the oldest forms of Greek. Over time, the *ablative* case (preserved in Latin) came to share the same form as the genitive. The *instrumental* and *locative* cases (also preserved in Latin) came to share the same form as the dative case. This leaves us with five cases in Hellenist Greek.

5.1.1 Nominative Case[1]

The nominative case is used to indicate the *subject* of a sentence or of an independent clause. The nominative case also has other uses: A few verbs, such as εἰμί, γίνομαι, and ὑπάρχω, do not take a direct object, but rather a *predicate.*[2] This predicate is always given in the *nominative*, not the accusative case.

The nominative case is the foundational case in the Greek case system. The so-called "oblique" cases, namely accusative, genitive, and dative, are distinguished from the nominative case as a group. The accusative case is the foundational case of the oblique cases.

5.1.2 Accusative Case

The original meaning of the accusative is *motion toward.* However, the most common use of the accusative is to indicate the *direct object* of a transitive verb. Some verbs regularly have two accusatives (e.g., verbs of asking, teaching, naming, and swearing): One accusative specifies a person and the other accusative specifies a thing. For example, in Jesus' question, "Why do you call *me good*?"[3] "me" and "good" are both in the accusative case in Greek.

---

1 Strictly speaking, the nominative and vocative are not cases, for case implies dependence.

2 Either a noun or an adjective. You may wonder how one determines which nominative is the subject and which is the predicate nominative. If only one word is a personal pronoun, demonstrative pronoun, or relative pronoun, it is the subject. If only one has a definite article, that articular noun is the subject. Otherwise, whichever noun comes first is the subject.

3 τί με λέγεις ἀγαθόν (Mark 10:18). Verbs of "teaching" (e.g., διδάσκω) and "asking" (e.g., αἰτέω) take *two* accusatives, both of which are objects of the verb.

5.1.3 Genitive Case

The genitive case often indicates some sort of dependent or derivative status of a term in relation to the preceding term. Originally, this case signified *motion away from*, or more generally, *separation from*. But in the GNT, one of the most common uses of the genitive is to express possession (e.g., "the people *of God*"). The "genitive of possession" is strictly defined in terms of belonging (i.e., "the people belonging to God"). There are also many other uses of the genitive, such as the so-called genitive of kind, which specifies the genus of a thing (e.g., "baptism of repentance").

5.1.4 Dative Case

The dative case originally signified *rest in* a place. In the GNT, the dative case is often used to specify an indirect object, that is, to indicate the person or thing to, or for, which something is done or given (e.g., "I will repay all things *to you*").[4]

The means by which, or the cause through which, something is done can also be expressed by the dative case. For example, "I have baptized you *with* (i.e., by means of) water."[5] This is termed the "instrumental" dative. It expresses an action performed by something. The dative case is also used after certain Greek verbs where one would not expect them based on English usage.[6] As a starting point, when you meet the dative, try using helping words such as "to," "for," "in," or "with."

5.1.5 Vocative Case

This is the case of direct address (e.g., "O brothers and sisters," "O foolish Galatians" [Gal 3:1]). Words in the vocative case are always set off by commas. Sometimes words in the vocative are introduced with ὦ (O!). The vocative case is often identical to the nominative case.

5.2 DECLINING NOUNS

To decline a noun means to modify its endings in order to specify its respective cases. Oscar Wilde once humorously declared, "I would rather decline two drinks

---

4 πάντα ἀποδώσω σοι (Matt 18:26).

5 ἐγὼ ἐβάπτισα ὑμᾶς ὕδατι (Mark 1:8).

6 Among these verbs that take an object in the dative case are the following:

ἀκολουθῶ + dat.	I follow sby
ἀποκρίνομαι + dat.	I answer sby
διακονῶ + dat.	I serve sby
ἐγγίζω + dat.	I draw near to sby/sthg
ἐπιτιμῶ + dat.	I rebuke sby/sthg
πιστεύω + dat.	I believe sby/in sthg

than one Greek noun." But take no notice of Wilde. He obviously did not spend as much time learning Greek as you have!

In the paradigms (tables) that follow, the names of the cases will be abbreviated with the letters N, G, D, A, V, as follows:

N Nominative
G Genitive
D Dative
A Accusative
V Vocative

One of the most important implications of these case endings is that the Greek language exhibits a much greater freedom of word order than does English. Written language, by its very nature, involves the arrangement of words, one after the other, in linear sequences. The Greek declensional endings allowed Greek authors to order words in a great variety of ways according to the emphases and interests of the author. In contrast, English words – with their minimal inflection – must follow a much more predictable order.

Why is this important? If you begin translating a Greek sentence word by word into English, your translation will probably not make good sense. Before translating, you must *first analyze the Greek sentence grammatically*. This is how to begin:

1. determine whether there is an explicit subject (in nominative case)
2. identify the main verb
3. determine whether there is a direct object (in accusative case)
4. determine whether there is an indirect object (in dative case)
5. identify words that coordinate clauses like καί, δέ, ἀλλά, μέν, ἵνα, ὥστε, and so on.

If you practice these skills now, while the sentences for Greek translation are simple, you will be much better prepared to translate the longer, more complicated sentences that you will encounter later in this book and in the GNT.

5.3 MASCULINE NOUNS OF THE SECOND DECLENSION

With a few exceptions, all of the nouns in the second declension are masculine or neuter in grammatical gender.[7] The nominative form of masculine nouns ends in -ος, whereas the nominative form of neuter nouns ends in -ον. For example, ἄνθρωπος ("person") and λόγος ("message") are masculine and τέκνον ("child") and

[7] The following second declension words are feminine: νόσος, ψῆφος, ὁδός, σύνοδος, τροφός, ἄβυσσος, ἀλάβαστρος (Mark 14:3), ἄμφοδον, βάτος, ληνός (Rev 14:20), στάμνος, and τρίβος.

ἔργον ("deed") are neuter. In the case of second declension nouns, the ending of the lexical form will tell you whether a given noun is masculine or neuter (e.g., κόσμος is masculine; τέκνον is neuter). The masculine nouns of the second declension are declined according to the following endings:

	Singular	*Plural*
N	-ος	-οι
G	-ου	-ων
D	-ῳ	-οις
A	-ον	-ους
V	-ε	-οι

Thus, if we decline the masculine second declension noun κόσμος ("world"), the following paradigm is formed:

⊕	*Sg.*		*Pl.*	
N	κόσμος	(**kos**-mos)[8]	κόσμοι	(**kos**-mi)
G	κόσμου	(**kos**-mou)	κόσμων	(**kos**-mon)
D	κόσμῳ	(**kos**-mo)	κόσμοις	(**kos**-mis)
A	κόσμον	(**kos**-mon)	κόσμους	(**kos**-mus)
V	κόσμε	(**kos**-me)	κόσμοι	(**kos**-mi)

Remember, the iota subscript in the dative singular is only an editorial mark. In a real manuscript, the word κόσμῳ would be written without an iota subscript or accents like:[9]

κοcμω

Nonetheless, the editorial addition of the iota subscript helps us distinguish the singular *dative* case ending of the noun from the first-person, present active indicative ending of a verb like λύω.

5.4 NEUTER NOUNS OF THE SECOND DECLENSION

Many of the endings of neuter nouns of the second declension are the same as the masculine nouns. You should take note of the differences as they occur in the

[8] Remember that before a voiced consonant (i.e., β, γ, δ, λ, μ, ν, ρ), σ is pronounced like ζ.

[9] Note that in many uncial manuscripts, both medial sigma and final sigma are written like **c**. This is called a *lunate* sigma.

nominative singular and in the nominative plural and accusative plural.

	Singular	*Plural*
N	-ον	-α
G	-ου	-ων
D	-ῳ	-οις
A	-ον	-α
V	-ον	-α

Thus, if we decline the neuter second declension noun τέκνον ("child"), the following paradigm results:

⊕	*Sg.*	*Pl.*
N	τέκνον (**tek**-non)	τέκνα (**tek**-na)
G	τέκνου (**tek**-nou)	τέκνων (**tek**-non)
D	τέκνῳ (**tek**-no)	τέκνοις (**tek**-nis)
A	τέκνον (**tek**-non)	τέκνα (**tek**-na)
V	τέκνον (**tek**-non)	τέκνα (**tek**-na)

Note the following for second declension nouns:

- The nominative, accusative, and vocative endings of neuter nouns are identical in the singular and in the plural forms.
- Even though many of the declensional endings for masculine and neuter nouns are the same, the grammatical gender of the noun will allow you to distinguish masculine nouns from neuter nouns. For example, the lexical form (which is by definition in the nominative case) of τέκνον ends in -ον. Therefore, you know it must be a neuter noun. The *cases* of τέκνον can either be nominative or accusative, depending on the literary context, but its *gender* can only be neuter. It cannot be masculine accusative.
- The final α in the ultima of the nominative and accusative plural neuter noun is always short (e.g., τέκνα). As the following section demonstrates, this information is helpful when thinking about the position of accents on nouns.

5.5 ACCENTING NOUNS

5.5.1 General Rule: The general rules for accenting nouns do not determine which syllable must be accented. Instead, they determine which syllables *cannot* be accented; for the general rules for accenting nouns, see Sections 2.4.1–2.4.10.

5.5.2 The accent will remain on the same syllable as in the nominative singular form, except when the general rules require the accent to move. Thus, the *accent on the nominative singular form of nouns must be memorized as part of the spelling of the word*. It cannot be predicted.

5.5.3 In both the first and second declension, *when* the ultima (i.e., the last syllable) takes an acute accent in the nominative singular form, it will change to a circumflex accent in the genitive and dative forms, in both the singular and plural. Elsewhere, the ultima will carry an acute accent (or grave, when followed by another word). This rule also applies to the definite article (Section 5.7).

5.6 PROCLITICS AND ENCLITICS

5.6.1 Proclitics

A proclitic is a word that "leans forward" on to the word which *follows* to such an extent that it usually has no accent. The nominative forms of the definite articles (ὁ, ἡ, οἱ, αἱ), some conjunctions (εἰ, ὡς), prepositions (εἰς, ἐκ, ἐν), and negative particles (οὐ, οὐκ, οὐχ) are all proclitics. For this reason, you should pronounce them as if they were joined to the word that follows.

5.6.2 Enclitics

An "enclitic" is a word that "leans on" the word which *precedes* to such an extent that it appears to have no accent of its own. Enclitics can be one- or two-syllable words. As previously discussed, disyllabic forms of εἰμί (i.e., not second sg.) are also enclitics (Section 3.10.1). Many pronouns (μοῦ, μοί, μέ, σοῦ, σοί, σέ, see Sections 8.1–2), indefinite adverbs (πού, ποτέ, πώς), and indefinite forms of τις (see Section 15.5) are also enclitics and thus often appear in texts without accents. They normally throw their accents off onto the preceding word, according to the following rules:

1. If the previous word has an accent on the antepenult or a *circumflex* on the penult, then the word will receive an additional accent on its ultima from the enclitic (e.g., ἄνθρωπός μου, πνεῦμά ἐστιν, εἶχέν τις).
2. If the preceding word has an *acute* accent on the penult, then a monosyllabic enclitic will simply lose its accent (e.g., ὁ λόγος μου/προσώπου σου), but a disyllabic enclitic (e.g., ἐστίν) will retain its accent (e.g., ὁ λόγος ἐστὶν ἀγαθός).
3. When an enclitic begins a clause, it must retain its accent (e.g., τινὲς δὲ τῶν ἐκεῖ . . .).

4. When enclitics shift their accents to the ultima of the previous word, the accent remains acute. It does not change to a grave accent (e.g., τὸν ἄγγελόν μου).

5.7 THE DEFINITE ARTICLE

The definite article ("the") always agrees with the noun it modifies: Masculine nouns are preceded by masculine articles, feminine nouns by feminine articles, and neuter nouns by neuter articles. Thus, if you are ever unsure of the gender of a particular noun, the preceding definite article will indicate the gender of the word in question.

Because articles must agree with their noun in gender, number, and case, there are twenty-four possible forms of the article! Fortunately, the endings of definite articles are the same or very similar to their corresponding second declension nouns. In this lesson, we will learn the forms of masculine and neuter articles.

	Sg.				*Pl.*			
⊕	*m.*		*nt.*		*m.*		*nt.*	
N	ὁ	(o)	τό	(to)	οἱ	(i)	τά	(ta)
G	τοῦ	(tou)	τοῦ	(tou)	τῶν	(ton)	τῶν	(ton)
D	τῷ	(to)	τῷ	(to)	τοῖς	(tis)	τοῖς	(tis)
A	τόν	(ton)	τό	(to)	τούς	(tous)	τά	(ta)

The nominative forms of the masculine and feminine definite article (e.g., ὁ, ἡ, οἱ, αἱ) are proclitics. They have no accent because each is read so closely with the following word as to *lean* on it and rely on its accent.

Also bear in mind that the acute accent (ʹ) on these articles will always become grave (ˋ) when followed by another word (e.g., τὸ τέκνον). Of course, in real Greek text, the article is *always* followed by another word. The following example illustrates how these definite articles can be added to masculine and neuter nouns of the second declension:

	Sg.		*Pl.*	
	m.	*nt.*	*m.*	*nt.*
N	ὁ κόσμος (the world)	τὸ τέκνον (the child)	οἱ κόσμοι (the worlds)	τὰ τέκνα (the children)
G	τοῦ κόσμου (of the world)	τοῦ τέκνου (of the child)	τῶν κόσμων (of the worlds)	τῶν τέκνων (of the children)
D	τῷ κόσμῳ (to/for the world)	τῷ τέκνῳ (to/for the child)	τοῖς κόσμοις (to/for the worlds)	τοῖς τέκνοις (to/for the children)
A	τὸν κόσμον (the world)	τὸ τέκνον (the child)	τοὺς κόσμους (the worlds)	τὰ τέκνα (the children)

The article is sometimes used in Greek where it is not required in English. For example, it is often used with abstract nouns and proper names. For example, ὁ Ἰησοῦς (o-i-i-**sous**) is translated "Jesus," not "*the* Jesus." Similarly, ὁ Παῦλος (o-**pav**-los) is translated "Paul," not "*the* Paul."

5.8 IMPORTANT USES OF ὅτι

The term ὅτι can have a variety of meanings, as outlined below. Its meaning must always be determined on the basis of context alone.

5.8.1 ὅτι As a Marker of Indirect Speech

Verbs of saying introducing indirect speech are often followed by the conjunction ὅτι ("that"). In English, we find similar constructions:

> εἶπόν σοι ὅτι εἶδόν σε...
> ("I said to you that I saw you..." [John 1:50])

5.8.2 ὅτι As a Marker of Direct Speech

The conjunction ὅτι can also be used to introduce *direct* speech following verbs of saying. In such cases, ὅτι should be left *untranslated*, with quotation marks following:

> ἀμὴν ἀμὴν λέγω σοι ὅτι ὃ οἴδαμεν λαλοῦμεν...
> ("Truly, truly I say to you, – 'What we know we say...' " [John 3:11])

5.8.3 Causal ὅτι

The conjunction ὅτι can also have a causal use, meaning "because" or "since."[10]

> καὶ οὐκ ἤφιεν λαλεῖν τὰ δαιμόνια, ὅτι ᾔδεισαν αὐτόν.
> ("And he did not allow the demons to speak because they knew him." [Mark 1:34])

> Ῥαχὴλ ... οὐκ ἤθελεν παρακληθῆναι, ὅτι οὐκ εἰσίν.
> ("Rachael...refused to be consoled because they [her children] are no more." [Matt 2:18, quoting Jer 31:15])

[10] Other causal conjunctions include διότι ("because"), ἐπεί, and ἐπειδή ("since").

5.8.4 ὅτι Marking Explanatory Clauses ("that . . . ").

αὕτη δέ ἐστιν ἡ κρίσις ὅτι τὸ φῶς ἐλήλυθεν εἰς τὸν κόσμον καὶ ἠγάπησαν οἱ ἄνθρωποι μᾶλλον τὸ σκότος ἢ τὸ φῶς·
("And this is the judgment, that the light has come into the world and people loved darkness more than the light." [John 3:19])

5.8.5 Verbs of thinking, knowing, believing, hoping, and hearing are often followed by ὅτι, as they are in English (e.g., "I think *that* . . . ", "I know *that* . . . ", "I hear *that* . . . "):

οἴδαμεν ὅτι ἀπὸ θεοῦ ἐλήλυθας διδάσκαλος
("We know that you are a teacher come from God." [John 3:2])

μεμαρτύρηκα ὅτι οὗτός ἐστιν ὁ υἱὸς τοῦ θεοῦ.
("I have testified that this is the Son of God." [John 1:34])

θεωρῶ ὅτι προφήτης εἶ σύ
("I see that you are a prophet."[John 4:19])

5.9 THE FUNCTION OF PREPOSITIONS

Prepositions are little words like "in," "on," and "for", which link together other words in a sentence to specify how they are interrelated. They are normally positioned before nouns and pronouns and supply information about time, place, or direction.

In Greek, prepositions are followed by the genitive, dative, or accusative case, depending on the preposition and the intended meaning. Some prepositions consistently take one particular case. For example, ἐν ("in") is always followed by the dative case. Other prepositions can be followed by two, or even three, different cases, acquiring different meanings according to the case that follows and the literary context.

Prepositional phrases can function like attributive adjectives. For example the phrase οἱ ἐν τῇ οἰκίᾳ ἄνθρωποι means the "people *in the house*." Similarly, it is very common to find a definite article followed by a prepositional phrase *without* any accompanying noun. For example, οἱ ἐν τῇ οἰκίᾳ also means "the (people) *in the house*."

The use of prepositions is among the most idiomatic features of all languages, including Greek. The vocabulary lists in this text will suggest some typical glosses (i.e., English translations) for each preposition to help you get started. However, *these English glosses cannot be substituted mechanically for a given preposition*. In actual fact, any Greek preposition can be rendered into many different English prepositions depending on the context. Thus, one must always consider carefully the literary context and idiomatic English usage before translating them. In actual pratice, it will often be necessary for you to consult a lexicon to determine the most appropriate translation for a preposition in a specific Greek text.

5.9.1 Elision

When prepositions precede a word beginning with a vowel, they normally undergo elision. Elision is the deletion of a vowel at the end of a word before a word that begins with a vowel. An apostrophe marks the place where the vowel was deleted, or elided (e.g., ἀλλ᾽ ἐγώ = ἀλλὰ ἐγώ). Many of the most frequent prepositions undergo elision:

ἀπό → ἀπ᾽
διά → δι᾽
ἐπί → ἐπ᾽
μετά → μετ᾽
παρά → παρ᾽
ὑπό → ὑπ᾽

When a preposition such as ἐπί is followed by a word beginning with a vowel carrying a rough breathing, the preposition elides as above and the remaining stop becomes a fricative (e.g., ἐφ᾽ ἑαυτοῦ).

ἀπό → ἀφ᾽
ἐπί → ἐφ᾽
μετά → μεθ᾽
ὑπό → ὑφ᾽

As you know, words in Hellenistic Greek were never aspirated with an "h" sound, nor, of course, did they ever carry rough breathing marks (which are editorial marks). However, *the historical phenomenon of aspiration is preserved as a kind of "phantom" in the Hellenistic practice of aspirating stop consonants during elision* (cf. 2.7).

5.10 THE USE OF PREPOSITIONS WITH CASES

Now that we have learned about Greek cases, let us review some of the prepositions you have already memorized. Some prepositions consistently take one particular case. For example, ἐγγύς is always followed by the genitive case. Other prepositions can be followed by two, or even three, different cases. These prepositions acquire different meanings according to the case that follows. So far, we have learned the following prepositions:

- ἀνά (a-**na**) (w. acc.), each, each one, apiece
- διά (dhi-**a**) (w. gen.) through, by means of
  (w. acc.) because of, on account of
- κατά (ka-**ta**) (w. gen.) against, down from
  (w. acc.) according to
- ἐγγύς (e^{ng}-**gis**) (w. gen.) near, close to
- μετά (me-**ta**) (w. gen.) with
  (w. acc.) after (temporal), behind (spatial)
- πέραν (**pe**-ran) (w. gen.), beyond, across to, on the other side

5.11 THE USE OF PREPOSITIONS TO EXPRESS MOTION AND LOCATION

5.11.1 Motion and Location

Motion *toward* a place is often expressed by a preposition followed by the *accusative* case. For example:

πρός ("toward")
εἰς ("into")
ἐπί ("onto")
παρά ("[motion] to [a position] beside")[11]

Motion *away from* a place, or separation from something, is often expressed by a preposition followed by the *genitive* case.[12] For example:

ἀπό ("[away] from")
ἐκ ("from, out of")
παρά[13] ("from")

The place where something is situated, sitting, or located is often expressed by a preposition followed by the dative case.[14] For example:

ἐν ("in")
ἐπί ("on")
παρά ("beside," "with")[15]

---

[11] E.g., παριπάτει παρὰ τὴν θάλασσαν ("he walks beside the sea").
[12] This is termed the *ablative* use.
[13] E.g., ἄνθρωπος παρὰ τοῦ θεοῦ ("a person from God").
[14] This is termed the *locative* use.
[15] E.g., μένουσιν παρ' αὐτῷ ("they remain with him").

5.11.2 Genitive Expressing Agency

The person by whom the action of a passive verb is performed is expressed by the preposition ὑπό ("by"), indicating *agency.* This use of ὑπό is followed by the *genitive* case (e.g., ὑπὸ αὐτοῦ, "*by* him").

5.12 CASE ENDINGS EXPRESSING TIME

The case endings can be used, without prepositions, to express different meanings of time.

5.12.1 The accusative expresses *duration* of time:

δύο ἡμέρας (acc. pl.)	("for two days")
μένουσιν τὴν ἡμέραν ἐκείνην (acc. sg.)	("they remained that day")
καὶ ἦν ἐν τῇ ἐρήμῳ τεσσεράκοντα ἡμέρας (acc. pl.)	("he was in the desert for forty days" [Mark 1:13])

5.12.2 The dative case expresses the time *when* something happens (i.e., often a specific point in time).

τῇ τρίτῃ ἡμέρᾳ (dat. sg.) ("on the third day")

5.12.3 The genitive case expresses the time *within which* something happens (e.g., the thief comes *in* the night): "You must say that his disciples came *during* the night (gen., νυκτός) and stole him away while we were asleep." (Matt 28:13) (i.e., at some point during the whole night, then stole him).

5.13 GENITIVE OF COMPARISON

When two things are compared with one another, a comparative adjective is often used, followed by a noun in the genitive. This is termed the genitive of comparison, as the following example illustrates:

ὁ ἰσχυρότερός μου
"The one who is mightier *than I* " (Mark 1:7)

5.14 PARADIGM OF THE PROPER NAME "JESUS"

The proper name "Jesus" (i-i-**sous**) is the Greek translation equivalent of the Hebrew name "Joshua." Thus, the name of the sixth book of the Bible in the Septuagint is Ἰησοῦς, "Jesus"! The paradigm for "Jesus" is somewhat irregular because the root of this proper name actually ends in -ο (√ ιησο). This final -ο contracts with the second declension endings as follows:

	paradigm	*uncontracted form*
N	Ἰησοῦς	[Ἰησο-ος]
G	Ἰησοῦ	[Ἰησο-ου]
D	Ἰησοῦ	[Ἰησο-ῳ → Ἰησοω → Ἰησου]
A	Ἰησοῦν	[Ἰησο-ον]
V	Ἰησοῦ	[Ἰησο-ε]

Notice that the genitive, dative, and vocative forms are identical. Given the fact that this proper name often occurs with a definite article in Greek, the case of the article will allow you to determine the case of the name, as will the context.

5.15 VOCABULARY TO BE MEMORIZED

1. ἀμνός, ὁ (a-**mnos**), lamb
2. ἄνθρωπος, ὁ (**an**-thro-pos), a person (human being) of either sex (cf. German "Mensch"), but in context it often refers to a man
3. ἔργον, τό (**er**-gon), work, deed, task
4. θάνατος, ὁ (**tha**-na-tos), death (cf. "thanatology")
5. θεωρῶ (-έω) (the-o-**ro**), I see, watch, observe, perceive
6. ἐπαύριον (e-**pav**-ri-on), the next day (adv.)
7. ἴδε, ἴδου/ἰδού, ἴδετε[16] (**i**-dhe, i-**dhou**, **i**-dhe-te), look! see! (pointing word)
8. ἵνα (**i**-na) (conj.), in order that; that (explaining something)[17]
9. κύριος, ὁ (**ki**-ri-os), sir, master of a household; the LORD, as a designation for God (the LXX translates the divine name, YHWH, as ὁ κύριος); as applied to Jesus, the term κύριος is intentionally polysemous (cf. MGr, in which κύριος means "Mr.")
10. οὐρανός, ὁ (ou-ra-**nos**), sky, heaven[18]
11. σάββατον, τό (**sav**-va-ton), the Sabbath, week (John 20:1)[19] (cf. MGr, in which σάββατον means "Saturday")

---

[16] This word is accented with an acute on its ultima when it functions as a demonstrative particle or as an interjection, as is frequently the case in the GNT (e.g., Lk 17:23; Gal 1:20). It was originally the 2 aor. mid. impv. of ὁράω (i.e., ἰδοῦ).

[17] This is known as the *explanatory* or *epexegetic* ἵνα.

[18] Also used of God to avoid mention of the sacred name (e.g., "kingdom of heaven"); cf. Uranus, which is the "heavenly" planet.

[19] The word often appears in the plural form when the singular is intended, especially the dat. pl. τοῖς σάββασιν ("on the Sabbath").

12. τέκνον, τό (**tek**-non), child
13. τόπος, ὁ (**to**-pos), a place, location (cf. topography, toponym)
14. νόμος, ὁ (**no**-mos), the Torah, law
15. ὀπίσω (o-**pi**-so) (with gen.), after, behind
16. ὅπου (**o**-pou), where (non-interrogative)

6.

First Declension and the Definite Article

6.1 THE FIRST DECLENSION

In this lesson we shall study the first declension. Most of the nouns in this declension are feminine in gender. Feminine nouns of the first declension can be grouped into three classes, namely:

1. those having the vowel -η in the ending;
2. those having the vowel -α in the ending;
3. those having a mixed -α/-η pattern in the ending.

These different vowels in the endings occur only in the singular forms. The plural endings are identical in all three classes. We will refer to these three classes of first declension nouns as follows:

1. η-pure (also known as η-stem)
2. α-pure (also known as long α-stem)
3. α-impure (also known as short α-stem)

The first declension also includes a group of *masculine* nouns ending in -ης and -ας in the nominative singular: for example, μαθητής (disciple), νεανίας (young man) (cf. Section 6.7).

6.2 η-PURE NOUNS

In this class of nouns, the vowel in the singular endings is always -η.

Figure: Funerary relief (ancient Neapolis).

	Sg.	*Pl.*
N	-η	-αι
G	-ης	-ῶν
D	-ῃ	-αις
A	-ην	-ας
V	-η	-αι

Our example word is φωνή ("voice"):

⊕	*Sg.*		*Pl.*	
N	φωνή	(fo-**ni**)	φωναί	(fo-**ne**)
G	φωνῆς	(fo-**nis**)	φωνῶν	(fo-**non**)
D	φωνῇ	(fo-**ni**)	φωναῖς	(fo-**nes**)
A	φωνήν	(fo-**nin**)	φωνάς	(fo-**nas**)
V	φωνή	(fo-**ni**)	φωναί	(fo-**ne**)

Accents

- First declension nouns always carry a circumflex accent on the ultima in the genitive *plural* form, regardless of where the accent falls in the nominative singular (e.g., διαθήκη → διαθηκῶν).[1]
- The α of the accusative plural ending (-ας) of all first declension nouns is always *long*, which prevents the antepenult from ever being accented.

6.3 α-PURE NOUNS

First declension noun stems ending in ε, ι, or ρ have an α (instead of an η) in the singular endings. These nouns have slightly different endings. In this class of nouns, the vowel in the singular endings is usually a long α:[2]

	Sg.	*Pl.*
N	-α	-αι
G	-ας	-ῶν
D	-ᾳ	-αις
A	-αν	-ας
V	-α	-αι

[1] The genitive plural of the first declension is always accented with a circumflex because -ων is actually a contraction of -άων.

[2] There are some α-pure, first declension nouns that have a short α in the nominative, accusative, and vocative singular. For example, ἀλήθεια (in this lesson's vocabulary), ἀσθένεια (cf. Chapter 17), and διάνοια (Chapter 19) all belong to a group of abstract nouns ending in -εια or -οια, which are derived from third declension adjectives (e.g., ἀληθής, -ές; ἀσθενής, -ές). A very small number of first declension stems end in -ρ but are declined according to the α-impure pattern (e.g., μάχαιρα, -ης; πλήμμυρα, -ης).

Notice that the genitive singular and the accusative plural of α-pure nouns have the same ending. One can distinguish -ας (gen. sg.) from -ας (acc. pl.) by the article preceding the noun: Is the article τῆς or τάς? (see section 6.5) In the absense of an article, you must rely on context to distinguish these endings. Our example word is ἡμέρα ("day"):

⊕	*Sg.*		*Pl.*	
N	ἡμέρα	(i-**me**-ra)	ἡμέραι	(i-**me**-re)
G	ἡμέρας	(i-**me**-ras)	ἡμερῶν	(i-me-**ron**)
D	ἡμέρᾳ	(i-**me**-ra)	ἡμέραις	(i-**me**-res)
A	ἡμέραν	(i-**me**-ran)	ἡμέρας	(i-**me**-ras)
V	ἡμέρα	(i-**me**-ra)	ἡμέραι	(i-**me**-re)

6.4 α-IMPURE NOUNS

Noun stems ending in either σ, consonant blends (ξ, ζ), double consonants (e.g., λλ, σσ), or αιν- have mixed endings, with α in the nominative, accusative, and vocative, and η in the genitive and dative:[3]

	Sg.	*Pl.*
N	-α	-αι
G	-ης	-ῶν
D	-ῃ	-αις
A	-αν	-ας
V	-α	-αι

Our example word of an α-impure noun is δόξα ("fame, honor, glory"):

⊕	*Sg.*		*Pl.*	
N	δόξα	(**dho**-ksa)	δόξαι	(**dho**-kse)
G	δόξης	(**dho**-ksis)	δοξῶν	(dho-**kson**)
D	δόξῃ	(**dho**-ksi)	δόξαις	(**dho**-kses)
A	δόξαν	(**dho**-ksan)	δόξας	(**dho**-ksas)
V	δόξα	(**dho**-ksa)	δόξαι	(**dho**-kse)

- Note: In the α-impure class, α in the singular ending is usually *short*.

[3] Phrased differently, nouns where the nom. sg. ends in -α and is not immediately preceded by the letters ε, ι, or ρ have mixed endings.

6.5 DEFINITE ARTICLE FOR FEMININE NOUNS OF THE FIRST DECLENSION

The definite article ("the") in the first declension is the same for all three classes of nouns. It follows the pattern of the η-pure class. Notice the rough breathing (added by editors) in the nominative forms:

	Sg.		*Pl.*	
N	ἡ	(i)	αἱ	(e)
G	τῆς	(tis)	τῶν	(ton)
D	τῇ	(ti)	ταῖς	(tes)
A	τήν	(tin)	τάς	(tas)

6.6 COMPLETE PARADIGM OF THE DEFINITE ARTICLE

If we combine the paradigm of the feminine article with those of the masculine and neuter articles, the following paradigm is formed:

		Sg.			*Pl.*	
⊕	*m.*	*fm.*	*nt.*	*m.*	*fm.*	*nt.*
N	ὁ	ἡ	τό	οἱ	αἱ	τά
G	τοῦ	τῆς	τοῦ	τῶν	τῶν	τῶν
D	τῷ	τῇ	τῷ	τοῖς	ταῖς	τοῖς
A	τόν	τήν	τό	τούς	τάς	τά

The addition of the definite article to first and second declension nouns produces the following table:

		Sg.			*Pl.*	
	m.	*fm.*	*nt.*	*m.*	*fm.*	*nt.*
N	ὁ κόσμος	ἡ φωνή	τὸ τέκνον	οἱ κόσμοι	αἱ φωναί	τὰ τέκνα
G	τοῦ κόσμου	τῆς φωνῆς	τοῦ τέκνου	τῶν κόσμων	τῶν φωνῶν	τῶν τέκνων
D	τῷ κόσμῳ	τῇ φωνῇ	τῷ τέκνῳ	τοῖς κόσμοις	ταῖς φωναῖς	τοῖς τέκνοις
A	τὸν κόσμον	τὴν φωνήν	τὸ τέκνον	τοὺς κόσμους	τὰς φωνάς	τὰ τέκνα

6.7. MASCULINE NOUNS OF THE FIRST DECLENSION

Within the first declension, there is an important group of *masculine* nouns. Nouns in this group include some professions, such as μαθητής ("disciple"), προφήτης (*prophet*) and κλέπτης ("thief"), and many (masculine) proper names, such as Ἰωάννης ("John"). All of these nouns take masculine articles. However, their endings are very similar to the endings of feminine, first declension nouns:

	Sg.	*Pl.*
N	-ης	-αι
G	-ου	-ῶν
D	-ῃ	-αις
A	-ην	-ας
V	-η/-α[4]	-αι

Our example word is μαθητής ("disciple"). Note that in this group of nouns, the article often has a *different* form than the ending on the noun. Nonetheless, they still agree in gender, number, and case:

⊕	*Sg.*		*Pl.*	
N	ὁ μαθητής	(o-ma-thi-**tis**)	οἱ μαθηταί	(i-ma-thi-**te**)
G	τοῦ μαθητοῦ	(tou ma-thi-**tou**)[5]	τῶν μαθητῶν	(ton ma-thi-**ton**)
D	τῷ μαθητῇ	(to ma-thi-**ti**)	τοῖς μαθηταῖς	(tis ma-thi-**tes**)
A	τὸν μαθητήν	(ton ma-thi-**tin**)	τοὺς μαθητάς	(tous ma-thi-**tas**)
V	(ὦ) μαθητά	(ma-thi-**ta**)	(ὦ) μαθηταί	(ma-thi-**te**)

As you might expect, masculine nouns ending in ε, ι, or ρ also have stems ending with α instead of η. We can use νεανίας ("young man") as an example:

N νεανίας (ne-a-**ni**-as)
G νεανίου
D νεανίᾳ
A νεανίαν
V νεανία

Some proper names also fall under this category: for example, Ἀνδρέας, -έου ("Andrew"), Ἠσαΐας, -ΐου ("Isaiah").[6]

6.8 SUBSTANTIVE USE OF THE DEFINITE ARTICLE

The definite article was originally a demonstrative pronoun. This explains why the definite article can function substantively like a noun and even substitute for personal pronouns. For example, when ὁ, ἡ, and οἱ are not followed by a noun, they can actually be translated as "he," "she," and "they," respectively. Likewise, ὁ δέ is often found in texts meaning "and he," or "but he." Similarly, ὁ μέν … ὁ δέ are frequently used to coordinate two sentences, with the meaning "the one … the other …," just as οἱ μέν … οἱ δέ … means "some … others …"

[4] The voc. ends in short -α if the nom. sg. ends in -της, but otherwise ends in -η.
[5] This -ου ending is borrowed from the second declension.
[6] Note many proper names of Hebrew origin have -ᾶ as a genitive ending: e.g., Κηφᾶς, Κηφᾶ; Ἰωνᾶς, Ἰωνᾶ; Βαρναβᾶς, Βαρναβᾶ; Ἰούδας, Ἰούδα (both "Judah, Judas"); Σατανᾶς, Σατανᾶ.

6.9 ACCENTING FIRST DECLENSION NOUNS

When the ultima of a nominative singular first declension noun is accented with an acute accent, this accent will change to a circumflex accent in the genitive and dative forms (sg. and pl.). Elsewhere it will be acute (or grave, when followed by another word).

But, as noted above, in the case of the genitive plural form, the ultima is always accented and always carries a circumflex, regardless of where the accent occurs in other cases, because -ων is actually a contraction of -άων.

	Sg.	*Pl.*
N	φωνή	φωναί
G	φωνῆς	φωνῶν
D	φωνῇ	φωναῖς
A	φωνήν	φωνάς
V	φωνή	φωναί

6.10 VOCABULARY TO BE MEMORIZED

1. ἀδελφός, ὁ (a-dhel-**fos**), brother; ἡ ἀδελφή, sister; in plural: οἱ ἀδελφοί, brothers and sisters[7]
2. ἀλήθεια, ἡ (a-**li**-thi-a),[8] truth
3. ἀληθινός, -ή, -όν (a-li-thi-**nos**), true, trustworthy, genuine (adj.)
4. ἁμαρτία, ἡ (a-mar-**ti**-a), sin, sinfulness
5. ἀπεκρίθη (a-pe-**kri**-thi), he answered (followed by the dat.)[9]
6. ἀρχή, ἡ (ar-**khi**), beginning
7. διὰ τοῦτο (dhi-**a tou**-to), therefore
8. δόξα, ἡ (**dho**-ksa), fame, glory, honor, reputation
9. ἐγώ (e-**go**), the pronoun "I" (nom.)
10. εἰς (is) (with acc.), into, to, as; the so-called telic use of εἰς expressed the goal or purpose of an action ("for")[10]
11. ἐκ, ἐξ[11] (ek, eks), (with gen.), from, out of

[7] BDAG, 18, (1).

[8] Contrary to the general rule, abstract α-pure nouns, which are derived from adjectives ending in -ης/-ες, and whose stems end in -ει, have short α in the ending (not long) in the singular nom. and acc. forms (Smyth 219.2 b). This allows the antepenult of ἀλήθεια to be accented.

[9] We will learn the full paradigm for this form later in this course (Chapter 17).

[10] In the GNT, εἰς is sometimes used interchangeably with ἐν, with the result that εἰς is used in contexts where one would expect ἐν ("in").

[11] ἐξ when followed by a word beginning with a vowel. The preposition ἐξ, like ἐν, εἰς, and ἐκ, is a *proclitic*. In other words, it has no accent because it is closely connected with the word that follows. Other proclitics include εἰ, ὡς, οὐ, οὐκ, ὁ, ἡ.

12. ἐκκλησία (ek-kli-**si**-a), an assembly of people, a Christian congregation of people[12]
13. ἐν (en), (with dat.), in, among, with;[13] when, while, during (concerning time when sthg happens)
14. ἐξουσία, ἡ (e-ksou-**si**-a), authority
15. ζωή, ἡ (zo-**i**), life
16. ἦν (in),[14] he/she/it was; this is the third sg. imperfect (past) form of εἰμί
17. ἴδιος (**i**-dhi-os), -α, -ον, one's own, belonging to one (cf. "idiomatic")
18. μαθητής (ma-thi-**tis**), ὁ, disciple, pupil (in Attic Greek)
19. ὁδός, ἡ, (o-**dhos**), road, journey, way (note the unexpected feminine gender)
20. οὐδέ (ou-**dhe**), not even, and not, nor; οὐδέ ... οὐδέ ... neither ... nor ...
21. παρά (pa-**ra**): (1) (with gen.) from, by, with; (2) (with dat.) with, in the presence of; (3) (with acc.) to beside, along
22. περί (pe-**ri**), (1) (with gen.) about, concerning; (with acc.) around
23. πρός (pros), (with acc.) toward, with (in John and Paul)
24. σκοτία, ἡ (sko-**ti**-a), darkness
25. φωνή, ἡ (fo-**ni**), voice, a sound

---

[12] The term ἐκκλησία is etymologically related to the noun κλῆσις ("calling," "vocation") and the verb καλῶ ("I call").

[13] When used by Paul and John, ἐν often designates a close personal relationship (cf. Gal 2:4, 3:8, 3:14; Phil 3:9, 4:1).

[14] The paradigm of this verb will be learned in Chapter 12.

7.

Adjectives, Demonstrative Pronouns, and Comparison

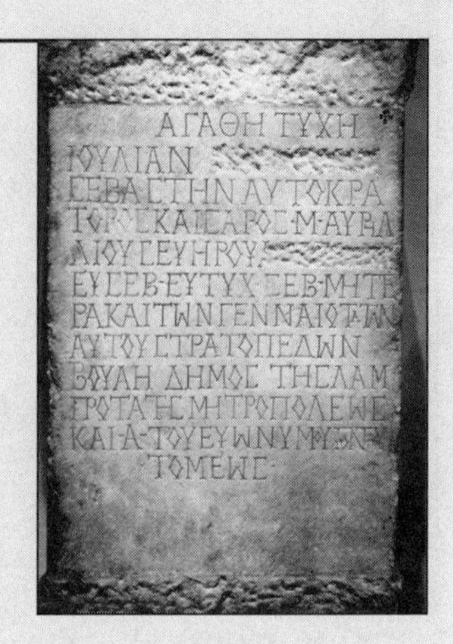

7.1 ADJECTIVES

As in the case of articles, adjectives must also agree with the nouns they modify (in gender, number, and case). Thus, many adjectives – like the definite article – have twenty-four possible forms. But do not despair: Most adjectives of the first and second declension have the same endings as second declension nouns. If we add the adjectival endings to the adjective ἀγαθός ("good"), the following paradigm is formed:

		Sg.			*Pl.*	
⊕	*m.*	*fm.*	*nt.*	*m.*	*fm.*	*nt.*
N	ἀγαθός	ἀγαθή	ἀγαθόν	ἀγαθοί	ἀγαθαί	ἀγαθά
G	ἀγαθοῦ	ἀγαθῆς	ἀγαθοῦ	ἀγαθῶν	ἀγαθῶν	ἀγαθῶν
D	ἀγαθῷ	ἀγαθῇ	ἀγαθῷ	ἀγαθοῖς	ἀγαθαῖς	ἀγαθοῖς
A	ἀγαθόν	ἀγαθήν	ἀγαθόν	ἀγαθούς	ἀγαθάς	ἀγαθά
V	ἀγαθέ	ἀγαθή	ἀγαθόν	ἀγαθοί	ἀγαθαί	ἀγαθά

First declension (feminine) forms of adjectives, like first declension nouns, can also be grouped into three classes: η-pure, α-pure, and α-impure. In the example above, ἀγαθή is an η-pure adjective. The feminine adjective δικαία (from δίκαιος, -α, -ον), meaning "just," is an example of an α-pure adjective. Because the stem of this adjective ends in ι (δικαι-), it must decline according to an α-pure, not η-pure, pattern. All adjectival stems ending in either ε, ι, or ρ will follow the α-pure pattern in the feminine singular. There is no need to reproduce the masculine and neuter endings here. The feminine (α-pure) forms of this adjective are as follows:

Figure: Inscription on stele: "For good fortune…" (Thrace, *IBM* II 176). Can you read the word *ajgaqhv* in the first line?

	Sg.	*Pl.*
N	δικαία	δίκαιαι
G	δικαίας	δικαίων[1]
D	δικαίᾳ	δικαίαις
A	δικαίαν	δικαίας
V	δικαία	δίκαιαι

The penult of the feminine singular forms is accented instead of the antepenult (which is the original position of the accent in the masc. form, δίκαιος), because the α of the α-pure endings is long. As you know, the antepenult cannot be accented when the ultima is long. Therefore, the accent must move to the penult. Because the -αι plural ending (in the nom. and voc. cases) is short, the accent can return to its original position, over the antepenult, in the nominative and vocative plural forms.

7.2 THE USE OF THE ADJECTIVE

When an adjective is associated with a definite article and a noun, the following rules apply:

7.2.1 Attributive Adjectives

Attributive adjectives directly modify nouns. *An attributive adjective is often preceded by a definite article.* There are three possible configurations, with little difference in meaning:

First Attributive Position

In this case, the attributive adjective is found *between* the article and the noun, as it often is in English syntax. This is termed the *first attributive position*:

ὁ ἀγαθὸς ἀδελφός ("the good brother")

Second Attributive Position

In this case, the attributive adjective *follows* the noun and has its own article. This is termed the *second attributive position*:

ὁ ἀδελφός ὁ ἀγαθὸς ("the good brother").

[1] Unlike first declension nouns, first declension adjectives are not accented automatically with a circumflex on the ultima.

This second example does not follow English word order. If you do not recognize this syntactical construction, you will not be able to translate it.

Third Attributive Position

In this case, the attributive adjective follows the noun and has its own article, but the noun lacks an article.[2] This is termed the *third attributive position*: for example, ἀδελφὸς ὁ ἀγαθός ("the good brother"). This construction is commonly used with proper names.

7.2.2 Predicate Adjectives

In this case, the adjective is *not* preceded by a definite article. As above, the adjective may come before or after the noun it modifies, with very little difference in meaning. For example:

a) First Predicate Position: ἀγαθὸς ὁ ἀδελφός
b) Second Predicate Position: ὁ ἀδελφὸς ἀγαθός

Both of these phrases mean "the brother (is) good," or "the brother who is good."[3] Note that in *neither* case is the adjective preceded by an article.

However, if the accompanying noun lacks an article (i.e., is anarthrous), then the situation is ambiguous. It then becomes necessary to rely on context to determine whether the adjective is functioning attributively or predicatively.

There is an exception to the above rules. As we shall see, a small group of special adjectives are found in the predicate position, even though they function attributively (e.g., οὗτος, ἐκεῖνος, ὅλος, and sometimes πᾶς). We will discuss these words in subsequent lessons.

7.2.3. Substantival Adjectives

A solitary adjective preceded by an article can also function as a noun. The article preceding the adjective turns it into a substantive. We have this same grammatical structure in English (e.g., Jesus came to save *the poor*).

- ὁ ἀγαθός "the good man"
- ἡ ἀγαθή: "the good woman"
- τὰ ἀγαθά (nt. pl.): "the good things"

---

2 This is more common with attributive participles than with adjectives.

3 E.g., μακάριοι οἱ πτωχοὶ τῷ πνεύματι (*Blessed* [are] the poor with respect to the human spirit [Matt 5:3]); καλὸν τὸ ἅλας (Salt [is] *good* [Mark 9:50]).

7.3 POSSESSIVE ADJECTIVES

Greek uses *possessive* adjectives to express ownership in the first- and second-person singular. They are declined like other first and second declension adjectives. These are frequently used for emphasis.

- ἐμός, ἐμή, ἐμόν (my, mine): e.g., ἐμὴ ἐξουσία (my authority)
- σός, σή, σόν (your, yours): e.g., σὸς μαθητής (your disciple)
- ἡμέτερος, -α, -ον (our)
- ὑμέτερος, -α, -ον (your [pl.])

Try not to confuse these *adjectival* forms with the possessive pronouns we will study in Chapter 8.

7.4 IRREGULARLY INFLECTED (HETEROCLITE) ADJECTIVES

Two common adjectives require special mention, namely πολύς ("much"/ pl. "many") and μέγας ("large, great"). The genitive and dative forms of these adjectives in the masculine and neuter, singular and plural, are completely regular, as are their feminine forms. However, the nominative and accusative singular forms of the masculine and neuter are *irregular*. Nonetheless, with a little attention, even these can be easily mastered.

πολύς, πολλή, πολύ ("much"/ pl. "many")

		Singular			*Plural*	
	m.	*fm.*	*nt.*	*m.*	*fm.*	*nt.*
N	πολύς	πολλή	πολύ	πολλοί	πολλαί	πολλά
G	πολλοῦ	πολλῆς	πολλοῦ	πολλῶν	πολλῶν	πολλῶν
D	πολλῷ	πολλῇ	πολλῷ	πολλοῖς	πολλαῖς	πολλοῖς
A	πολύν	πολλήν	πολύ	πολλούς	πολλάς	πολλά

1. πολύς, πολλή, and πολύ are used with non-countable nouns to mean "much":
   - γῆν πολλήν (much soil [Matt 13:5])
   - ἐν τρόμῳ πολλῷ (by much trembling [1 Cor 2:3])
2. πολλοί, πολλαί, πολλά, are used with countable nouns to mean "many":
   - πολλοὶ λεπροί (many lepers [Luke 4:27])
   - ὄχλοι πολλοί (many crowds [Luke 5:15]
   - δαιμόνια πολλά (many demons [Luke 8:30])
3. πολλοί by itself means "many people" (e.g., Luke 1:14); the English expression "hoi polloi" comes directly from οἱ πολλοί (i-pol-li).

4. πολλῷ μᾶλλον and οὐ πολλῷ μᾶλλον are very common expressions meaning "much more" and "not much more", respectively (e.g., Matt 6:30).
5. The comparative form of πολύς is πλείων or πλέων (m./fm.), πλέον (nt.) ("more")[4] and the superlative form is πλεῖστος, -η, -ον ("most").

μέγας, μεγάλη, μέγα **("large, great")**

	Singular			*Plural*		
	m.	*fm.*	*nt.*	*m.*	*fm.*	*nt.*
N	μέγας	μεγάλη	μέγα	μεγάλοι	μεγάλαι	μεγάλα
G	μεγάλου	μεγάλης	μεγάλου	μεγάλων	μεγάλων	μεγάλων
D	μεγάλῳ	μεγάλῃ	μεγάλῳ	μεγάλοις	μεγάλαις	μεγάλοις
A	μέγαν	μεγάλην	μέγα	μεγάλους	μεγάλας	μεγάλα

The comparative from of μέγας is μείζων, (m./fm.) μεῖζον (nt.) ("greater") and the superlative form is μέγιστος, -η, -ον ("greatest").[5]

7.5 DEMONSTRATIVE PRONOUNS: "THIS" AND "THAT"

οὗτος, αὕτη, τοῦτο **("this")**

The demonstrative pronoun, meaning "this," is declined like first and second declension nouns, with only a few changes to remember:

1. All forms begin with *taf* (τ), *except* for the nominative singular and plural forms of the masculine and feminine. These latter forms have a rough breathing mark (added by editors).
2. The feminine genitive plural form, τούτων, is identical to the masculine and neuter genitive plural forms.
3. The neuter singular, in the nominative and accusative, lacks a final *ni* (ν); it is τοῦτο, not τοῦτον.
4. The neuter plural form, ταῦτα, is also somewhat unexpected. It occurs frequently in texts with the meaning "these things."

	Sg.			*Pl.*		
⊕	*m.*	*fm.*	*nt.*	*m.*	*fm.*	*nt.*
N	οὗτος	αὕτη	τοῦτο	οὗτοι	αὗται	ταῦτα
G	τούτου	ταύτης	τούτου	τούτων	τούτων	τούτων
D	τούτῳ	ταύτῃ	τούτῳ	τούτοις	ταύταις	τούτοις
A	τοῦτον	ταύτην	τοῦτο	τούτους	ταύτας	ταῦτα

[4] This is a third declension adjective (see Chapter 15).

[5] μειζότερος ("greater") also began to occur in the first century.

ἐκεῖνος, ἐκείνη, ἐκεῖνο ("that")

The demonstrative pronoun, meaning "that," is declined like first and second declension nouns, with a few changes to remember.

1. The feminine genitive plural, ἐκείνων, is identical to the masculine and neuter genitive plural forms.
2. The neuter nominative and accusative singular forms of ἐκεῖνος also lack a final ν.

		Sg.			*Pl.*	
⊕	*m.*	*fm.*	*nt.*	*m.*	*fm.*	*nt.*
N	ἐκεῖνος	ἐκείνη	ἐκεῖνο	ἐκεῖνοι	ἐκεῖναι	ἐκεῖνα
G	ἐκείνου	ἐκείνης	ἐκείνου	ἐκείνων	ἐκείνων	ἐκείνων
D	ἐκείνῳ	ἐκείνῃ	ἐκείνῳ	ἐκείνοις	ἐκείναις	ἐκείνοις
A	ἐκεῖνον	ἐκείνην	ἐκεῖνο	ἐκείνους	ἐκείνας	ἐκεῖνα

ὅδε, ἥδε, τόδε ("this")

The demonstrative pronoun, ὅδε, is more emphatic than οὗτος but is used in the New Testament less frequently. Its paradigm is easy to form. Simply, take the paradigm of the definite article and add -δε (e.g., τοῦδε, τῷδε, τῇσδε, τῇδε, τήνδε, τάδε, etc.).

7.6 USE OF THE DEMONSTRATIVE PRONOUN

The demonstrative pronoun is not preceded by an article. It is employed in the *predicative* position but is translated as if it were in the attributive position. For example:

αὕτη ἡ ζωή ("this life")
ἐκεῖνος ὁ ἄνθρωπος ("that person")

Demonstrative pronouns can also be used in the place of a noun, especially in the case of people. For example:

οὗτός ἐστιν υἱός μου (Matt 3:17)
"this [person] is my son"

Thus, οὗτος and αὕτη can often be translated as "this man/this one" and "this woman," respectively, or as "he" and "she."

7.7 REFERENCE: COMPARATIVE AND SUPERLATIVE ADJECTIVES

There are two regular ways of forming comparative and superlative adjectives.

1. The usual way to form a comparative adjective is to add -τερος, -τερα, -τερον to the adjectival stem (declined like regular first and second declension adjectives);
2. The usual way to form a superlative adjective is to add -τατος, -τατη, -τατον to the adjectival stem (declined like regular first and second declension adjectives).

We can illustrate this using πιστός ("trustworthy") as an example:

1. Comparative ("more trustworthy"): πιστότερος, πιστοτέρα, πιστότερον
2. Superlative ("most trustworthy"): πιστότατος, πιστοτάτη, πιστότατον

The second way of forming comparatives and superlatives is to add -(ι)ων, -(ι)ονος, etc. to form a comparative adjective, and to add -ιστος, -ιστη, -ιστον to form a superlative: e.g., ταχύς ("fast"), ταχίων ("faster"), τάχιστος ("fastest"). In Chapter 15.8 we will study μείζων ("larger, greater"), which is the comparative of μέγας ("large, great"). Its superlative form is μέγιστος.

Some frequently occurring adjectives such as ἀγαθός and κακός have irregular comparatives and superlatives, as they do in English (cf. good → better → best; bad → worse → worst). This is also true for μέγας, μικρός, and πολύς.

7.8 VOCABULARY TO BE MEMORIZED

1. εἰ (i), if (do not confuse εἰ with the verb εἶ, meaning "you are")
2. εἶπεν (**i**-pen), he/she said, εἶπον, I said, they said; sometimes spelled, εἶπαν, they said (past tense of λέγω)
3. 'Ηλίας (I-**li**-as), Elijah
4. καθώς (ka-**thos**), just as, as

Adjectives

5. ἀγαθός, -ή, -όν (a-ga-**θos, -i,** -ον), good, beneficial, generous
6. ἄξιος, -α, -ον (**a**-ksi-os, -a, -on), worthy, deserving
7. δίκαιος, -α, -ον (**dhi**-ke-os, -a, -on), ethically just or fair, righteous, upright
8. ἕκαστος, -η, -ον (**e**-ka-stos, -i, -on), each, every

9. ἔρημος (m./fm.), -ον (nt.) (**e**-ri-mos, -on), deserted (adj. of two terminations);[6] in the GNT, this lexeme usually appears in its substantival form, ἡ ἔρημος, meaning the "wilderness, desert" (e.g., John 1:23, Matt 24:26)
10. Ἰουδαῖος, -α, ον (i-ou-**dhe**-os, -a, -on), Jewish/Judean (adj.); as a noun, Ἰουδαῖοι, Jews/Judeans
11. μέγας, μεγάλη, μέγα (**me**-gas, me-**ga**-li, **me**-ga), large, great
12. μέσος, -η, -ον (**me**-sos, -i, -on), middle, in the middle
13. πιστός, -ή, -όν (pi-**stos**, -**i**, -**on**), trustworthy, faithful[7]
14. ποῖος, ποία, ποῖον (**pi**-os, -a, -on), what, which, what kind of (interrogative pronoun)
15. πολύς, πολλή, πολύ (po-**lis**, pol-**li**, po-**li**), much (sg.), many (pl.)
16. πρῶτος, -η, -ον (**pro**-tos, -i, -on), first, foremost (ordinal number) (cf. 18.10)
17. οὗτος, αὕτη, τοῦτο (**ou**-tos, **af**-ti, **tou**-to), this, this one
18. ἐκεῖνος, -η, -ο (e-**ki**-nos, e-**ki**-ni e-**ki**-no), that (note that the nt. ends in -ο not -ον)
19. ἐμός, ἐμή, ἐμόν (e-**mos**, -**i**, -**on**), my, mine
20. ἡμέτερος, -α, -ον (i-**me**-te-ros, -a, -on), our
21. σός, σή, σόν (sos, si, son), your, yours
22. ὑμέτερος, -α, -ον (i-**me**-te-ros, -a, -on), your (pl.)

---

6 Some adjective like this one have identical forms in the masculine and feminine. These are known as adjectives of "two terminations" (i.e., fm. forms are the same as the m. forms).

7 This term was originally related to the practice of making oaths; it concerns one who can be "trusted" to take an oath and is "faithful" to fulfill the agreement undertaken.

8. Personal Pronouns, Relative Pronouns, and Reflexive Pronouns

Greek pronouns also decline. The declensions of the first-person and second-person pronouns bear little similarity to the declensions we have studied in previous lessons, with the exception of the genitive forms.

Most first-person and second-person singular personal pronouns are enclitics (cf. Section 5.6). As you know, enclitics throw their accent back on the last syllable of the previous word (except when standing at the beginning of a sentence). Thus, the accent of an enclitic can be found on the previous word. For this reason, pronouns without accents should be pronounced as if it were part of, or joined to, the previous word.

8.1 FIRST-PERSON PRONOUN (SINGULAR AND PLURAL)

There are two sets of first-person singular pronouns in the oblique cases: an enclitic form (e.g., μου) and accented form (e.g., ἐμοῦ).

⊕	*Sg.*		*Pl.*	
N	ἐγώ	(e-**go**)	ἡμεῖς	(i-**mis**)
G	μου, ἐμοῦ	(mou, e-**mou**)	ἡμῶν	(i-**mon**)
D	μοι, ἐμοί	(mi, e-**mi**)	ἡμῖν	(i-**min**)
A	με, ἐμέ	(me, e-**me**)	ἡμᾶς	(i-**mas**)

The unaccented (enclitic) forms, μου, μοι, με, are the most frequently occurring forms. The accented forms, ἐμοῦ, ἐμοί, ἐμέ, are employed to express emphasis.

Figure: Tripartite scene, depicting a horseman holding a whip (Apa, Taurus mountains, *IKonya* 139).

8.2 SECOND-PERSON PRONOUN (SINGULAR AND PLURAL)

⊕	*Sg.*		*Pl.*	
N	σύ	(si)	ὑμεῖς	(i-**mis**)
G	σου, σοῦ	(sou)	ὑμῶν	(i-**mon**)
D	σοι, σοί	(si)	ὑμῖν	(i-**min**)
A	σε, σέ	(se)	ὑμᾶς	(i-**mas**)

As in the case of the first-person pronoun, the unaccented, enclitic forms, σου, σοι, σε, are the most frequently occurring forms in the New Testament. The accented forms are employed to express emphasis. (Since accents were not written in the original documents, their addition requires an editorial decision.)

Expressing Possession

The first-person, genitive forms, μου (ἐμοῦ) and ἡμῶν, often express possession and mean "my" and "our." Similarly, the second-person genitive forms, σου (σοῦ) and ὑμῶν, can express possession and mean "your" (sg.) and "your" (pl.).

As explained in Section 7.3, possession can also be expressed using the possessive adjectives, ἐμός, ἐμή, ἐμόν (my), and σός, σή, σόν (your). Be careful not to confuse the possessive adjectives, which belong to the first and second declension, with these personal pronouns, which (as we shall see) actually belong to the third declension (cf. Chap. 14).

8.3 THIRD-PERSON PRONOUN

The third-person pronoun is declined like the first and second declension nouns that we studied in previous lessons. But there is one important exception. Note that the neuter singular forms in the nominative and accusative lack a final ν (αὐτό not αὐτόν). This change can be compared with the third-person neuter pronoun, τοῦτο.

			Sg.			
⊕	*m.*		*fm.*		*nt.*	
N	αὐτός	(af-**tos**)	αὐτή	(af-**ti**)	αὐτό	(af-**to**)
G	αὐτοῦ	(af-**tou**)	αὐτῆς	(af-**tis**)	αὐτοῦ	(af-**tou**)
D	αὐτῷ	(af-**to**)	αὐτῇ	(af-**ti**)	αὐτῷ	(af-**to**)
A	αὐτόν	(af-**ton**)	αὐτήν	(af-**tin**)	αὐτό	(af-**to**)

	Pl.					
	m.		*fm.*		*nt.*	
N	αὐτοί	(af-**ti**)	αὐταί	(af-**te**)	αὐτά	(af-**ta**)
G	αὐτῶν	(af-**ton**)	αὐτῶν	(af-**ton**)	αὐτῶν	(af-**ton**)
D	αὐτοῖς	(af-**tis**)	αὐταῖς	(af-**tes**)	αὐτοῖς	(af-**tis**)
A	αὐτούς	(af-**tous**)	αὐτάς	(af-**tas**)	αὐτά	(af-**ta**)

- You should parse all of the above as follows: specify the person (1, 2, 3), number (sg., pl.) and case.

8.4 USES OF αὐτός

As you know, the Greek verb can specify the subject by its ending (e.g., ἀκούω, "*I* hear," ἀκούομεν "*we* hear," ἀκούεις, "*you* hear," ἀκούετε, "*you* [pl.] hear"). Thus, the *nominative* forms of the personal pronoun are *not* required to express the subject of the sentence or clause as they are in English. When these nominative personal pronouns *are* used in this manner, they express emphasis or contrast.[1]

The genitive forms (αὐτοῦ, αὐτῆς, αὐτῶν, etc.) are commonly used to express possession, that is, "his, her, its, their" (e.g., τῇ ἀγάπῃ αὐτοῦ, "for *his* love"). The genitive, dative, and accusative forms of αὐτός can also be used in place of a noun of the same case. The forms αὐτῷ and αὐτόν can function as indirect and direct objects, respectively ("to/for him," "him"). Of course, Greek prepositions require specific cases, and if αὐτός follows a preposition, it must take the specific case required by it.

The third-person pronoun has a greater range of uses than those mentioned above. These various uses can be summarized as follows:

8.4.1 Predicative Use ("Self")

The third-person pronoun, αὐτός, often appears in the *predicative* position (and thus is *not* preceded by an article). In such cases, it is used to intensify the noun and is translated as "himself, herself, themselves," and so on: for example, αὐτὸς ὁ ἀπόστολος ("the apostle *himself*").

8.4.2 Attributive Use ("Same")

When a form of αὐτός appears in the attributive position (and thus is preceded by an article), it is translated as "same": for example, ὁ αὐτὸς ἀπόστολος ("the *same* apostle").

[1] When a gen. form follows the verb ἀκούω, it indicates the person or source of the sound, whereas the acc. case denotes the object or thing that is heard. However, in Hellenistic Greek, these distinctions became blurred.

8.4.3 Personal Pronoun for Emphasis

The nominative forms of αὐτός can be used, without a noun, to emphasize the implied subject: for example, αὐτὸς γινώσκει ("he *himself* knows"), αὐτοὶ λέγομεν ("we *ourselves* say").

8.4.4 Personal Pronoun

In the so-called oblique cases (i.e., genitive, dative, and accusative cases), a form of αὐτός may stand in place of a noun: for example, λέγω αὐτῷ ("I say *to him*"), ἀκούω αὐτήν ("I hear *her*"). The genitive form, αὐτοῦ/αὐτῶν, is often used to express possession in the third person (e.g., ἔργον αὐτοῦ, "*his* deed," ἔργα αὐτῶν, "their works").

8.5 THE RELATIVE PRONOUN (WHO, WHICH, WHAT)

The relative pronoun is declined like the article, except the initial *taf* (τ) is missing. It is the practice of editors to add rough breathing marks to the relative pronoun, although this has no effect on their pronunciation.

		Sg.			*Pl.*	
⊕	*m.*	*fm.*	*nt.*	*m.*	*fm.*	*nt.*
N	ὅς	ἥ	ὅ	οἵ	αἵ	ἅ
G	οὗ	ἧς	οὗ	ὧν	ὧν	ὧν
D	ᾧ	ᾗ	ᾧ	οἷς	αἷς	οἷς
A	ὅν	ἥν	ὅ	οὕς	ἅς	ἅ

Use of the Relative Pronoun

8.5.1 The relative pronoun always agrees with its antecedent in gender and number, but not case (cf. Section 8.5.2). For example, the antecedent of the relative pronoun ᾧ would be a masculine or neuter, singular noun (or pronoun).

8.5.2 The *case* of the relative pronoun is often determined by its grammatical function in the clause in which it is found, and not by its antecedent. For example, a relative pronoun would be in the nominative case when it functions as the subject of the verb, and in the accusative case when it functions as the object of the verb. However, this rule often does not apply to relative pronouns in the genitive and dative cases (cf. Section 8.5.3).

8.5.3 Attraction of the Relative: When the antecedent of the relative pronoun is in the genitive or dative case, the case of the relative pronoun is normally *attracted* to the case of its antecedent. In other words, it takes on the same case as its antecedent, *regardless of the relative pronoun's grammatical function*. For example, if the antecedent is genitive (e.g., τέκνου) or dative (e.g., τέκνῳ), the relative pronoun would conform to this case by becoming, respectively, genitive (οὗ) or dative (ᾧ), regardless of its function in its own clause. This phenomenon is known as the *attraction of the relative*.

8.5.4 Relative pronouns are *not* used to express questions (e.g., who? which?).

8.6 RECIPROCAL PRONOUN ἀλλήλων (m., fm., nt.)

The reciprocal pronoun ἀλλήλων is employed to express an action that *reciprocates* between two or more people. This pronoun never occurs in the nominative case. Therefore, it is cited in lexica and the vocabulary list in the genitive plural form.

G	ἀλλήλων	(a-**li**-lon)	"of one another"
D	ἀλλήλοις	(a-**li**-lis)	"to/for one another"
A	ἀλλήλους	(a-**li**-lous)	"one another"

8.7 REFLEXIVE PRONOUNS

The reflexive pronoun is a combination of the personal pronoun with "self" added (e.g., himself, herself, themselves). They are formed by adding a prefix (ἐμ-, σε-, or ἑ-) to the various forms of αὐτός.

8.7.1 Reflexive pronouns do not possess nominative forms because they specify a verbal action that refers back to the subject: for example, βλέπω ἐμαυτόν ("I see myself"). Therefore, they are listed in lexica in their genitive singular forms.

8.7.2 The plural forms of the first-, second-, and third-person reflexive pronouns are identical. Because the forms are identical, one must rely on context to determine their meanings.

First-Person Reflexive Pronoun ("myself, ourselves")

	Sg.		*Pl.*	
	m.	*fm.*	*m.*	*f.*
G	ἐμαυτοῦ	ἐμαυτῆς	ἑαυτῶν	ἑαυτῶν
D	ἐμαυτῷ	ἐμαυτῇ	ἑαυτοῖς	ἑαυταῖς
A	ἐμαυτόν	ἐμαυτήν	ἑαυτούς	ἑαυτάς

Second-Person Reflexive Pronoun ("youself, yourselves")

	Sg.		*Pl.*	
	m.	*fm.*	*m.*	*f.*
G	σεαυτοῦ	σεαυτῆς	ἑαυτῶν	ἑαυτῶν
D	σεαυτῷ	σεαυτῇ	ἑαυτοῖς	ἑαυταῖς
A	σεαυτόν	σεαυτήν	ἑαυτούς	ἑαυτάς

Third-Person Reflexive Pronoun ("himself, herself, itself, themselves")

	Sg.			*Pl.*		
	m.	*fm.*	*nt.*	*m.*	*f.*	*nt.*
G	ἑαυτοῦ	ἑαυτῆς	ἑαυτοῦ	ἑαυτῶν	ἑαυτῶν	ἑαυτῶν
D	ἑαυτῷ	ἑαυτῇ	ἑαυτῷ	ἑαυτοῖς	ἑαυταῖς	ἑαυτοῖς
A	ἑαυτόν	ἑαυτήν	ἑαυτό	ἑαυτούς	ἑαυτάς	ἑαυτά

Note:

- Note the lack of a final ν in the nt. acc. forms of ἑαυτό (cf. ἀυτό, τοῦτο).
- The genitive forms, ἑαυτοῦ, ἑαυτῆς, and ἑαυτοῦ, are sometimes used in the place of αὐτοῦ, αὐτῆς, αὐτοῦ, to express possession in the third person.

8.8 VOCABULARY TO BE MEMORIZED

1. ἅγιος, -α, -ον (**a**-yi-os, -α, -ον), set apart for God, consecrated, holy; οἱ ἅγιοι, (God's) consecrated people, 'saints'; τὸ ἅγιον πνεῦμα, the Holy Spirit
2. ἀληθῶς (a-li-**thos**), truly (adv.) (cf. ἀλήθεια, ἀληθινός, -ή, -όν)
3. ἄν (an), particle indicating contingency, uncertainty, possibility (do not translate)
4. γινώσκω (yi-**no**-sko), I know[2]
5. ἡμέρα, ἡ (i-**me**-ra), day[3]
6. Ἰσραηλίτης, ὁ (is-ra-i-**li**-tis), Israelite (m. first declension noun)
7. ὅς (os), ἥ(i), ὅ(o), who, which, what (relative pronoun); "who" should be used when the antecedent refers to a person, and "which" should be used when the antecedent refers to a thing, regardless of the gender of the relative pronoun

[2] We will study the future form of this verb in Sections 10.4.2; 11.6 (Box 1).

[3] In MGr, the greeting καλημέρα means "good day" or "good morning."

8. πνεῦμα, τό (**pnev**-ma), a wind, breath, human spirit, one's inner self (as part of one's psychological domain, cf. Section 18.9); a ghost, Spirit/breath (of God)[4] (cf. pneumonia, pneumatology)
9. ποῦ (pou), interrogative adv. where? at/to what place? (cf. non-interrogative ὅπου)
10. ὥρα, ἡ (**o**-ra), moment, hour of the day, a short indefinite period of time

Pronouns

11. ἀλλήλων (al-**li**-lon), one another, each other (reciprocal pronoun); this word never appears in the nom. case, or in the singular. It only occurs in the plural form and thus is listed in lexica in the gen. pl. form; similarly, ἐμαυτοῦ, ἑαυτοῦ, and σεαυτοῦ never occur in the nom. case (see below).
12. αὐτός, -ή, -ό (af-**tos**, af-**ti**, af-**to**), he, she, it, etc.; himself, herself, itself, etc. (intensive); same (attributive position)
13. ἑαυτοῦ, -ῆς, -οῦ, (e-af-**tou**, e-af-**tis**, e-af-**tou**) himself, herself, itself (reflexive pronoun); his, hers, etc. (possessive pronoun)
14. ἐμαυτοῦ, -ῆς (e-maf-**tou**, -**tis**), myself, my own
15. σεαυτοῦ, -ῆς (se-af-**tou**, -**tis**), yourself
16. σύ (si), you (sg.)
17. ἡμεῖς (i-**mis**), we
18. ὑμεῖς (i-**mis**), you (pl.)[5]

Prepositions

19. ἀπό, ἀπ', ἀφ' (a-**po**, ap, af), (w. gen.) from, away from; ἀπό becomes ἀπ' when followed by a word beginning with a vowel, and ἀφ' when followed by a word beginning with a vowel carrying a rough breathing.
20. ἐπί, ἐπ'/ἐφ' (e-**pi**, ep, ef), (1) (w. gen.) on, upon; (2) (w. dat.) on, on the basis of; (3) (w. acc.) on, around.[6]
21. πρό (pro) (with gen.), before (a time or place)
22. ὑπό, ὑπ', ὑφ ' (i-**po**, ip, if), (1) (with gen.), by (with passive verbs, expressing agency); (2) (with acc.), under, below (cf. hypodermic, lit. "under the skin").[7]

---

4 We will learn the declension for this word in Section 15.1.

5 I.e., pronounced the same as ἡμεῖς.

6 ἐπί becomes ἐπ' when followed by a word beginning with a vowel carrying a smooth breathing, and ἐφ' when followed by a word beginning with a vowel carrying a rough breathing. ἐπί with the genitive can also mean "in the time of."

7 ὑπό becomes ὑπ' when followed by a word beginning with a vowel, and ὑφ' when followed by a word beginning with a vowel carrying a rough breathing.

9.

First Aorist Active Indicative

The simple past tense in Greek is termed the *aorist* tense. The term "aorist" is derived from the Greek adjective ἀόριστος, meaning "without boundaries" or "unbounded." In other words, the aorist tense describes a past action, without further definition or qualification.

The aorist tense is formed in two different ways. These two ways are called, respectively, the *first* aorist and the *second* aorist.[1] These two aorist forms are translated the same way. They are simply two different ways of forming a past tense, namely a regular way and an irregular way. As an analogy, compare the formation of past tenses in English. The regular way of forming a past tense is to add the suffix "-ed" to the verb stem:

watch → watched
walk → walked

The irregular way of forming an English past tense involves a minor, or major, stem change:

eat → ate
goes → went

The regular past tense in English corresponds to the Greek *first* aorist, while the irregular past tense in English is comparable to the Greek *second* aorist.[2]

Most Greek verbs form *either* a first aorist *or* a second aorist past tense, but not both. Therefore, one of your tasks will be to become familiar with the particularities

---

[1] Some grammars use the terms *weak* aorist (= first aorist) and *strong* aorist (= second aorist).

[2] We will deal with the second aorist in Chapter 10.

Figure: Relief of figure of a man, recumbent on a couch, with his wife and son (ancient Tyriaion, central Turkey, *IKonya* 144).

of frequently occurring Greek verbs. Whether a given verb forms a first aorist or a second aorist must be memorized on a verb-by-verb basis.

9.1 THE "ASPECT" OF THE AORIST

As previously noted, the term "aspect" refers to the *kind* of action depicted by the verb. Of course, the consideration of the aspect of a given verb should never be separated from the specific context in which it appears. This being said, each tense has its own particular aspect associated with it.

The aspect of the aorist tense is aoristic. It expresses the simple (or summary) occurrence of a verbal action. The term "aoristic" means that the verbal action is presented as a completed and undifferentiated process. Thus, the aorist tense is often used when the specification of other more descriptive aspects is not required.

In the indicative mood, the aorist tense almost always expresses an action that takes place in the past. Thus, the aorist tense is often used in the gospel narratives: for example, "Jesus said," "they went," "he taught," and so on. In each case, the nature of the verbal action is undefined (e.g., whether the action is progressive, puntiliar, repetitive, etc.) and is simply portrayed as a completed action.

9.2 FORMATION OF THE FIRST AORIST ACTIVE TENSE

To form the *first* aorist active tense, observe the following steps:

1. Isolate the verb stem by removing -ω from the lexical form (e.g., λύω → λυ-).
2. If the stem begins with a consonant, add a *syllabic augment* ε to the beginning of the stem (ἐ + λυ → ἐλυ-).[3] This ε augment is an indicator of past time (in the indicative mood). If the stem begins with a vowel, an augment is not added. Instead, the initial vowel is lengthened as follows:[4]

α → η	ο → ω
ε → η	υ → υ
η → η	ω → ω
ι → ι[5] (sometimes ει)	

For example, the verb ἀκού-ω (I hear) would become ἤκου-. Obviously, in the case of η and ω, no lengthening occurs because they are naturally long.

3 This is termed a syllabic augment because the prefixed ε adds a syllable.

4 Technically speaking, this lengthening is a *temporal augment*, because the time required to pronounce the initial syllable is increased when the vowel is lengthened.

5 E.g., ἰσχύω → ἴσχυσα.

If the verb begins with a double vowel, whose second vowel is ι, the first vowel is usually lengthened and the ι is written subscript under the lengthened vowel. If the second vowel is υ, the first vowel is lengthened:

αι → ῃ   αυ → ηυ
ει → ῃ   ευ → ηυ
οι → ῳ

The double vowels οι and ευ do not always lengthen. They sometimes remain the same (e.g., οἰκοδομέω → οἰκοδόμησεν [Acts 7:47]; εὐδοκέω → εὐδόκησεν [Luke 12:32], εὐλογέω → εὐλόγησεν [Heb 7:6]) as they often do in MGr.

3. Attach the first aorist *tense formative* -σα and the secondary endings. Past tenses (in the indicative mood) take secondary endings. The secondary active endings are as follows:

	Singular	*Plural*
1	-ν	-μεν
2	-ς	-τε
3	-	-ν

As applied to the first aorist, there is only one unexpected change: In the first-person singular, no ending is used.[6]

Sg.		
1	-σα	no ending used
2	-σα + ς > -σας	
3	-σα > -σε(ν)	no ending is added, but α (of σα) changes to ε and a movable ν is sometimes added
Pl.		
1	-σα + μεν > -σαμεν	
2	-σα + τε > -σατε	
3	-σα + ν > -σαν	

Now let us look at an example. To form the first aorist of λύω, one must add an *augment* to the verb stem (ἐλυ-), and the first aorist tense formative (ἐλυσα-), and then the personal endings, as follows:

First Aorist Active Indicative of λύω

⊕		*Sg.*			*Pl.*	
1	ἔλυσα	(**e**-li-sa)	[I untied]	ἐλύσαμεν	(e-**li**-sa-men)	[we untied]
2	ἔλυσας	(**e**-li-sas)	[you untied]	ἐλύσατε	(e-**li**-sa-te)	[you (pl.) untied]
3	ἔλυσε(ν)	(**e**-li-se[n])	[he/she/it untied]	ἔλυσαν	(**e**-li-san)	[they untied]

[6] According to Smyth, -ν was originally -μ. After the consonant σ, it became α. Hence ἔλυσα (fr. ἐλησμ) (Smyth, 464a, cf. 20b, 35c).

As you know, the accent of verbs in the indicative mood is *recessive*, meaning it is placed as far back from the end of the word (i.e., to the left) as the general rules permit. The α of the first aorist tense formative is always short, as is the ε in the ultimas of the third sg. and first and second pl. Therefore, the antepenult is accented throughout the example above.

9.3 AUGMENTING AND ACCENTING COMPOUND VERBS

A compound verb has a prepositional prefix attached to the verb stem. For example, ἀποστέλλω and ἀπολείπω both have a prefixed ἀπό, and ἐκβάλλω and ἐκδικέω have a prefixed ἐκ, and εἰσέρχομαι and εἰστρέχω have a prefixed εἰς. In the Hellenistic period, it was common practice to add one, two, or sometimes even three prepositions, to the beginning of a verb to create verbs with greater specificity.

When adding the past-tense augment (ε) to such compound verbs, the augment is inserted *after* the preposition (and immediately before the verb stem), and the final vowel of the preposition is deleted.[7] For example:

ἀπολύω → ἀπέλυσα

A few of these prepositional prefixes undergo a change when the augment is added. For example:

ἐκ + ε → ἐξε-
κατα + ε → καθε- (not consistent)[8]

Accenting Compound Verbs: An accent cannot precede the augment. Therefore, compound verbs are never accented on the prepositional prefix.

9.4 THE FIRST AORIST OF CONTRACT VERBS

As in the case of the future tense, the aorist tense of contract verbs is easy to form because there are no vocalic contractions. To form the first aorist of a contract verb, simply observe the following steps:

1. Add the augment or lengthen the initial vowel (as above).
2. Lengthen the *final* stem vowel of the verb stem (ε → η, α → η, ο → ω).

[7] There are exceptions to this rule: e.g., the verb προφητεύω forms its aorist as ἐπροφήτευσα, not – as one would have expected – as πρεφήτευσα.

[8] E.g., κατέλαβεν.

3. Add the usual first aorist endings. This can be illustrated using the verbs ποιῶ (-έω), ἀγαπῶ (-άω), and πληρῶ (-όω):

ἐ + ποιε	→ ἐποιη-	+ σα =	ἐποίησα	(e-**pi**-i-sa)	[I did/made]
ἀγαπα	→ ἠγαπη-	+ σα =	ἠγάπησα	(i-**ga**-pi-sa)	[I loved]
ἐ + πληρο	→ ἐπληρω-	+ σα =	ἐπλήρωσα	(e-**pli**-ro-sa)	[I filled/fulfilled]

Figure 9.1. Figure of a woman, with lentoid eyes, with carved mirror to the lef (*IKonya* 172).

9.5 FIRST AORIST STEMS OF VERBS ENDING IN LIQUID CONSONANTS

As you know, some verb stems end in the so-called liquid consonants, λ, μ, ν, and ρ. As in the case of the future tense, these liquid consonants *cannot be followed by* σ. This creates a problem because -σα is the tense formative of the first aorist tense. For this reason, when a verb stem ends in either λ, μ, ν, or ρ, only -α (not -σα) is added. For example, the first aorist of the verb ἐγείρω (I raise) is formed as follows:

ἐγειρ- → ἤγειρ + α → ἤγειρα (I raised)

To compensate for the lack of σ, the aorist verb stem will often change in some way. For example, the previous vowel in the stem may lengthen into a double vowel (e.g., μένω → ἔμεινα). This phenomenon is termed "compensatory lengthening." Here is the first aorist paradigm of μένω, a liquid verb:

First Aorist Active Indicative of μένω ("I remain")

	Sg.		*Pl.*	
1	ἔμεινα	(**e**-mi-na)	ἐμείναμεν	(e-**mi**-na-men)
2	ἔμεινας	(**e**-mi-nas)	ἐμείνατε	(e-**mi**-na-te)
3	ἔμεινε(ν)	(**e**-mi-ne[n])	ἔμειναν	(**e**-mi-nan)

Sometimes, other changes will also take place. As in the case of the future tense, some verbs will not only lengthen the previous vowel but also change the *present* stem to differentiate it from the aorist stem. For example, some verbs double the final consonant of the *present* verb stem:

Present	*First Aorist*	*Future*
ἀποστέλλω (a-po-**stel**-lo) (I am sending)	ἀπέστειλα (a-**pe**-sti-la) (I sent)	ἀποστελῶ (a-po-ste-**lo**) (I will send)

In this case, the real stem of ἀποστέλλω is ἀποστέλ- (which is preserved in the future form).

Some verbs add a vowel such as *iota* (ι) to the present stem. In the case of the verb αἴρω, the real stem is αρ-, which is preserved in the first aorist and future forms (in the first aor. form, the intial α has been lengthend to η):

Present	*1 Aorist*	*Future*
αἴρω (**e**-ro) (I am taking)	ἦρα (**i**-ra) (I took)	ἀρῶ (I will take)

9.6 FIRST AORIST FORMS OF VERBS ENDING IN LABIALS, VELARS, AND DENTALS

You have already been introduced to labial, velar, and dental consonants:

	unvoiced stops	*voiced fricatives*	*unvoiced fricatives*
labial	π	β	φ
velar	κ	γ	χ
dental	τ	δ	θ

What we observed in the case of the formation of the future tense is also true of the first aorist: The addition of -σα (the first aorist tense formative) to verbal stems ending in labials, velars, and dentals produces predictable morphological changes (cf. Section 3.11). These changes can be summarized as follows:

π, β, φ + σα = ψα
κ, γ, χ + σα = ξα
τ, δ, θ, ζ + σα = σα

Here are some examples. When the labial consonants, π, β, φ, combine with the σ of the first aorist -σα tense formative, they form the consonantal blend ψ. For example, in the case of βλέπω and γράφω:

βλεπ- →	ἐ + βλεπ + σα	ἔβλεψα	(**e**-vle-psa)	[I saw]
γραφ- →	ἐ + γραφ + σα	ἔγραψα	(**e**-gra-psa)	[I wrote]

When the velar consonants, κ, γ, χ, combine with σ, they form the consonantal blend ξ. Take, for example, ὑπάρχω, which in the third-person singular means "there is."

ὑπαρχ- → ὑπ + αρχ + σε ὑπῆρξε (ip-**ir**-kse) [there was]

When a dental consonant (τ, δ, θ, and ζ) comes up against σ, the dental *drops out.*[9] For example, in the case of βαπτίζω, σῴζω, and δοξάζω, the following changes occur. Bear in mind that verbs whose present stem ends in -ιζ or -αζ have a final dental (or occasionally a velar) concealed in the verbal root. Thus, in the case of βαπτίζω and δοξάζω, the roots are actually √ βαπτιδ and δοξαδ- :

βαπτιζ	ἐ + βαπτιδ + σα	ἐβάπτισα	(e-va-**pti**-sa)	[I baptized]
δοξαδ	ἐ + δοξαδ + σα	ἐδόξασα	(e- **dho**-ksa-sa)	[I honored/praised]
σῳζ-	ἐ + σῳζ + σα	ἔσωσα	(**e**-so-sa)[10]	[I saved]

9.7 PARADIGM OF οἶδα ("I KNOW")

This verb οἶδα (**i**-dha) is an unusual verb. Its grammatical form is perfect in tense. But, in terms of meaning, οἶδα is translated as if it were a present-tense verb, meaning "I know" (not "I have known"). You have not learned the perfect endings yet, but in most cases, they are identical to the first aorist active endings above (except without the σ). The paradigm for οἶδα is as follows:

Perfect Active Indicative of οἶδα

⊕	*Sg.*	*Perfect*	
1	οἶδα	(**i**-dha)	(I know)
2	οἶδας	(**i**-dhas)	(you know)
3	οἶδε(ν)	(**i**-dhe[n])	(he/she/it knows)
	Pl.		
1	οἴδαμεν	(**i**-dha-men)	(we know)
2	οἴδατε	(**i**-dha-te)	(you [pl.] know)
3	οἴδασι(ν)	(**i**-dha-si[n])	(they know)

[9] The longer explanation for this phenomenon is as follows: The dental actually assimilates to σ, and the resulting σσ reduces to σ. Not every instance of σσ in the GNT does not assimilate to σ owing to Attic influences.

[10] This verb can have the stem σω- and σωι- .

9.8 THE USE OF οὐ AND μή IN QUESTIONS

Questions expecting the answer "yes" are negated with οὐ, οὐκ, or οὐχ (and sometimes οὐχί). For example:

> Οὐχ οὗτός ἐστιν Ἰησοῦς ὁ υἱὸς Ἰωσήφ, οὗ ἡμεῖς οἴδαμεν τὸν πατέρα καὶ τὴν μητέρα (John 6:42)
> "Isn't this Jesus, the son of Joseph, whose father and mother we know?"
> (expected answer: "yes, of course it is!")
>
> Questions expecting the answer "no" are negated with μή. For example:
>
> Μὴ καὶ ὑμεῖς θέλετε ὑπάγειν (John 6:67)
> "Surely you don't also want to go, do you?
> (expected answer: "No, of course not!")

9.9 OBJECTIVE GENITIVE AND SUBJECTIVE GENITIVE

Two very important uses of the genitive case are known as the *objective* and *subjective* genitive.

9.9.1 Subjective Genitive

This use of the genitive case can be explained as follows. As an example, we will use the phrase "comfort *of the Holy Spirit*" (Acts 9:31). First, imagine the *non-genitive* noun as a verbal idea. In our example, "comfort" implies the verbal idea of "comforting." *If*, the *genitive* term would better serve as the *subject* of the verbal action, in the sense of *initiating* this verbal action, then the genitive term is a *subjective genitive*. Thus, "comforting *of the Holy Spirit*" implies the comfort *given by* the Holy Spirit. Thus, "of the Holy Spirit" is a subjective genitive.

Similarly, in the expression, "the love *of Christ*" (Rom 8:35), the genitive term "of Christ" initiates the action of "love"; hence it means "Christ's love (for us)," not "love for Christ" (at least in the context of Rom 8:30–31). Here are some more examples:

> "bond *of peace*" (Eph 4:3) → "bond produced by peace"
> "labour *of love* and endurance *of hope*" (1 Thess 1:3) → "labour produced by love and endurance produced by hope"

9.9.2 Objective Genitive

The objective genitive can be explained as follows. As an example, we will use the phrase "blasphemy *of the Spirit*" (Matt 12:31). Once again, imagine the non-genitive noun as a verbal idea. In this example, "blasphemy" implies the verbal idea of "blaspheming."

Next, think of the noun in the genitive as the *recipient* (direct object) of this verbal action, or that this verbal action is directed toward the term in the genitive. In our example, "*of the Spirit*" implies blasphemy, which is "directed toward the Spirit." Thus, "of the Holy Spirit" is an objective genitive.

Similarly, in the phrase "fear of the Romans" (τὸν φόβον τῶν Ῥωμαίων), "fear" implies the action of "fearing" that is "directed toward the Romans," who are the feared object. Here are some other examples:

"zeal *of God*" (Rom 10:2) → "being zealous for God"
"witness *of the Messiah*" (1 Cor 1:6) → "witnessing that is directed toward the Messiah"

Sometimes it is difficult to decide between the objective and subjective genitive. For example, ἡ ἀγάπη τοῦ θεοῦ could be either a subjective genitive (God's love [for us]) or an objective genitive ([our] love for God).

- Note: The simple genitive of possession is distinct from the subjective genitive because that which is possessed does not involve a verbal idea or action.

9.10 VOCABULARY TO BE MEMORIZED

1. αἴρω (**e**-ro), I take, take up, take away; fut. ἀρῶ, 1 aor. ἦρα (ι has been added to the present stem; the real stem is αρ-)
2. γάμος, ὁ (**ga**-mos), wedding, wedding banquet
3. ἕως (**e**-os), (1) conj. until (with any tense), while (with pres. ind. only); (2) prep. (with gen.) to, until, as far as
4. γυνή, ἡ (yi-**ni**), voc. sg. γύναι(**yi**-ne), woman, wife (not first declension)[11]
5. διάκονος, ὁ (dhi-**a**-ko-nos), household steward, assistant, waiter, deacon, servant (cf. Section 21.6)
6. ζῆλος, ὁ (**zi**-los), zeal, jealousy (cf. English "zealot")
7. ἤδη (**i**- dhi), already, now
8. ἥκω (**i**-ko), I have come, I am present; fut. ἥξω, 1 aor. ἦξα
9. ἱερόν, τό (i-e-**ron**), temple, temple precincts
10. ναός, ὁ (na-**os**), inner part of temple, including the Jewish temple
11. καλός, -ή, -όν (ka-**los, -i, -on**), good, useful, fine (cf. "caligraphy")

[11] This is a third declension word (cf. Chapter 14).

12. μή (mi), not (often used with non-indicative verbs; cf. οὐ); also used to negate questions expecting the answer "no" (cf. Section 9.8)
13. νεκρός, -ά, -όν (ne-**kros, -i, -on**), dead, lifeless; pl. οἱ νεκροί, the dead (cf. "necrosis, necrotic"; the term "necropolis" [νεκρά + πόλις] is literally a "city of the dead," that is, a cemetery).
14. νῦν (nin), now, at the present time
15. οἶδα (**i**-dha), I know, understand, perceive (this verb is perfect in tense, but should be translated in the present tense); fut. εἰδήσω
16. οἶκος, ὁ (**i**-kos), house, household (cf. Section 21.6) (cf. "economy")
17. οἰκία, ἡ (i-**ki**-a), house, household (cf. Section 21.6)
18. οἶνος, ὁ (**i**-nos), wine (cf. "oinophile," meaning "wine lover")
19. οὕτω, οὕτως (**ou**-to, **ou**-tos), 1) (as adv.) thus, so, in this way; 2) (as adj.) such; 3) as follows
20. ὅταν (**o**-tan), when, whenever (combination of ὅτε + ἄν)
21. οὔπω (ou-**po**), not yet
22. πάσχα, τό (**pas**-kha), the Passover (festival), Passover meal (indeclinable)
23. πόθεν (**po**-then), from where? where? (interrogative adv.)[12]
24. σημεῖον, τό (si-**mi**-on), a sign or distinguishing mark, a portent (cf. "semiology," the study of signs) (John 1:19–12:20 is known as the "book of signs [σημεῖα]")
25. τρίτος, -η, -ον (**tri**-tos, -i, -on), third (cf. "tripod", "Trinity")

Box 1. Some Unexpected First Aorists Forms of Previously Learned Verbs

- θέλω, ἠθέλησα (i-**θe**-li-sa): the original root of this verb is √ εθελε-. This root shows up in the first aorist form but it is abbreviated to θελ- in the present form.
- καλω (-έω), ἐκάλεσα (e-**ka**-le-sa) (remember the final ε of the root does not lengthen)

[12] The termination -θεν signifies "movement away from."

10.

Verbal Roots, Principal Parts, and Second Aorist Active Indicative

10.1 VERBAL ROOTS

All languages have unexpected or irregular features, and Greek is no exception. For example, the stems of some Greek verbs undergo changes when forming different tenses. In order to deal with this phenomenon, it is important to understand the difference between verbal *stems* and *roots*.

The verbal root represents the original stock of a verb, from which most of its forms developed. In other words, a root is the most basic form of a verb. In this textbook, we will indicate these verbal roots with the symbol √. For example, the root of λύω is √ λυ.

The term "stem" refers to the basic form of a verb in a particular tense. In some cases, a verb's root and stem are identical. In other cases, the stem of a verb may be slightly different from the root. For example, the stem of βαπτίζω ("I baptize") is βαπτιζ-, but its root is actually √ βαπτιδ-.[1] Similarly, the root of αἴρω is √ αρ.[2] In some instances, one root will be *substituted* for an entirely different root in the paradigm of the same verb. Consider the following examples of root substitutions in forming the future tense:

Lexical Form	*Present Root*	*Future Root*	*Future Indicative*
λέγω (I say)	√ λεγ	√ ερ[3]	ἐρῶ[4] (I will say)
ὁρῶ (-άω) (I see)	√ ορα[5]	√ οπ	ὄψομαι (I will see)

1 Verbs whose present stem ends in -ιζ or -αζ have a concealed final dental or velar γ in the stem.

2 Some present-tense stems add an iota to the root (√ αρ → αἴρ-).

3 Actually √ ϝερ. Though the ancient Greek letter digamma *F* died out long before the Hellenistic age, a 'phantom' digamma continues to influence some forms of the words which originally included it.

4 Position of the accent tells us it behaves like a contract verb, ἐρέω.

5 Actually √ ϝορα.

Figure: Marble circular base with funerary inscription of 'Mussidius Fronto' (*IKonya* 69).

10.2 UNDERSTANDING PRINCIPAL PARTS

Some Greek verbs have irregular forms in their various tenses. In many instances, these changes cannot be predicted. Moreover, Greek lexica do not list all the irregular forms separately. For example, to translate ἐρῶ or ὄψομαι in the GNT, you must look up λέγω and ὁρῶ (-άω), respectively, in a lexicon. How, then, can one keep track of these many stem changes and root substitutions?

The solution to this problem lies in becoming familiar with the *principal parts* of irregular verbs. Principal parts are really summaries of the stems of a verb in its various tenses. If you know a verb's principal parts, then you should be able to predict all forms of that verb, throughout all of its tenses, voices, and moods.

To help you with this, this book provides a table of the principal parts of some of the most common irregular verbs (see Appendix 1). Theoretically, every verb can have as many as six principal parts, though in practice many verbs have fewer.

Though the verb λύω is not irregular, it is used here by way of illustration. Its six principal parts are as follows:

1	2	3	4	5	6
λύω	λύσω	ἔλυσα	λέλυκα	λέλυμαι	ἐλύθην

By convention, these six prinicipal parts represent the following tenses and voices of the *indicative* form of the verb:

1. present, active *or* middle
2. future, active *or* middle
3. first aorist *or* second aorist, active *or* middle
4. perfect active
5. perfect, middle *or* passive
6. first or second aorist passive

From these six principal parts, the following additional tenses are formed:

1. → present passive, imperfect active, middle or passive
2. —
3. —
4. → pluperfect active
5. → pluperfect, middle *or* passive
6. → future passive

Note that the aorist passive and future passive are formed using the sixth principal part. This will allow you to distinguish easily between the middle and passive forms of this verb in these two tenses.

10.3 SECOND AORIST ACTIVE INDICATIVE

As explained in Chapter 9, the second aorist is an irregular way of forming a past tense. The aspect of the second aorist is the same as the first aorist, namely aoristic.

The second aorist *always* involves a stem change. This might involve a minor change (comparable in English to "he sings" → "he sang"), or it might involve a total stem change (comparable in English to "he goes" → "he went").

If you do not know the stem of the aorist active form of a verb, you can find it by consulting a table of principal parts or the lexical entry of the verb. The aorist active form can be found in the third column of a table of principal parts. In a lexicon, the first-person singular first aorist stem will end in -σα (-ψα, -ξα, or -α in the case of liquid verbs), and end in -ον, in the case of second aorist verbs (e.g., λέγω → εἶπ<u>ον</u>).

Forming the second aorist active tense:

1. If the stem begins with a consonant, add the syllabic augment ε to the second aorist stem, according to the same rules you learned for the first aorist. If the stem begins with a vowel, lengthen the vowel (i.e., temporal augment), as you would for a first aorist verb.
2. Add the following secondary personal endings, which use ο or ε as connecting vowels.

	Sg.	*Pl.*
1	-ον	-ομεν
2	-ες	-ετε
3	-ε(ν)	-ον

We will use λέγω ("I say") as an example. The third principal part of λέγω is εἶπον. Thus, the verbal root has changed from √ λεγ→ √ ειπ (actually √ ϝειπ).[6] The second aorist active indicative paradigm of εἶπον is as follows (i.e., augment + second aorist stem + ο/ε + secondary active endings):

⊕	*Sg.*		*Pl.*	
1	εἶπον	(I said)	εἴπομεν	(we said)
2	εἶπες	(you said)	εἴπετε	(you [pl.] said)
3	εἶπε(ν)	(he/she/it said)	εἶπον	(they said)

[6] ει does not lengthen to η in aorist tense because the original stem began with a digamma consonant (F).

Note the following:

- The second aorist does *not* employ -σα as a tense formative.
- The first-person singular and third-person plural have identical forms. They can only be distinguished on the basis of context.
- The third-person singular has no ending but only the connecting vowel -ε. It may be followed by a movable ν.

10.4 SECOND AORIST FORMS OF ἔχω AND γινώσκω

10.4.1 As you will recall, the root of ἔχω ("I have") is not √ εχ-, but √ σεχ or √ σχ.[7] This √ σχ root reappears in the second aorist form of ἔχω, which is ἔσχον.

1	ἔσχον	ἔσχομεν
2	ἔσχες	ἔσχετε
3	ἔσχε(ν)	ἔσχον

10.4.2 The root of γινώσκω is actually √ γνο, whose final vowel often lengthens to √ γνω. In Attic Greek, the initial consonant is reduplicated (γνω → γιγνω-). In other words, the lexical form used to be γιγνώσκω. By the Hellenistic period, the second γ dropped out, leaving γινώσκω.[8] Thus, the original present stem of this verb, γιγνώσκω, has a reduplicated initial consonant and -σκ added to the root, which is √ γνο/γνω.

In the second aorist, this verb is *athematic*. In other words, no connecting vowel (ο/ε) is used to connect the personal endings to the verb stem. The second aorist forms are created by adding the secondary endings directly to the augmented second aorist stem ἐγνω-, *without a connecting vowel*.[9] In the third-person plural, -σαν, taken from the first aorist ending, is used as an ending instead of -ον. Here is the second aorist paradigm of γινώσκω:

Singular

1	ἔ + γνω + ν →	ἔγνων	(I knew)
2	ἔ + γνω + ς →	ἔγνως	(you knew)
3	ἔ + γνω →	ἔγνω[10]	(he/she/it knew)

Plural

1	ἔ + γνω + μεν →	ἔγνωμεν	(we knew)
2	ἔ + γνω + τε →	ἔγνωτε	(you [pl.] knew)
3	ἔ + γνω + σαν →	ἔγνωσαν[11]	(they knew)

[7] √ σχ is possibly a result of vowel gradation or syncope (Smyth 493).

[8] Cf. Attic verb γίγνομαι, which becomes γίνομαι in the GNT.

[9] Although some authors argue that these athematic (or root) aorists should form a third group of aorists, owing to the lack of a connection vowel.

[10] I.e., no ending; do not confuse with first singular of present indicative.

[11] The expected form, ἔγνων, never occurs in the GNT.

10.5 VOCABULARY TO BE MEMORIZED

1. ἄγω (**a**-go), I lead, bring, go; fut. ἄξω; the second aorist form is ἤγαγον (The stem of ἄγω is αγ-. In the second aorist, it has undergone a reduplication to form αγαγ-, which becomes ηγαγ- when augmented.)
2. ὑπάγω (ip-**a**-go), I go away, depart to (this is a prefixed form of the verb ἄγω; as such, it has the same basic principal parts)
3. αἰώνιος, -ον (e-**o**-ni-os, -on), eternal (of quality), unending, everlasting (adj. of two terminations) [12]
4. ἄνωθεν (**a**-no-then), (with gen.) from above; again
5. ἀποστέλλω (a-po-**stel**-lo), I send; fut. ἀποστελῶ, 1 aor. ἀπέστειλα (cf. ἀπόστολος)[13]
6. βασιλεία, ἡ (va-si-**li**-a), a kingdom, an empire (cf. "basilica")
7. γραφή, ἡ (gra-**fi**), scripture, a passage of scripture (sg.), the Hebrew Scriptures (pl.)
8. δεῖ (dhi) (followed by acc.), an impersonal verb meaning "it is necessary"; for example, δεῖ με means "it is necessary for me," or "I must"
9. δεύτερος, -α, -ον (**dhef**-te-ros, -α, -ον), second (cf. πρῶτος, -η, -ον/τρίτος, -η, -ον)
10. ἐάν (e-**an**), (a contraction of εἰ and ἄν), if, even if (takes subjunctive mood); sometimes ἐάν simply has the same meaning as ἄν
11. ἐὰν μή (e-**an** mi) unless, except (often followed by the subjunctive mood)
12. ἑορτή, ἡ (e-or-**ti**), a (religious) festival, feast
13. κρίνω (**kri**-no), I judge, decide, determine; fut. κρινῶ, 1 aor. ἔκρινα
14. κρίσις, ἡ (**kri**-sis),[14] judgment, condemnation (cf. "crisis")[15]
15. λαμβάνω (lam-**va**-no), I take, take hold of, receive; fut. λήμψομαι, 2 aor. ἔλαβον
16. πείθω (**pi**-tho), I persuade, convince; fut. πείσω, 1 aor. ἔπεισα
17. πίπτω (**pi**-pto), I fall, fall down; second aor. ἔπεσον (the fut. form will be learned in Chapter 11)
18. πνῶ (-έω) (pno), I blow (of wind); first aor. ἔπνευσα[16]
19. πῶς (pos), how? in what way? (interrogative particle)

---

[12] I.e., feminine forms have the same endings as the masculine forms.

[13] Remember that the stem is actually ἀποστελ- . A second λ has been added to the present stem, and the first aorist stem has undergone compensatory lengthening of the stem vowel.

[14] This is a third declension noun, whose declension we will learn in Chapter 14.

[15] Barth famously developed κρίσις theology in his commentary of Paul's *Letter to the Romans* (*Der Römerbrief*). In this book he announced a "*krisis* of knowledge" (Rom 9:30–10:3), a "*krisis* of human freedom" (14:1–15:13), and the arrival of a crisis in time, which he termed a "zero hour" (Stunde Null), in which one experiences "abandonment and doubt and uncertainty (Barth, *Church Dogmatics: IV. The Doctrine of Reconciliation*, 2nd ed. [London/New York: T. & T. Clark International, 1956], 431).

[16] The root of πνέω is πνεϝ, which results in uncontracted plural endings πνέομεν and πνέουσι. πνέω belongs to the same group of verbs as πλῶ (-έω) ("I sail"), whose stem also originally ended in a digamma (πλεϝ). Consequently, ε + ω/ο/ου generally does not contract in 1st sg. and pl. in the pres. and impf. ind.

20. φέρω (**fe**-ro), I bring, carry; fut. οἴσω; the aorist function of this verb has been taken over by ἤνεγκα (**i**-ne^{ng}-ga),[17] the unaugmented stem of which is ἐνεγκ-.

Second Aorist Forms of Previously Learned Verbs

- γινώσκω → ἔγνων
- εὑρίσκω → εὗρον (no lengthening of initial vowel)
- ἔχω, ἔσχον
- λέγω, the aorist function has been taken over by εἶπον: sometimes this verb takes first aorist endings (εἶπα, εἶπας, εἶπαν).
- ὁράω, the aorist function has been taken over by εἶδον; sometimes this verb takes first aor. endings (εἴδαμεν, εἴδατε, εἶδαν).

---

[17] Outside of GNT, also appears as ἤνεγκον.

11.

Present Middle and Passive Indicative, Future Middle Indicative, and Future Indicative of the Verb “to be”

11.1 THE MEANING OF THE PASSIVE VOICE

In the active voice, the subject of the verb performs an action on an object (e.g., “he finds the book”). The passive voice is essentially the opposite of the active voice: namely, the subject is the recipient of the action of the verb (e.g., “he is found”).

When the passive voice is employed, the preposition ὑπό (followed by the genitive case) is frequently employed to indicate the agency “by whom” or “by which” the action is accomplished: for example, “the word was spoken *by* the Lord (ὑπὸ κυρίου).” Thus, the presence of ὑπό can help you identify the use of the passive voice.

11.2 THE MIDDLE VOICE

In addition to the active and passive voices, Greek has a so-called *middle* voice. In Attic Greek (fifth to fourth centuries BC), the middle voice had a variety of special meanings. The most common of these meanings was that of doing something *for* oneself, or with some kind of self-interest. For example:

Active Voice	*Middle Voice*
φέρω (I bring)	φέρομαι (I bring *for myself*, i.e., I win)
διδάσκω (I teach)	διδάσκομαι τὸν υἱόν (I have my son taught)

Figure: Relief of husband and wife, with a mattock and sickle pictured to the left, and two household objects pictured to the right (*IKonya* 168).

By the Hellenistic period, the function of the middle voice had more or less fallen into disuse. Consequently, the distinction between the active and middle had become quite blurred by the time the New Testament was being written. Commenting on this phenomenon, C. F. D. Moule remarks:

> The fact remains that the distinction [between the active and middle voice] has become blurred by the N.T. period, and, as a rule, it is far from easy to come down from the fence with much decisiveness on either side in an exegetical problem if it depends on the voice.[1]

This being said, there are certainly examples of the continuing use of the middle voice in the GNT such as the following:

Active		*Middle*	
ἀπόλλυμι	I ruin, destroy	ἀπόλλυμαι	I perish, am ruined
ἐνδύω	I dress, clothe	ἐνδύομαι	I put on, wear
ἐξαιρῶ (-έω)	I take out, tear out	ἐξαιροῦμαι	I rescue, deliver, save
ἐξομολογῶ (-έω)	I agree	ἐξομολογοῦμαι	I confess, acknowledge
μετατίθημι	I put in another place	μετατίθεμαι	I change my mind, turn away

Nevertheless, in mainstream Hellenistic Greek and non-literary Greek, the force of the middle voice was used with decreasing frequency over time because this voice was becoming "lexicalized." In other words, when an author wanted to express an active voice, he would often choose one particular verb. When he wanted to express involvement, or reflexivity, he would choose a *different* verb. This is a complicated topic. But for the present, let us follow this simple guideline: In the majority of cases, *the middle voice of thematic verbs should be translated as an active voice.*[2]

11.3 DEPONENT VERBS

A *deponent* verb is a verb that is middle or passive in form but active in function. A verb can be completely deponent (i.e., middle or passive in all its parts) or partially deponent (i.e., middle or passive in only one or more of its principal parts). The

[1] C. F. D. Moule, *An Idiom Book of the New Testament Greek* (Cambridge: Cambridge University Press, 1953), 24.

[2] Over the last decade, the function of the middle voice in the GNT has become one of the more contested features of language. For the present, suffice to say that, from an exegetical perspective, one should never appeal to the force of a middle voice on the basis of morphology alone. There must be other contextual indicators before one can claim that a middle sense is intended.

term "deponent" describes the *function* of a word, not its form. For this reason, the term "deponent" should not be used when parsing verbs because parsing is an analysis of *morphology* (i.e., form), not function. When parsing, *never* use the term "deponent." Instead, use the terms "middle" or "passive."

When parsing deponent verbs, never parse a verb as "middle or passive" or as "middle/passive." In every case, a verb will either be middle or passive, but not both. Therefore, *you* must figure out which voice is being used: Is it middle or is it passive? We will return to this subject below.

11.4 FORMATION OF THE PRESENT PASSIVE INDICATIVE TENSE

The original primary passive endings are as follows:

	Sg.	*Pl.*
1	-μαι	-μεθα
2	-σαι	-σθε
3	-ται	-νται

As in the case of the active voice, these endings are attached to the present stem using either ο or ε as a connecting vowel (i.e., present stem + ο/ε + primary passive endings). However, there is one exception: The second-person singular, -σαι, undergoes a transformation to -ῃ in the present tense.[3] Thus, the present *passive* of λύω is:

Present Passive Indicative of λύω

⊕	*Sg.*	*Pl.*
1	λύομαι	λυόμεθα
2	λύῃ	λύεσθε
3	λύεται	λύονται

Given that the English meaning of these forms is not very interesting, let us look at the present passive form of πιστεύω:

	Sg.		*Pl.*	
1	πιστεύομαι	(I am believed)	πιστευόμεθα	(we are believed)
2	πιστεύῃ	(you are believed)	πιστεύεσθε	(you [pl.] are believed)
3	πιστεύεται	(he/she/it is believed)	πιστεύονται	(they are believed)

[3] The σ becomes intervocalic (between the ε connecting vowel and the vowel of the suffix) and drops out. The ε then contracts with αι and ι is written as a subscript by editors: λυ + ε + σαι → λυεαι → λυηι → λυῃ.

11.5 FORMATION OF THE PRESENT MIDDLE INDICATIVE TENSE

The middle endings are identical to the passive endings in the present tense. We shall illustrate the present-tense middle endings using a different verb, namely ἔρχομαι (**er**-kho-me).

Present Middle Indicative of ἔρχομαι *(I come, I go)*

⊕	*Sg.*		*Pl.*	
1	ἔρχομαι	(I come/go)	ἐρχόμεθα	(we come/go)
2	ἔρχῃ	(you come/go)	ἔρχεσθε	(you [pl.] come/go)
3	ἔρχεται	(he/she/it come/goes)	ἔρχονται	(they come/go)

11.6 DISTINGUISHING MIDDLE FORMS FROM PASSIVE FORMS IN THE PRESENT AND FUTURE INDICATIVE TENSES

The middle voice can be confusing to students because the endings are identical to the passive endings in the present, imperfect, and perfect tenses. This problem is easily addressed if you keep the following two general guidelines in mind:

1. Most thematic verbs in the GNT that have an *active* form in a particular tense do *not* have a corresponding middle form *in the same tense.*
2. Conversely, most thematic verbs in the GNT that have a *middle* form in a particular tense do not normally have a corresponding active form in the same tense (e.g., ἔρχομαι).

There are certainly exceptions to these two guidelines, and advanced students should develop a more nuanced understanding of the function of the middle voice. But as *general* guidelines, these principles will help you distinguish between most morphologically ambiguous forms. Bearing these two guidelines in mind, here are some basis instructions to help you deal with this subject.

First, remember the six principal parts:

1. present, active *or* middle
2. future, active *or* middle
3. first *or* second aorist, active *or* middle
4. perfect active
5. perfect, middle *or* passive
6. first or second aorist passive

If the first or second principal part of a verb is *middle* in that tense (i.e., it ends in -ομαι), then translate it actively (e.g., ἔρχομαι, "I come/go").

A Greek verb can be active in one principal part but middle in another principal part, especially if there is a significant stem change. For example, the following verbs are active in the first principal part and middle in the second principal part. The distinction between active and middle principal parts is obvious because the first principal part (present tense) ends in -ω and the second principal part (future tense) ends in -ομαι (or -οῦμαι):[4]

Present		*Future*	
ἀποθνῄσκω	(I die)	ἀποθανοῦμαι (acts like contract verb in fut.)	(I will die)
γινώσκω	(I know)	γνώσομαι (the stem is γνω-)	(I will know)
λαμβάνω	(I take)	λήμψομαι	(I will take)
ὁράω	(I see)	ὄψομαι (stem οπ)	(I will see)
πίπτω	(I fall)	πεσοῦμαι (acts like contract verb in fut.)	(I will fall)

There are a few verbs whose middle form has an entirely different meaning than that of the active form. For example:

ἄρχω (I rule)	ἄρχομαι (I begin)
ἅπτω (I light/kindle a fire)	ἅπτομαι (I touch, take hold of)

This is not an exception to the guidelines above. In this case, the active and middle forms should be treated as separate lexical items with distinct meanings.

To sum up: Owing to the decline of the distinctive use of the middle voice in the Hellenistic period, many of the verbs you will encounter will either have:

- an active and passive form but no middle form in a particular tense, *or*
- a middle form and no corresponding active or passive form.

You will not be able to distinguish between many middle and passive endings on the basis of the verbal ending alone. But if you know the lexical form and principal parts of a particular verb, you can easily distinguish between a middle form and a passive form. For example, the ending -ω of the lexical form of βλέπω (**vle**-po) tells you that this is an *active* verb because -ω is an active ending ("I see"). Therefore, βλέπεται (**vle**-pe-te) must be present *passive* ("he is seen"), not present middle.

On the other hand, when the lexical form (first principal part) ends in -ομαι, such as the verb, γίνομαι (**yi**-no-me), it is a *middle* verb in the present. Now, it is true that -ομαι can hypothetically be either a middle ending or a passive ending, but the

4 If the first, second, or third principal part of a verb is *active*, and you encounter a middle form of the verb in the same tense, be aware that some verbs are in the process of changing from active verbs to middle verbs in the first century AD. For example, the GNT sometimes uses the active verbs, εὐαγγελίζω and φοβέω, but in the majority of instances, it prefers the middle forms, εὐαγγελίζομαι and φοβέομαι. In these cases, the middle voice should be translated *actively* (i.e., "I preach the gospel," "I fear," etc.). When in doubt, let your lexicon be your guide!

lexical form (which you find in your vocabulary lists and in a Greek lexicon) is, *by definition*, always active or middle, not passive. Therefore, the *lexical* form γίνομαι cannot be passive. It must be middle. In light of this, if you encounter the form γίνεται (third sg.), it *must* be middle because you know, on the basis of the lexical form, that γίνομαι is a middle verb.

Here is another example: The lexical form, λαμβάνω (lam-**va**-no) ends in -ω. This fact tells you that λαμβάνω is an *active* verb ("I receive"). Therefore, λαμβάνομαι must be passive ("I am received"), not middle. As you can see, you should not attempt to parse an unfamiliar form of a verb without first knowing the lexical form and the relevant principal parts of the verb you are parsing. If this seems a little confusing, it will become clearer with practice.

11.7 FORMATION OF THE FUTURE MIDDLE INDICATIVE

We will consider the future passive verbal forms in Chapter 17 because they are formed on a different stem (the sixth principal part). The future *middle* is formed almost the same way as the present middle. As you will recall, the future *tense formative* consonant is σ. To form the future middle tense, simply add the tense formative -σ to the verbal stem (of the second principal part), followed by the present middle endings (i.e., future stem + σ + ο/ε + primary middle endings).

We will use ἔρχομαι as an example. The verbal root of ἔρχομαι changes completely from √ ερχ in the present middle tense (cf. ἔρχομαι, "I come/go") to √ ελευθ in the future middle (second principal part). The final dental consonant (θ) disappears when the σ tense consonant is added (ἐλεύσομαι, "I will come"):

Future Middle Indicative of ἔρχομαι

⊕	*Sg.*		*Pl.*	
1	ἐλεύσομαι	(I will come/go)	ἐλευσόμεθα	(we will come/go)
2	ἐλεύσῃ	(you will come/go)	ἐλεύσεσθε	(you [pl.] will come/go)
3	ἐλεύσεται	(he/she/it will come/go)	ἐλεύσονται	(they will come/go)

11.8 FUTURE INDICATIVE OF εἰμί ("I AM")

The root of εἰμί is actually √ εσ. This root reappears in the future paradigm. The future of εἰμί employs many of the same middle endings you already know. Only the third-person singular form is unexpected:

⊕	*Sg.*		*Pl.*	
1	ἔσομαι	(I will be)	ἐσόμεθα	(they will be)
2	ἔσῃ	(you will be)	ἔσεσθε	(you [pl.] will be)
3	ἔσται[5]	(he/she/it will be)	ἔσονται	(they will be)

[5] No connecting vowel.

11.9 PRESENT MIDDLE AND PASSIVE FORMS OF CONTRACT VERBS

Contract verbs follow the same rules of vowel contraction in the middle and passive as they do in the active voice. As it turns out, the example verbs for contract verbs used in Chapter 4 are all active verbs. Therefore, in the present tense, they form *passive*, not middle, forms. The following verbs are all *passive* verbs. Their endings are provided here for future reference:

Present Passive Indicative Forms of ποιέω, ἀγαπάω, πληρόω

	-εω	-αω	-οω
Sg.			
1	ποιοῦμαι	ἀγαπῶμαι	πληροῦμαι
	[-ε + ο + μαι]	[-α + ο + μαι]	[-ο + ο + μαι]
2	ποιῇ	ἀγαπᾶσαι	πληροῖ[6]
	[-ε + ῃ]	[-α + ε + σαι][7]	[-ο + + ῃ]
3	ποιεῖται	ἀγαπᾶται	πληροῦται
	[-ε + ε + ται]	[-α + ε + ται]	[-ο + ε + ται]
Pl.			
1	ποιούμεθα	ἀγαπώμεθα	πληρούμεθα
	[-ε + ο + μεθα]	[-α + ο + μεθα]	[-ο + ο + μεθα]
2	ποιεῖσθε	ἀγαπᾶσθε	πληροῦσθε
	[-ε + ε + σθε]	[-α + ε + σθε]	[-ο + ε + σθε]
3	ποιοῦνται	ἀγαπῶνται	πληροῦνται
	[-ε+ ο + νται]	[-α + ο + νται]	[-ο + ο + νται]

11.10 PRESENT MIDDLE PARADIGM OF δύναμαι ("I AM ABLE, I CAN")

The verb δύναμαι (**dhi**-na-me) is middle (deponent) in the present tense. However, its conjugation is somewhat unusual. It is an *athematic* verb. In other words, the personal endings are added to the verbal stem δύνα- *without* any connecting vowel. We have previously observed this phenomenon with the second aorist of γινώσκω. Thus, the present middle forms are as follows:

[6] This form is identical to the third sg. pres. act. ind.

[7] In this case, the original primary passive ending, -σαι, is retained.

Sg.

1	δυνα- + μαι	→	δύναμαι	(I can)
2	δυνα- + σαι or ῃ	→	δύνασαι or δύνῃ	(you can)
3	δυνα- + ται	→	δύναται	(he/she/it can)

Pl.

1	δυνα- + μεθα	→	δυνάμεθα	(we can)
2	δυνα- + σθε	→	δύνασθε	(you [pl.] can)
3	δυνα- + νται	→	δύνανται	(they can)

11.11 VOCABULARY TO BE MEMORIZED

1. ἀναβαίνω (a-na-**ve**-no), I go up, ascend; fut. ἀναβήσομαι, 2 aor. ἀνέβην (this verb is also athematic in the 2 aor.; for the principal parts of this verb, see Section 25.11, s.v. βαίνω (this uncompounded verb does not occur in the GNT)

   Note: Hellenistic Greek routinely formed hundreds and hundred of new verbs by adding prepositions to the beginning of simple verbs. These are termed compound verbs. For example, the verbs ἀναβαίνω and καταβαίνω are compounded forms of βαίνω (whose basic meaning is "go"), with the addition of the prepositions ἀνά and κατά. In some cases, the addition of a preposition creates a new, unexpected meaning. For example, the verb ἀναγινώσκω, which is a prefixed form of γινώσκω, does not mean "I know up," but rather "I read."
2. καταβαίνω (ka-ta-**ve**-no), I go down, descend; fut. καταβήσομαι, 2 aor. κατέβην (this verb is also athematic in the 2 aor. cf. Section 25.11, s.v. βαίνω)[8]
3. ἀποκρίνομαι (a-po-**kri**-no-me) (w. dat.), I answer, reply (we have already learned a past tense deponent form of this verb, ἀπεκρίθη. We will learn more about this form in Chapter 17)
4. ἄρχω (**ar**-kho), I rule, govern; fut. ἄρξω, 1 aor. ἦρξα; the middle form of this verb, ἄρχομαι (**ar**-kho-me), has a completely different meaning, "I begin"; fut. ἄρξομαι (cf. ἀρχή).
5. ἀσπάζομαι (a-**spa**-zo-me), I greet, I say goodbye
6. γίνομαι (**yi**-no-me), I become, I am, it happens (in third sg.), I arrive (somewhere); fut. γενήσομαι. Like εἰμί, γίνομαι takes a predicate (in nom. case), not a direct object. (We will learn the second aor. form of this verb in Section 13.4)[9]
7. γῆ, ἡ (yi), the earth, land, country, region[10]

---

[8] But 3rd pl. is normally κατέβη<u>σαν</u> (as is ἀνέβησαν, cf. ἔγνωσαν).

[9] The original present form of γίνομαι was γίγνομαι. As previously noted, a few Classical verbs, such as γίγνομαι and γιγνώσκω, reduplicated their initial consonant in the present tense. In HGr the second γ drops out, forming γίνομαι.

[10] The paradigm for this lexeme is as follows: γῆ (γέα), γῆς (γεας), γῇ (γεᾳ), γῆν (γεαν); this is really an α-pure word.

8. δύναμαι (**dhi**-na-me), I can, am able (often followd by infin.); fut. δυνήσομαι. This athematic verb does not have a first aorist. Instead, it appears in the impf. form, ἐδυνάμην (alternatively written ἠδυνάμην).
9. ἔρχομαι (**er**-kho-me), I come, I go (i.e., does not specify direction); fut. ἐλεύσομαι (e-**lef**-so-me), 2 aor. ἦλθον (**il**-thon, √ ελθ)
10. μᾶλλον (**mal**-lon), more, rather; μᾶλλον ... ἤ, more/rather ... than
11. μισῶ (-έω), I hate, despise, disregard; fut. μισήσω, 1 aor. ἐμίσησα (cf. misanthrope, misogynist)
12. ὀργή, ἡ (or-**yi**), anger, wrath
13. πονηρός, -ά, -όν (po-ni-**ros**, -a, -on BOLDED), evil, bad
14. σύν (sin) (with dat.) with, together with, in company with (cf. syn- and sym- words in English such as "symphony")
15. σφραγίζω (sfra-**yi**-zo), I mark with a seal or stamp (σφραγίς), I set my seal upon, I mark to indicate ownership; first aor. ἐσφράγισα
16. ὑπέρ (i-**per**), (1) (with gen.) for, on behalf of; about, concerning; (2) (with acc.) over and above, beyond (in spatial terms, it contrasts with ὑπό [below, under])
17. ὑψῶ (-όω) (i-**pso**), I lift up, I exalt (sby); fut. ὑψώσω, 1 aor. ὕψωσα
18. φίλος, ὁ (**fi**-los), a friend
19. φυλακή, ἡ (fi-la-**ki**), prison, jail
20. ὥστε (**o**-ste) (conj.), so that, with the result that (do not confuse this marker of a result clause with ἵνα, the marker of a purpose clause, meaning "in order that")

Future Middles of Some Previously Learned Verbs

The following three verbs are active in the present tense but middle in the future tense:

Present	*Future*	*Future Root*
γινώσκω	γνώσομαι	√ γνω (cf. 10.4.2)
ὁράω	ὄψομαι	√ οπ-
πίπτω	πεσοῦμαι	√ πετ

πίπτω is a very unusual verb. It is the only verb in the GNT that forms its future with the Doric tense formative -σε. The root is apparently √ πετ. When πετ combines with σ, the final τ drops out forming πεσέ (+ ο + μαι). Then ε of the tense formative contracts with the thematic vowel ο/ε (e.g., πεσοῦμαι).

12.

Imperfect Active Indicative and Imperfect of the Verb "to be"

12.1 ASPECT OF THE IMPERFECT

The aspect of the imperfect tense is *imperfective*. In other words, the action is understood to be in progress, without reference to its final completion. Such an action may infer attempting, continuing, setting about, or beginning an action, depending on the context. As such, different English expressions are be required to translate the imperfect tense in different passages. For example, an imperfect tense might be translated by such English phrases as:

was (do)ing
was trying to (do)
began (doing)
used to (do)

12.2 USES OF THE IMPERFECT

In contrast to the aorist tense, the imperfect tense is usually employed selectively with a more nuanced range of connotations. When you encounter a verb in the imperfect tense, you should treat it with special care and try to determine whether a more nuanced meaning is implied, on the basis of context. Here are some possibilities:

12.2.1 Progressive Imperfect

Describes an *ongoing* past action ("he was. . . . ing")

Figure: Stele with carved figures (Hatunsaray, central Turkey, *IKonya* 113).

12.2.2 Customary Imperfect

Describes a regularly occurring action in the past over an extended period of time ("he used to . . . , she continually . . . ").[1]

12.2.3 Iterative Imperfect

Describes a *repeated* action in the past over a period of time (e.g., "he repeatedly . . . ").

12.2.4 Conative Imperfect

Describes an action that was *attempted* but not completed (e.g., "he tried to . . . ," "she attempted to . . . ").

12.2.5 Inceptive Imperfect

Describes the beginning of a past action (e.g., "he began doing something . . . ").[2]

12.2.6 Imperfect with Verbs of "Saying"

Verbs of "saying" (e.g., ἔλεγεν) often occur in the imperfect tense, especially if they introduce a speech of some length. In such cases, the emphasis is not on the fact that "such and such" a thing was said, but on the exposition of what was said. These imperfects can be translated as simple past tenses ("he said").

12.2.7 Imperfect in Indirect Discourse

Indirect discourse in the Greek language preserves the original tense of the direct discourse. In contrast, when changing direct discourse into indirect discourse, English pushes the tense back. For example, if John says: "I *am going* to the library," and someone asks you what John said, you would reply, "John said that he *was going* to the library." Notice how the present tense verb "am going" was changed to the past tense "was going" in English, when the verb introducing the indirect discourse shifted into the past tense (i.e., John *said*).

Greek does not make this change. Therefore, the imperfect tense in Greek indirect discourse (which is already a past tense) must be translated into English using the pluperfect tense (i.e., one tense further back into the past). So if John says: "I *was going* to the library," and someone asks you what John said, you would reply, "John *said* that he *had gone* to the library."

---

1 Also termed the *habitual* imperfect.

2 Also known as the *ingressive* imperfect; cf. Daniel Wallace, *Greek Grammar: Beyond the Basics* (Grand Rapids: Zondervan, 1996), 544.

12.3 FORMING THE IMPERFECT ACTIVE INDICATIVE

1. The imperfect tense is formed using the *present* verbal stem (i.e., the first principal part, which is also the lexical form). Therefore, there will be *no stem change* in most cases. If you know the present stem, you also know the imperfect stem.
2. If a verb is active in the present tense, it will be active in the imperfect. Similarly, if it is middle in the present tense, it will be middle in the imperfect.
3. If the stem begins with a consonant, add a syllabic augment, ε, according to the same rules as the aorist tense. If the stem begins with a vowel, lengthen the vowel, as in the case of the aorist tense.
4. The imperfect has the same endings as the second aorist (in the indicative mood), namely secondary personal endings, using ο or ε as a connecting vowel.

	Sg.	*Pl.*
1	-ον	-ομεν
2	-ες	-ετε
3	-ε(ν)	-ον

However, unlike the second aorist, the imperfect tense does not undergo a stem change. Therefore, *the only way to distinguish an imperfect tense from a second aorist is by the stem change*. The imperfect will preserve the stem of the present tense. The second aorist will change the stem.

Imperfect Active Indicative of λύω

	Sg.	*Pl.*
1	ἔλυον	ἐλύομεν
2	ἔλυες	ἐλύετε
3	ἔλυε(ν)	ἔλυον

12.4 IMPERFECT ACTIVE INDICATIVE OF εἰμί

The imperfect active paradigm of εἰμί is as follows:

⊕	*Sg.*		*Pl.*	
1	ἤμην	(I was)	ἦμεν[3]	(we were)
2	ἦς[4]	(you were)	ἦτε	(you [pl.] were)
3	ἦν	(he/she/it was)	ἦσαν	(they were)

[3] ἤμεθα (middle form) is an alternative form of ἦμεν (cf. Gal 4:3).

[4] ἦσθα in Matt 26:69 and Mark 14:67.

12.5 IMPERFECT ACTIVE INDICATIVE OF ἔχω

As you will recall, the root of ἔχω is actually √ σεχ. But the imperfect form of ἔχω is εἶχον. This can be explained as follows. The expected imperfect form would be ἔσεχον. The σ in this form is intervocalic and drops out, leaving ε + ε to contract to form ει (ἔσεχον → ἔεχον → εἶχον). When the imperfect endings are added, the following conjugation results:

	Sg.		*Pl.*	
1	εἶχον	(I had)	εἴχομεν	(we had)
2	εἶχες	(you had)	εἴχετε	(you [pl.] had)
3	εἶχε(ν)	(he/she/it had)	εἶχον	(they had)

We have now learned the following four tenses of this verb:

Present	ἔχω	(I have)	= first principal part
Imperfect	εἶχον	(I used to have)	
Future	ἕξω	(I will have)	= second principal part
Second aorist	ἔσχον	(I had)	= third principal part

12.6 VOCABULARY TO BE MEMORIZED

1. ἀναγγέλλω (an-a^{ng}-**gel**-lo), I announce, proclaim, report (but in John's Gospel it can also mean "I interpret"); fut. ἀναγγελῶ, 1 aor. ἀνήγγειλα (cf. ἄγγελος) (this verbal stem undergoes the same changes as ἀποστέλλω)
2. δέχομαι (**de**-kho-me), I receive, accept
3. διψῶ (-άω) (dhi-**pso**), I am thirsty; fut. διψήσω, 1 aor. ἐδίψησα (cf. the English word "dipsomaniac," i.e., an alcoholic)
4. δωρεά, -ᾶς, ἡ, (dho-re-**a**), gift
5. ἐνθάδε (en-**tha**-dhe), here, in this place (common term used on Greek tombstones: "*Here* lies [so-and-so]")
6. ἐνώπιον (e-**no**-pi-on), (with gen.) before, in the presence of
7. ἐπάνω (e-**pa**-no), (with gen.) on, over, above
8. εὐαγγέλιον, τό (ev-a^{ng}-**ge**-li-on), a joyful announcement, good news
9. ζητῶ (-έω) (zi-**to**), I seek, look for; fut. ζητήσω; first aor. ἐζήτησα
10. θεάομαι (the-**a**-o-me), I see, look at, watch, observe; fut. θεάσομαι
11. πάλιν (**pa**-lin), again, once more[5]
12. πέντε (**pen**-de), five (cardinal number, indeclinable)

[5] Cf. the English word "palindrome" literally means to "run/return again" (the word "-drome" is based on the Greek work meaning 'running' or "returning").

13. πίνω (**pi**-no), I drink; fut. πίομαι, 2 aor. ἔπιον (cf. Section 22.10)
14. πλησίον[6] (pli-**si**-on), (with gen.) near; when πλησίον is accompanied by an article, ὁ πλησίον, it becomes a substantive meaning "neighbor" or "fellow human being"
15. πηγή, ἡ (pi-**yi**), a spring of water, a well
16. προσεύχομαι (pros-**ef**-kho-me), I pray; fut. προσεύξομαι
17. ῥῆμα, τό (**rhi**-ma), what is said, a Greek word, a saying, a proclamation (this is a third declension word, cf. Section 15.1)
18. τοιοῦτος, -αύτη, -οῦτο(ν) (ti-**ou**-tos, -**af**-ti, -**ou**-ton), of such a kind, such as this (cf. paradigm for οὗτος)
19. χαίρω (**khe**-ro), I rejoice, am glad; fut. χαρήσομαι (fut. tense preserves the true root, which is χαρ-)
20. χαρά, ἡ (kha-**ra**), joy, happiness

δεῖ

As you know, this impersonal verb only occurs in the third person form, δεῖ (from δέω). It conjugates in imperfect tense as ἔδει ("it was necessary").

6 πλησίον is the neuter form of πλησίος, -α, -ον.

13.

Imperfect Middle and Passive Indicative and First and Second Aorist Middle Indicative

13.1 IMPERFECT PASSIVE INDICATIVE

As in the case of the active voice, the imperfect passive also employs *secondary* endings, not primary endings.[1] These endings are as follows:

	Sg.	*Pl.*
1	-μην	-μεθα
2	-σο	-σθε
3	-το	-ντο

When forming the imperfect passive indicative, these passive secondary endings are attached to the present stem, using either ο or ε as a connecting vowel (augment + present stem + ο/ε + secondary passive endings). However, there is one exception: The second-person singular, -σο, undergoes a transformation to -ου.[2] Thus, the imperfect passive paradigm of λύω is:

Imperfect Pasive Indicative of λύω

⊕	*Sg.*	*Pl.*
1	ἐλυόμην	ἐλυόμεθα
2	ἐλύου	ἐλύεσθε
3	ἐλύετο	ἐλύοντο

[1] Secondary endings are used for verbs expressing past tense: e.g., imperfect, aorist, and pluperfect.
[2] The intervocalic σ drops out, and the remaining ο contracts with the previous ε connecting vowel to produce -ου: -ε-σο → -ε-ο → -ου.

Figure: Carved figures of three men and one woman, with lentoid eyes (Kusca, central Turkey, *IKonya* 130).

To facilitate the memorization of these endings, it is helpful to compare them to the passive endings of the present tense:

	Present Passive Ind.	*Imperfect Passive Ind.*
	Sg.	*Sg.*
1	λύομαι	ἐλυόμην
2	λύῃ	ἐλύου
3	λύεται	ἐλύετο
	Pl.	*Pl.*
1	λυόμεθα	ἐλυόμεθα
2	λύεσθε	ἐλύεσθε
3	λύονται	ἐλύοντο

By way of providing a more interesting example of the use of the imperfect passive indicative, let us examine the paradigm for βλέπω:

Imperfect Passive Indicative of βλέπω

	Sg.	
1	ἐβλεπόμην	(I was being seen)
2	ἐβλέπου	(you were being seen)
3	ἐβλέπετο	(he/she/it was being seen)
	Pl.	
1	ἐβλεπόμεθα	(we were being seen)
2	ἐβλέπεσθε	(you [pl.] were being seen)
3	ἐβλέποντο	(they were being seen)

13.2 IMPERFECT MIDDLE INDICATIVE

As explained above, if a verb is middle (deponent) in the present tense, it will also be middle in the imperfect. Thus, the present middle, ἔρχομαι ("I come/go"), forms an imperfect middle, ἠρχόμην. The imperfect middle and passive endings are the same.

In the case of the middle verb ἔρχομαι, the intitial vowel is lengthened from ἐρχ- → ἠρχ- :

Imperfect Middle Indicative of ἔρχομαι

⊕	*Sg.*		*Pl.*	
1	ἠρχόμην	(I was going)	ἠρχόμεθα	(we were going)
2	ἤρχου	(you were going)	ἤρχεσθε	(you [pl.] were going)
3	ἤρχετο	(he/she/it was going)	ἤρχοντο	(they were going)

13.3 FIRST AORIST MIDDLE INDICATIVE

As in the case of the imperfect middle, aorist middle verbs also employ secondary endings. Just as some verbs form either a first aorist active or a second aorist active, it is also true that other verbs form either a first aorist middle or a second aorist middle. The second aorist middle has the same endings as the imperfect middle. Remember, the basic middle endings are:

	Sg.	*Pl.*
1	-μην	-μεθα
2	-σο	-σθε
3	-το	-ντο

To form the first aorist middle, simply add the syllabic augment (ε), or lengthen the initial vowel, add the -σα tense consonant, and then the secondary endings, to the verb stem of the third principal part (augment + aorist stem + σα + secondary middle endings). There is one exception: The second-person singular form is -σω (not σο):[3]

	Sg.	*Pl.*
1	-σάμην	-σάμεθα
2	-σω	-σασθε
3	-σατο	-σαντο

Thus, the first aorist middle paradigm of θεάομαι ("I see, look at") is as follows:

First Aorist Middle Indicative of θεάομαι

⊕	*Sg.*		*Pl.*	
1	ἐθεασάμην	(I looked at)	ἐθεασάμεθα	(we looked at)
2	ἐθεάσω	(you looked at)	ἐθεάσασθε	(you [pl.] looked at)
3	ἐθεάσατο	(he/she/it looked at)	ἐθεάσαντο	(they looked at)

The following verbs form first aorist middles:

Present tense	*First Aorist Middle*	
ἀποκρίνομαι	ἀπεκρινάμην (liquid stem)	(I answered)[4]
ἄρχομαι	ἠρξάμην (-χ + σ→ ξ)	(I began)
ἀσπάζομαι	ἠσπασάμην (-ζ + σ→ σ)	(I greeted)
προσεύχομαι	προσηυξάμην (-χ + σ→ ξ)	(I prayed)

---

3 The second σ of -σα-σο is intervocalic and drops out, leaving -σα-ο, which contracts to -σω (-σασο → -σαο → -σω).

4 More often, this verb forms a passive deponent (cf. Chapter 17).

13.4 SECOND AORIST MIDDLE INDICATIVE

The second aorist middle indicative is also formed using the stem of the third principal part. It has an augment and the *same endings as the imperfect active indicative* (using ο or ε as a connecting vowel). Therefore, as in the case of the aorist active forms, the only way to distinguish an imperfect middle from a second aorist middle is by the stem change. For example, γίνομαι (**yi**-no-me) forms a second aorist middle, ἐγενόμην (e-ye-**no**-min) in contrast to the impf. form ἐγινόμην. Note how the stem has changed from γίν- to γεν- in the second aorist. The complete paradigm of ἐγενόμην is as follows:

Second Aorist Middle Indicative of γίνομαι

⊕	*Sg.*		*Pl.*	
1	ἐγενόμην	(I became)	ἐγενόμεθα	(we became)
2	ἐγένου	(you became)	ἐγένεσθε	(you [pl.] became)
3	ἐγένετο	(he/she/it became)	ἐγένοντο	(they became)

If the third principal part ends in -σάμην, the verb is *first* aorist middle in form. But if the third principal part ends in -όμην, it is a *second* aorist middle. In either case, you should usually translate these aorist middle verbs as active verbs.

We will not discuss the aorist *passive* indicative in this lesson because it is formed from the sixth principal part, and has different endings than the aorist middle (see Chap. 17).

13.5 VOCABULARY TO BE MEMORIZED

1. ἀπέρχομαι (ap-**er**-kho-me), I depart, go away; fut. ἀπελεύσομαι, 2 aor. ἀπῆλθον
2. διέρχομαι (dhi-**er**-kho-me), I go or pass through; fut. διελεύσομαι, 2 aor. διῆλθον
3. ἐξέρχομαι (eks-**er**-kho-me), I come or go out or forth, get out; fut. ἐξελεύσομαι, 2 aor. ἐξῆλθον

Box 1: Learning Compound Forms of ἔρχομαι

The compound forms of ἔρχομαι (e.g., ἀπέρχομαι, διέρχομαι, εἰσέρχομαι, etc.) have principal parts that are almost identical to those of the *unprefixed* form, ἔρχομαι. As a learning strategy, if you should learn the principal parts of ἔρχομαι the compound forms of this verb will be easy to identify.

4. ἄρτος, ὁ, bread, loaf, food
5. δηνάριον, τό, denarius (a Roman silver coin); usually occurs in the pl. δηνάρια, denaria (temporary and seasonal laborers were paid about 1 denarius per day)
6. εἰρήνη, ἡ (i-**ri**-ni), peace
7. ἐπαίρω (e-**pe**-ro), I raise, lift up; 1 aor. ἐπῆρα (ἐπι + αἴρω) (√ επαρ)
8. ἐρωτῶ (-άω) (e-ro-**to**), I ask (sby a question), request, beseech sby concerning sthg; fut. ἐρωτήσω, 1 aor. ἠρώτησα
9. ἐσθίω (es-**thi**-o), I eat; fut. φάγομαι, 2 aor. ἔφαγον (fut. and aor. are formed from a different stem, √ φαγ. Note also that fut. is mid. in form)
10. εὐαγγελίζομαι (ev-a^{ng}-ge-**li**-zo-me), I announce good news, proclaim, preach;[5] 1 aor. εὐηγγελισάμην (cf. εὐαγγέλιον)
11. θαυμάζω (θav-**ma**-zo), intrans. I marvel, wonder, am amazed; trans. I marvel, wonder at, admire; fut. θαυμάσομαι, 1 aor. ἐθαύμασα
12. θερίζω (the-**ri**-zo), I reap, harvest, gather; fut. θερίσω, first aor. ἐθέρισα
13. θερισμός, ὁ, (the-ris-**mos**), a harvest, a crop
14. καρπός, ὁ (kar-**pos**), grain, harvest
15. μήτι (**mi**-ti), used in questions to indicate negative answer expected
16. οὐκέτι (ou-**ke**-ti), no longer, no more (with ind. mood)
17. ὅσος, -η, -ον (**o**-sos, -i, -on), as much as (sg.), as many as (pl.), as great as (fig.), all
18. πράσσω (**pras**-so), I do, practice; fut. πράξω, 1 aor. ἔπραξα; as the fut. and aor. forms demonstrate, the stem of πράσσω conceals a hidden velar (√ πραγ).
19. συνάγω (si-**na**-go), I gather together, assemble (cf. συναγωγή); fut. συνάξω, 2 aor. συνήγαγον (cf. principal parts for ἄγω)
20. χώρα, ἡ (**kho**-ra), countryside, field (of crops), region
21. ψυχή, ἡ (psi-**khi**), life, person, one's innermost being, soul (only in Greek philosophical thought) (cf. Section 18.9) (cf. "psychology")

Box 2: First Aorist Middle Forms of Previously Learned Verbs

Present tense		*First aorist middle tense*	
ἀποκρίνομαι	→	ἀπεκρινάμην	(liquid verb)
ἄρχομαι	→	ἠρξάμην	
ἀσπάζομαι	→	ἠσπασάμην	(stem ends in dental)
δέχομαι	→	ἐδεξάμην	
θεάομαι	→	ἐθεασάμην	
προσεύχομαι	→	προσηυξάμην	

[5] This verb appears in the active form, εὐαγγελίζω, only rarely in the GNT (e.g., Rev 10:7, 14:6).

14.

Third Declension Nouns and Adjectives: Part 1

The third declension is really a category for all the nouns that do not belong to the first or second declension. In fact, some older Greek grammars actually divide this third declension into many different declensions.

This group of nouns requires special attention because many significant theological words, not to mention other high-frequency Greek words, decline according to a third declension pattern. Moreover, as we shall see, many of the paradigms of participles, as well as many adjectives, also follow the pattern of the third declension.

In many cases, the gender of third declension nouns cannot be predicted and must be memorized for each noun separately. But third declension nouns *do* take the same definite article as do first and second declension nouns. Therefore, if you are in doubt about the gender of a noun, the gender of the preceding article will be a reliable guide.

14.1 THIRD DECLENSION ENDINGS

In contrast to the first two declensions, the endings of the third declension exhibit much more diversity. Nonetheless, some of the general tendencies of the third declensional endings can be summarized as follows:

	masculine/feminine		*neuter*	
	sg.	*pl.*	*sg.*	*pl.*
N	-ς or none	-ες	—	-α
G	-ος	-ων	-ος	-ων
D	-ι	-σι(ν)	-ι	-σι(ν)
A	-α or -ν	-ας	—	-α
V	-ς or none	-ες	—	-α

Figure: Figure of a man, with lentoid eyes and plain cape (Kelhasan, central Turkey, *IKonya* 137).

In many cases, the nominative form cannot be predicted. However, *the genitive singular form preserves the actual noun stem (which can be found by removing the -ος ending)*. For example:

Nominative		*Stem*	*Genitive*
νύξ ("night")	→	νυκτ	νυκτός
παῖς ("child")	→	παιδ	παιδός
χάρις ("goodwill")	→	χαριτ	χάριτος
γυνή ("woman")	→	γυναικ	γυναικός

Therefore, when you memorize these third declension nouns, you must *memorize the genitive form as well as the nominative form*. Our primary example word for third declension nouns is ἄρχων ("ruler," m.). This word employs the endings listed above, which, when added to the stem ἀρχοντ form the following paradigm:

⊕	*Sg.*	*Pl.*
N	ἄρχων	ἄρχοντ-ες
G	ἄρχοντ-ος	ἀρχόντ-ων
D	ἄρχοντ-ι	ἄρχου-σι(ν)
A	ἄρχοντ-α	ἄρχοντ-ας
V	ἄρχον[1]	ἄρχοντ-ες

1. The nominative singular has no ending added to the stem. But because Greek words cannot end in τ, the final letter of the nominative stem ἄρχοντ drops off, and the previous stem vowel, ο, is lengthened in compensation to ω:

   ἄρχοντ → ἄρχον → ἄρχων

2. The final two stem consonants, ντ, are deleted when σι is added to form the dative plural. Compensatory lengthening of the preceding stem vowel then occurs:

   ἄρχοντ + σι → ἄρχοντσι → ἄρχοσι → ἄρχουσι

3. If you learn the paradigm of ἄρχων well, it will be much easier to identify the many variations that one encounters throughout the third declension, and it will also help you learn the paradigm of the present participle in Chapter 18.

---

[1] Vocative form is normally the pure stem.

14.2 THIRD DECLENSION STEMS ENDING IN DENTALS, VELARS, AND LABIALS

As we observed in the case of the future and aorist tenses, the addition of -σ to the stems of words ending in labials, velars, and dentals produces a series of predictable morphological changes. These rules also apply to third declension nouns. By way of illustration, here are the paradigms of four typical third declension nouns. The stems of the first three nouns end in dental consonants. The stem of the fourth ends in a velar. Notice in each case that the nominative form does not preserve the original stem:

	Nom.	*Stem*	*Gloss*
final τ (dental)	νύξ[2]	νυκτ	night
final τ (dental)	φῶς	φωτ	light
final δ (dental)	ἐλπίς	ελπιδ	hope
final κ (velar)	σάρξ	σαρκ	flesh

Paradigms

Sg.	*dental (fm.)*	*dental (nt.)*	*dental (fm.)*	*velar (fm.)*
N	νύξ (νυκτ-ς)	φῶς	ἐλπίς (ἐλπίδ-ς)	σάρξ (σαρκ-ς)
G	νυκτός	φωτός	ἐλπίδος	σαρκός
D	νυκτί	φωτί	ἐλπίδι	σαρκί
A	νύκτα	φῶς	ἐλπίδα	σάρκα
V	νύξ	φῶς	ἐλπί	σάρξ
Pl.				
N	νύκτες	φῶτα	ἐλπίδες	σάρκες
G	νυκτῶν	φώτων[3]	ἐλπίδων	σαρκῶν
D	νυξί(ν) (νυκτ-σι)	φωσί(ν) (φωτ-σι)	ἐλπίσι(ν) (ἐλπίδ-σι)	σαρξί(ν) (σαρκ-σι)
A	νύκτας	φῶτα	ἐλπίδας	σάρκας
V	νύκτες	φῶτα	ἐλπίδες	σάρκες

14.2.1 Observations

νύξ: The nominative singular and dative plural forms require special explanation. In the case of νύξ, the actual stem is νυκτ. When the -ς ending is added to the stem, the final τ drops off (remember τ, δ, θ, ζ + σ → σ); next, the now final κ combines

---

[2] νυκτ + ς → νυκς → νύξ.

[3] According to the rules for the accentation of monosyllabic nouns, an acute should fall on the penult in the gen. pl. However, φώτων is an exception to this rule.

with σ to form ξ (νυκτ-ς → νυκς → νύξ). In the dative plural, a similar change occurs, with νυκτ-σι becoming νυξί.

φῶς: The nominative and accusative forms of φῶς are identical in the singular and plural because it is a neuter noun.

ἐλπίς: The actual stem of ἐλπίς is ἐλπιδ. When the -ς ending is added to the stem, the final δ drops off (δ + σ → σ), and ἐλπίς is formed. In the dative plural, a similar change occurs, with ἐλπιδ-σι becoming ἐλπίσι.

σάρξ: The stem of σάρξ is σαρκ. When the -ς ending is added to this stem, the final κ combines with the -ς (remember κ, γ, χ + σ = ξ), and σάρξ is formed. In the dative plural, a similar change occurs, with σαρκ-σι becoming σαρξί.

14.2.2 Accentuation Rules

1. Monosyllables of the third declension (e.g., νύξ, σάρξ, φῶς) normally have the accent on the *ultima* in the genitive and dative, in both singular and plural (e.g., νυκτῶν), but on the *penult* in the accusative singular and plural, nominative plural forms (e.g., νύκτες).
2. Some long vowels take an acute in the nom. sg. (e.g., ἀγών, αἰών). However, the gen. pl. is normally accented with circumflex: [h]

nom. sg.	*gen. sg.*	*gen. pl.*
νύξ	νυκτός	νυκτῶν
σάρξ	σαρκός	σαρκῶν

14.3 THIRD DECLENSION STEMS ENDING IN ρ

In this section, we will examine three slightly different patterns of stems ending in ρ, using σωτήρ ("savior"), ἀνήρ ("man, husband"), and πατήρ ("father") as examples. The stems of these nouns are as follows:

nominative	*stem*
σωτήρ (m.)	σωτηρ
ἀνήρ (m.)	ανερ → ανδρ[4]
πατήρ (m.)	πατρ/πατερ-[5]

[4] The original stem, ανερ, undergoes syncope and loses its ε. A δ is then inserted between the resulting consonants, νρ, to facilitate pronunciation (ανερ → ανρ → ανδρ).

[5] The stem fluctuates between πατρ- and πατερ- (cf. μήτηρ, θυγάτηρ, γαστήρ [belly]).

Try not to let the very slight changes between these examples distract you from the reoccurring patterns in the overall paradigm:

	Sg.		
N	σωτήρ	ἀνήρ[6]	πατήρ
G	σωτῆρος	ἀνδρός	πατρός
D	σωτῆρι	ἀνδρί	πατρί
A	σωτῆρα	ἄνδρα	πατέρα
V	σῶτερ	ἄνερ	πάτερ
	Pl.		
N	σωτῆρες	ἄνδρες	πατέρες
G	σωτήρων	ἀνδρῶν	πατέρων
D	σωτῆρσι(ν)	ἀνδράσι(ν) (ἀνδρ-α-σι)	πατράσι(ν) (πατρ-α-σι)
A	σωτῆρας	ἄνδρας	πατέρας
V	σωτῆρες	ἄνδρες	πατέρες

In the case of ἀνήρ and πατήρ, -α is added to the stem in the dative plural, *prior to* attaching -σι. This addition prevents consonants from coming together (ἀνδρ-α-σι, πατρ-α-σι).[7]

The feminine noun χάρις (**kha**-ris), meaning "gratuitous service, grace, favor," requires special mention. There is one important exception to the above pattern, namely the accusative singular form is χάριν.[8] Noun stems that end in a dental, and are preceded by an unaccented vowel, tend to have ν in the accusative singular.

χάρις (fm.)

	Sg.	*Pl.*
N	χάρις	χάριτες
G	χάριτος	χαρίτων
D	χάριτι	χάρισι(ν)
A	χάριν	χάριτας
V	χάρι	χάριτες

[6] This noun follows the same pattern of accentuation as monosyllables of the third declension (cf. 14.2.2).

[7] Cf. μάρτυς (μάρτυρ-ς) (nom.), μάρτυρος (gen.), μάρτυρι (dat.), μάρτυρα (acc.); pl. μάρτυρες, μαρτύρων (gen.), μάρτυσι(ν) (dat.), μάρτυρας (acc.), μάρτυρες (voc.). Note how the final ρ drops off in the nom. sg. and dat. pl. before the addition of -ς and -σι, respectively.

[8] χάριτα only occurs twice in the GNT (Acts 24:27; Jude 1:4).

14.4 THIRD DECLENSION FEMININE STEMS ENDING IN VARIABLE ι/ε

Another class of third declension nouns have stems that end in a variable ι/ε. This group of nouns is feminine.[9] Our example word in πόλις (city). The stem of the nominative, accusative, and vocative singular cases ends in -ι (πολι-). But the stem of the remaining forms ends in -ε (πολε-).

Stems Ending in ι/ε πόλις (πολι-/πολε-)

	Sg.	*Pl.*
N	πόλις (πόλι-ς)	πόλεις (πόλε-ες)
G	πόλεως	πόλεων
D	πόλει (πόλε-ι)	πόλεσι(ν)
A	πόλιν	πόλεις (πόλε-ες)
V	πόλι	πόλεις

Note the following:

1. The genitive singular ending has lengthened from -ος to -ως. This explains why the accented antepenult appears to break the rules of accentuation.[10] The genitive plural is probably accented on the antepenult by analogy with the genitive singular.
2. Accusative ending is -ν (not -α).
3. The nominative and accusative plural forms have the same ending, -εις.

Other examples from this class of the third declension include πίστις ("faith, confidence") and δύναμις ("power, potential").

---

[9] Except ὄφις, -εως (m.) ("snake," "serpent") and σίναπι, -εως (nt.) ("mustard").

[10] The antepenult is accented in the genitive singular (πόλεως) despite the fact that the ultima is long. The accenting of the antepenult under these conditions is normally prohibited by the rules of accentuation. This irregularity can be explained on the basis of the earlier Homeric form. The original stem of this noun ended in η (πολη). Thus, the genitive singular form, πόληος (the Homeric form), was a legal form of accentuation. The antepenult could be accented because the ultima was short. Over time, the last two vowels underwent a transfer of quantity, becoming πόλεως (η → ε, ο → ω), with the accent remaining in its original position (Smyth, *Greek Grammar*, 270, 271, cf. 34).

14.5 REFERENCE: THIRD DECLENSION ADJECTIVE OF TWO TERMINATIONS: ἀληθής, -ές ("TRUE")

Some adjectives, like third declension nouns, have identical forms in the masculine and feminine. These are known as adjectives of two terminations. An important example of a third declension adjective of two terminations is ἀληθής, -ές. Because its stem ends in -εσ (αληθεσ-), many contractions occur with the endings. When found between two vowels, the σ of the stem becomes intervocalic and drops out, and then the remaining vowels contract.

	Sg.		*Pl.*	
	m./fm.	*nt.*	*m./fm.*	*nt.*
N	ἀληθής	ἀληθές	ἀληθεῖς (-έσ-ες)	ἀληθῆ (-έσ-α)
G	ἀληθοῦς (-έσ-ος)	ἀληθοῦς	ἀληθῶν (-έσ-ων)	ἀληθῶν
D	ἀληθεῖ (-έσ-ι)	ἀληθεῖ	ἀληθέσι(ν) (-έσ-σι)	ἀληθέσι(ν)
A	ἀληθῆ (-έσ-α)	ἀληθές	ἀληθεῖς (-έσ-ες)	ἀληθῆ (-έσ-α)
V	ἀληθές (pure stem)	ἀληθές	ἀληθεῖς (-έσ-ες)	ἀληθῆ (-έσ-α)

14.6 VOCABULARY TO BE MEMORIZED

1. ἀληθής (a-li-**this**) (m. and fm.), -ές (nt.), true, truthful (third decl.) (cf. ἀληθινός, -η, -ον [adj.], ἀλήθεια [noun])
2. ἄλλος, -η, -ο (**al**-los, -i, -o), another, other (cf. ἕτερος); ὁ ἄλλος, the other man, ἡ ἄλλη, the other woman
3. ἄρχων, ἄρχοντος, ὁ (**ar**-khon, **ar**-khon-dos), ruler, official, authority
4. δεῦτε (**dhef**-te), come!
5. ἕτερος, -α, -ον (**e**-te-ros, -a, on), different, another, one of two (cf. ἄλλος) ("heterodox, heterosexual")
6. ἔτι (**e**-ti), still, yet (adv.)
7. Μωϋσῆς, -έως (mo-**i**-sis, -**e**-os), Moses[11]
8. νύξ, νυκτός, ἡ (niks, ni-**ktos**), night
9. ὄρος, -ους, τό, mountain, hill (cf. Section 15.3)
10. πίστις, πίστεως, ἡ (**pi**-stis, **pi**-ste-os), confidence, faithfulness, faith, belief (cf. πιστός, -ή, -όν, πιστεύω)
11. πόλις, -εως (**po**-lis, -e-os), ἡ, city (so what is the meaning of the word "necropolis"?)

[11] Dat: Μωϋσεῖ (John 5:46) or Μωϋσῇ (Acts 7:44); Acc: Μωϋσέα (Luke 16:29) or Μωϋσήν (1 Cor 10:2); Voc.: Μωϋσῆν (Exod 3:4).

12. σάρξ, σαρκός, ἡ (sarks, sar-**kos**), flesh, physical body[12]
13. σωτηρία, ἡ (so-ti-**ri**-a) deliverance, rescue, salvation
14. σωτήρ, -ῆρος, ὁ (so-**tir**, -**i**-ros), savior, deliverer
15. ὕδωρ, ὕδατος, τό (**i**-dhor, **i**-da-tos), water (cf. "hydroelectric" means water-generated electicity)
16. χάρις, -ιτος, ἡ (**kha**-ris, -i-tos), gratuitous service (i.e., free from contractual obligations or counter service), grace, beneficient disposition, unmerited/undeserved goodwill toward someone, sign of favor, benefaction

Family

17. ἀνήρ, ἀνδρός, ὁ (a-**nir**, an-**dhros**) man, husband
18. γυνή, γυναικός, ἡ (yi-**ni**, yi-ne-**kos**), voc. γύναι, woman, wife
19. μήτηρ, -τρός, ἡ (**mi**-tir, mi-**tros**), mother (cf. Section 14.3)
20. πατήρ, -τρός, ὁ (pa-**tir**, pa-**tros**), father; in the plural form, πατέρες, often means "ancestors"

14.7 POLITICS AS A SEMANTIC FIELD: VOCABULARY REVIEW

- βασιλεύω — I rule
- βασιλεύς (gen. -έως) — king, emperor
- βασιλεία — kingdom, empire, domain
- βασιλικός, -ή, -όν — royal
- ἄρχων (gen. -οντος) — ruler, official, authority
- ἔθνος (gen. -νους) — nation, pl. Gentiles, nations
- λαός — people, people as a nation, populace
- ὄχλος — a crowd, a mob of common people
- πόλις (gen. -εως) — city

[12] Thus, a "sarcophagus" (ἡ σαρκοφάγος) is literally a "coffin" that "eats flesh".

15.

Third Declension Nouns and Adjectives: Part 2

15.1 THIRD DECLENSION NOUNS ENDING IN -μα

One important group of third declension nouns are those whose nominative singular forms end in -μα. This group of words is neuter. Their declensional endings can be summarized as follows:

	Sg.	*Pl.*
N	none	-α
G	-ος	-ων
D	-ι	-σι(ν)
A	none	-α

For example, the stem of ὄνομα ("name") is ὀνοματ-. The paradigm is as follows:

	Sg.	*Pl.*
N	τὸ ὄνομα	τὰ ὀνόματα
G	τοῦ ὀνόματος	τῶν ὀνομάτων
D	τῷ ὀνόματι	τοῖς ὀνόμασι(ν)
A	τὸ ὄνομα	τὰ ὀνόματα

1. Because a Greek noun cannot end with τ, the final τ of the stem, ὀνοματ, must drop off in the nominative and accusative singular forms.
2. As in the case of all neuter nouns, the nominative and accusative forms are identical, in the singular and plural.
3. The neuter nominative singular ending -μα contains a short α, allowing the antepenult to be accented (ὀνόματα).

Figure: Carved relief of a fish (*IKonya* 141).

4. Other examples from this class include:

- αἷμα ("blood")
- βρῶμα ("food")
- θέλημα ("will")
- πνεῦμα ("spirit")
- ῥῆμα ("word")
- σπέρμα ("seed")
- στόμα ("mouth")
- σῶμα ("body")

15.2 THIRD DECLENSION NOUNS ENDING IN -ε/ευ

Another group of third declension nouns have stems ending variably in -ε or -ευ. The stem ends in -ευ in the nominative singular, dative plural, and vocative singular. Our example word is βασιλεύς (va-si-**lefs**), meaning "king." As in the case of πόλις, the stem fluctuates between βασιλευ- in the nominative and vocative singular and dative plural, and βασιλε- everywhere else. The paradigm for βασιλεύς is as follows:

βασιλεύς (βασιλη/ε/ευ)

	Sg.	*Pl.*
N	βασιλεύς (-λευ-ς)	βασιλεῖς (-λε-ες)
G	βασιλέως (-λη-ος)[1]	βασιλέων
D	βασιλεῖ (-λε-ι)	βασιλεῦσι(ν) (-λευ-σι)
A	βασιλέα	βασιλεῖς (-λε-ες)
V	βασιλεῦ	βασιλεῖς

Other examples of this declension include γραμματεύς ("scribe"), ἱερεύς ("priest"), ἀρχιερεύς ("highpriest").

15.3 THIRD DECLENSION NEUTER NOUNS ENDING IN -ος

Words such as ἔθνος ("nation," pl. "Gentiles, nations"), γένος ("family, descendant"), and μέρος ("part, share") have nominative singular forms ending in -ος, which

[1] The primitive stem of this noun may have ended in ηϝ. The Greek letter ϝ (digamma/δίγαμμα) is an ancient letter that is no longer used in Attic and Hellenistic Greek. But a *phantom* digamma continues to exercise influence in the formation of some words. Diagamma (ϝ) generally drops out before vowels and vocalizes to υ before consonants, as we see in the nominative singular and dative plural.

could easily be mistaken for masculine second declension nouns. These are actually *neuter* nouns of the third declension. The stem of these nouns actually ends in -ες:

nom./acc.	*stem*
ἔθνος	εθνεσ
γένος	γενεσ
μέρος	μερεσ

In all cases, except the nominative and accusative singular, the final σ of the stem drops off (e.g., ἔθνεσ → ἔθνε-), resulting in the contraction of the now final -ε of the stem with the declensional ending. Given that many modifications and contractions occur in this paradigm, it is advisable to learn the final contracted forms. The paradigm for ἔθνος is as follows:

ἔθνος (stem: εθνεσ)

	Sg.		*Pl.*	
N	ἔθνος		ἔθνη	(ἔθνεσ-α → ἔθνε-α)
G	ἔθνους	(ἔθνεσ-ος → ἔθνε-ος)	ἐθνῶν	(ἐθνέσ-ων → ἔθνε-ων)
D	ἔθνει	(ἔθνεσ-ι → ἔθνε-ι)	ἔθνεσι(ν)	(ἔθνεσ-σι → ἔθνε-σι)
A	ἔθνος		ἔθνη	(ἔθνεσ-α → ἔθνε-α)
V	ἔθνος		ἔθνη	(ἔθνεσ-α → ἔθνε-α)

15.4 "3–1–3" TYPE ADJECTIVES

In Chapter 7, we discussed first and second declension adjectives. There are also adjectives that combine third declension endings with first declension endings. These are termed "3-1-3 type" adjectives. In other words, these adjectives are third declension in the masculine, first declension in the feminine, and third declension in the neuter.

15.4.1 πᾶς, πᾶσα, πᾶν (sg. "every," pl. "all")

The actual stem of πᾶς, πᾶσα, πᾶν is παντ. As in the case of all third declension words, one must also memorize the genitive masculine singular form, in addition to the masculine nominative form, because this form preserves the original stem. You should also memorize the feminine and neuter nominative forms.

πᾶς, πᾶσα, πᾶν (√ παντ)

⊕		*Sg.*			*Pl.*	
	m.	*fm.*	*nt.*	*m.*	*fm.*	*nt.*
N	πᾶς	πᾶσα	πᾶν	πάντες	πᾶσαι	πάντα
G	παντός	πάσης	παντός	πάντων	πασῶν	πάντων
D	παντί	πάσῃ	παντί	πᾶσι(ν)[2]	πάσαις	πᾶσι(ν)
A	πάντα	πᾶσαν	πᾶν	πάντας	πάσας	πάντα
V	πᾶς	πᾶσα	πᾶν	πάντες	πᾶσαι	πάντα

Observations:

1. The feminine singular forms are of the α-*im*pure class (cf. 6.4, δόξα).
2. The neuter nominative and accusative singular forms drop the τ from the stem παντ leaving παν, and the α lengthens in compensation. But the neuter nominative and accusative plural add α to the stem (πάντα).
3. As you would expect, the genitive and dative singular and plural forms of the neuter are identical to the masculine forms.

Uses of πᾶς, πᾶσα, πᾶν

1. When πᾶς is used in the *attributive* position, it denotes that the whole of something is regarded as a sum of its parts. In other words, the thing is to be taken as a whole: For example, ὁ πᾶς νόμος means "the *whole* law [in its entirety]."
2. The *predicate* use of πᾶς in the singular, *without* the article, can mean "every" or "each" (e.g., πᾶν ἔργον, "every deed").
3. The *predicate* use of πᾶς in the plural, *without* the article, can mean "all" (e.g., πάντες ἀδελφοί, "all brothers").
4. The *predicate* use of πᾶς, *with* the article, means "without exception" (e.g., πᾶς ὁ νόμος, "the entire law without exception").
5. This adjective is also frequently employed by itself as a substantive: for example, πᾶς ("everyone"), πάντες ("all people, everybody"), πάντα ("all things").

[2] When two consonants are deleted, as they are in the dative plural of the masculine and neuter, *compensatory lengthening* of the surviving stem vowel occurs: παντ → πα + σι → πᾶσι. The penult accented with a circumflex indicates that the α of πᾶσι is long.

15.4.2 οὐδείς, οὐδεμία, οὐδέν ("no, no one, nothing")

Another example of a "3-1-3" type adjective is οὐδείς:

⊕	*m.*	*fm.*	*nt.*
N	οὐδείς	οὐδεμία	οὐδέν
G	οὐδενός	οὐδεμιᾶς	οὐδενός
D	οὐδενί	οὐδεμιᾷ	οὐδενί
A	οὐδένα	οὐδεμίαν	οὐδέν

1. οὐδείς, οὐδεμία, and οὐδέν are only used with the indicative mood. With non-indicative moods, the alternative forms, μηδείς, μηδεμία, μηδέν, are used. It is declined in the same way.
2. As a substantive, this term means "no one" (m./fm.) and "nothing" (nt.).
3. The neuter accusative form, οὐδέν, can also function adverbially meaning "in no respect," or "in no way."

15.5 INDEFINITE PRONOUN: τις, τι

There is no indefinite article in Greek. The nearest equivalent is the indefinite pronoun, τις and τι, meaning "anyone, someone" (m./f.), and "something" (nt.), though the cordinal numbers, εἷς, μία, ἕν, are also used this way, as they are in MGr (cf.15.9). This is a pronoun of *two terminations*: In other words, the masculine and feminine forms are identical. It declines as a *third* declension adjective. The stem is actually τιν-.

τις, τι (τιν)

⊕	*m./fm.*		*nt.*	
Sg.				
N	τις		τι	
G	τινος	(τινός)	τινος	(τινός)
D	τινι	(τινί)	τινι	(τινί)
A	τινα	(τινά)	τι	
Pl.				
N	τινες	(τινές)	τινα	(τινά)
G	τινων	(τινῶν)	τινων	(τινῶν)
D	τισι(ν)	(τισί[ν])	τισι(ν)	(τισί[ν])
A	τινας	(τινάς)	τινα	(τινά)

There are several important factors to bear in mind:

1. The indefinite pronoun is normally an enclitic (cf. Section 5.6.2). As you know, enclitics throw their accent backon the last syllable of the previous word. For this reason, τις and τι should be pronounced as if they were part of the word that precedes them.
2. When the disyllabic forms *are* accented, the accent always falls on the *second* syllable (i.e., τινός, not τίνος). The monosyllabic forms are accented when standing first in a sentence.
3. In practice, τις and τι often function in a manner similar to the English indefinite article ("a," "an").

In Homer's *Odyssey*, the one-eyed Cyclops, named Polyphemus, asks for Odysseus' name. Odysseus gave himself a false name, Οὔτις, which is a combination of οὐ ("no") and τις ("someone"), in other words, "nobody!"[3]

15.6 THE INTERROGATIVE PRONOUN: τίς, τί

The paradigm of the interrogative pronoun, τίς and τί (who? which? what? why?), is almost identical to the indefinite pronoun. Therefore, special attention is required here to avoid confusing these two very similar words. This pronoun can be distinguished on the basis of its accentuation. In contrast to the indefinite pronoun, the interrogative pronoun is always accented.

	τίς, τί (τιν)	
⊕	*m./fm.*	*nt.*
Sg.		
N	τίς[4]	τί
G	τίνος	τίνος
D	τίνι	τίνι
A	τίνα	τί
Pl.		
N	τίνες	τίνα
G	τίνων	τίνων
D	τίσι(ν)	τίσι(ν)
A	τίνας	τίνα

---

[3] Od. 9.366, 408.

[4] The final ν drops out before the σ: τιν-ς → τις.

1. Note that this word is always accented on the *first* syllable.
2. The acute accent on the nominative singular forms does *not* change to a grave accent when followed immediately by another word.
3. The masculine and feminine nominative forms mean "who?" and the neuter nominative form can mean "what?'" or "why?'"

15.7 REVIEWING QUESTION WORDS

Over the previous lessons, we have learned the most commonly used question words. Let us review them here:

How?	πῶς	(do not confuse with the enclitic πώς which means "somewhere")
When?	πότε	(do not confuse with ποτέ which means "once, formerly")
Where?	ποῦ	(do not confuse with the enclitic πού, which means "somewhere")
Why?	τί	
Who?	τίς	
What?	τί	

15.8 COMPARATIVE ADJECTIVE OF TWO TERMINATIONS: μείζων, μεῖζον

The word μείζων ("greater, larger") is the comparative of μέγας ("large, great"). One way of forming a comparative adjective is to add -ων, -ονος, and so on, as illustrated by this paradigm:

μείζων, μεῖζον (μειζον)

	Singular		*Plural*	
	m./fm.	*nt.*	*m./fm.*	*nt.*
N	μείζων	μεῖζον	μείζονες[5]	μείζονα[6]
G	μείζονος	μείζονος	μειζόνων	μειζόνων
D	μείζονι	μείζονι	μείζοσι(ν)	μείζοσι(ν)
A	μείζονα[7]	μεῖζον	μείζονας[8]	μείζονα[9]
V	μεῖζον	μεῖζον	μείζονες[10]	μείζονα[11]

[5] Or μείζους.
[6] Or μείζω.
[7] Or μείζω.
[8] Or μείζους.
[9] Or μείζω.
[10] Or μείζους.
[11] Or μείζω.

1. When two things are compared with one another, a comparative adjective such as μείζων is often used, followed by a noun or pronoun in the genitive. This is termed the *genitive of comparison* ("greater than ...", cf. Section 5.13).
2. The superlative form of μέγας is μέγιστος, μεγίστη, μέγιστον ("greatest"). Its ending declines according to the pattern for the first and second declension adjectives.
3. The comparative of πολύς, πολλή, πολύ ("much, many"), is πλείων (m./fm.), πλεῖον (nt.),[12] meaning "more." It follows this same basic declensional pattern as μείζων.

15.9 CARDINAL NUMBERS

The cardinal numbers 1, 2, 3, 4 are declined like adjectives.

Number 1

The cardinal number 1 follows the "3-1-3" type adjectival paradigm. The actual stem of the masculine and neuter forms is εν.[13] Needless to say, this word has no plural forms!

εἷς, μία, ἕν

	m.	*fm.*	*nt.*
N	εἷς	μία	ἕν
G	ἑνός	μιᾶς	ἑνός
D	ἑνί	μιᾷ	ἑνί
A	ἕνα	μίαν	ἕν

1. In the case of the masculine nominative form (εἷς), the ν of the stem εν drops off when ς is added, and the preceding vowel lengthens in compensation (ἑν + ς → ἑνς → ἑς → εἱς).
2. Take note of the (editorial) rough breathing marks and accents. This will help you distinguish:
   - εἷς (= 1) from the preposition εἰς ("into")
   - ἕν (= 1) from the preposition ἐν ("in")
3. Note also that the masculine and neuter forms have third declension endings, whereas the feminine is first declension (α-pure).

---

[12] Alternative forms: πλέων, πλέον.

[13] Originally from the stem, σεμ. The initial σ dropped off and became a rough breathing (ἑν). Final μ became ν (apparently) because it cannot stand at the end of a word. Thereafter, third declension endings were added. Many other words follow this pattern, such as οὐδείς, οὐδεμία, and οὐδέν (a combination of οὐδέ + εἷς/μία/ἕν; cf. μηδείς, μηδεμία, μηδέν).

In the GNT, the cardinal numbers can also function as indefinite articles as they do in MGr:

εἷς ἀνήρ (a man)
μία γυνή (a woman)
ἓν τέκνον (a child)

You should now be able to translate the first clause of the Nicene Creed: Πιστεύω εἰς ἕνα θεὸν…καὶ εἰς ἕνα κύριον Ἰησοῦν Χριστὸν. How would you parse ἕνα?

Number 2

Most of the forms of the cardinal number 2 are identical, except for the dative plural, δυσί(ν). Needless to say, all its forms are plural:

	m./fm./nt.
N	δύο (**dhi**-o)
G	δύο
D	δυσί(ν) (**dhi**-si[n])
A	δύο

Number 3

The cardinal number 3 has identical forms in the masculine and feminine. Adjectives that follow this pattern are termed adjectives of two terminations.

	m./fm.	*nt.*
N	τρεῖς	τρία
G	τριῶν	τριῶν
D	τρισί(ν)	τρισί(ν)
A	τρεῖς	τρία

Number 4

The cardinal number 4 is also an adjective of two terminations.

	m./fm.	*nt.*
N	τέσσαρες	τέσσαρα
G	τεσσάρων	τεσσάρων
D	τέσσαρσι(ν)	τέσσαρσι(ν)
A	τέσσαρας	τέσσαρα

The cardinal numbers from 5 to 12, and from 15 to 199 are indeclinable: πέντε (5), ἕξ (6), ἑπτά (7), ὀκτώ (8), ἐννέα (9), δέκα (10), ἕνδεκα (11), δώδεκα (12), etc.[14]

Examples:

m.	*fm.*	*nt.*
εἷς ἀνήρ (one man)	μία γυνή (one woman)	ἕν τέκνον (one child)
δύο ἄνδρες (two men)	δύο γυναῖκες (two women)	δύο τέκνα (two children)
τρεῖς ἄνδρες (three men)	τρεῖς γυναῖκες (three women)	τρία τέκνα (three children)
τέσσαρες ἄνδρες (four men)	τέσσαρες γυναῖκες (four women)	τέσσαρα τέκνα (four children)
πέντε ἄνδρες (five men)	πέντε γυναῖκες (five women)	πέντε τέκνα (five children)
ἕξ ἄνδρες (six men)	ἕξ γυναῖκες (six women)	ἕξ τέκνα (six children)

15.10 VOCABULARY TO BE MEMORIZED

1. βασιλεύς, -έως, ὁ (va-si-**lefs**, -**e**-os), king (cf. βασιλεία)
2. ἔθνος, -ους, τό (**eth**-nos, -ous), nation pl., τὰ ἔθνη, "the Gentiles"
3. θέλημα, -ατος, τό (**the**-li-ma, -a-tos), will (as a noun), desire (as a noun) (cf. θέλω)
4. μείζων, -ον (**mi**-zon, -on), larger, greater (comp. of μέγας)
5. ὄνομα, -ατος, τό (**o**-no-ma, -a-tos), name (noun)
6. ὅστις (m.), ἥτις (fm.), ὅτι (nt.)[15] (**o**-stis, **i**-tis, **o**-ti), who, which, whoever, whichever (try not to confuse the nt. form of ὅστις with ὅτι meaning "because" or "that"). These relative pronouns are declinable (cf. τις, τι).
7. οὐδείς, οὐδενός (m. gen); οὐδεμία (fm.), οὐδέν (nt.) (ou-**dhis**, ou-dhe-**nos**; ou-dhe-**mi**-a, ou-**dhen**), no one, nothing, no (used with ind.)
8. μηδείς, μήδενός (m. gen); μηδεμία (gen.), μηδέν (mi-**dhis**, mi-dhe-**nos**; mi-dhe-**mi**-a, mi-**dhen**), no one, nothing (used with non-indicative moods)
9. πᾶς, παντός (m. gen); πᾶσα (fm.), πᾶν (nt.) (pas, pan-**dos**; **pa**-sa, pan), (1) without the article "each, every"; pl. all; (2) with the article entire, whole, all; (3) everyone, all things
10. ἅπας, ἅπασα, ἅπαν (**a**-pas, **a**-pa-sa, **a**-pan), this is an intensive form of πᾶς, πᾶσα, πᾶν
11. πλείων (m./fm.), πλείονος (m./fm. gen.), πλεῖον (nt.) (**pli**-on, **pli**-on-os, **pli**-on), more; comparative of πολύς
12. σκότος, -ους, τό (**sko**-tos, -ous), darkness (cf. σκοτία) (for paradigm, see ἔθνος, -ους, Section 15.3)
13. σπέρμα, -ατος, τό (**sper**-ma, -a-tos), seed (of plants, cf. Section 21.7); in plural form it often means "descendants" or "children"; in Johannine literature, notably

[14] The numbers 13 and 14 both decline (δεκατρεῖς, -τρία; δεκατέσσαρες, -α).
[15] But sometimes written ὅ τι to avoid confusion.

also "nature" or "character," such that one can speak of the "divine σπέρμα" in human beings.

14. σῶμα, -ματος, τό (**so**-ma, -ma-tos), body, physical body
15. τίς, τί (tis, ti), who? which? what? why? (interrogative)
16. τις, τι (tis, ti), anyone, anything, someone, something, some, any, a certain, a/an (enclitic indefinite pronoun)

Numbers (οἱ ἀριθμοί)

17. εἷς (m.), μία (fm.), ἕν (nt.) (is, **mi**-a, en), one (do not confuse εἷς with εἰς, and ἕν with ἐν)
18. δύο, δυσί(ν) (dat.) (**dhi**-o, dhi-**si**[**n**]), two
19. τρεῖς (m., fm.), τρία (nt.) (tris, **tri**-a), three
20. τέσσαρες (m., fm.), τέσσαρα (nt.) (**tes**-sa-res, **tes**-sa-ra), four

You have previously learned:

- πέντε (**pen**-de), five (indeclinable)
- ἕξ (eks), six (indeclinable)

16.

Perfect and Pluperfect Active, Middle, and Passive Indicative

16.1 REVIEW OF THE THREE GREEK ASPECTS

As you know, there are three aspects. Each of these aspects is associated with a particular tense, as follows:

Aoristic aspect	→ first and second aorist tenses, and sometimes present and future tenses
Imperfective aspect	→ imperfect, and often the present and future tenses
Perfective aspect	→ perfect and pluperfect tenses

These three Greek aspects can be explained using the analogy of a parade. Imagine yourself as a newspaper reporter in a helicopter flying over a parade. From this bird's-eye view you are able to view the parade in its entirety as a complete or undifferentiated totality, without further definition. This perspective can be compared to the aoristic aspect of the aorist tense.

Now, consider your changed perspective if you were a spectator standing on the street with others, watching the parade as it passed by you. You would view

Figure: Panel relief on sarcophagus (Istanbul Archaeological Museum).

Figure: Two women flanked by the carvings of spindle and distaff (Kadinhani, central Turkey, *IKonya* 146).

the action as an *event in progress*. This corresponds to the imperfective aspect of the imperfect tense. Finally, think of yourself as the administrator in charge of planning this parade. You have worked on this project for the previous year. When you watch the parade, you now perceive it from the perspective of all of your previous actions, and months of planning, which made this day possible. In other words, you view the parade in its perfective aspect, that is, as an outcome in the present arising from prior actions. This is the connotation of the perfective of the perfect tense.[1]

16.2 THE PERFECTIVE ASPECT

The aspect of the perfect tense is termed perfective. The perfective aspect conceives of a verbal action as a present state of affairs that has resulted from a *prior* action: for example, ᾠκοδόμηκα τὴν οἰκίαν ("I have built the house" [and it is still standing]).[2] Similarly, in the statement "the heavenly kingdom *has come near*,"[3] the verb "has come near" is in the perfect tense. Its aspect implies that the establishment of the "kingdom of God" in the past has ongoing consequences for those living in the present. Thus, one must often take special notice of the use of the perfect tense because it can introduce a verbal action in a more defined or complex way than the aorist tense does.

The perfective aspect is sometimes referred to as the "stative" aspect. It can be used to describe a present *state* resulting from a past action. For example, the verb οἶδα is perfect in tense. It means "I know" (i.e., I am in a present state of knowing something because of having come to know something in the past). Similarly, as we shall see, the passive form of the verb γράφω ("I write") and the active form of ἵστημι ("I stand," cf. Chapter 20) often appear in the GNT in the perfect tense, but they are translated using the English *present* tense: "It is written" and "I am standing."

perfect of γράφω → a book *is* (now) written (because of the past action of it having been written)
perfect of ἵστημι → I *am* presently standing (because of the past action of having stood myself up)

Thus, the Greek perfect tense is often translated into English using the helping words "has" or "have" (e.g., "he has said," "they have said"). But in the case of stative verbs, it is often preferable to translate them using the present tense.

1 Cf. Stanley E. Porter, *Verbal Aspect in the Greek of the New Testament, with Reference to Tense and Mood* (New York: Peter Lang, 1989), chs. 2, 4, 5, 9.

2 Cf. 1 Kings 8:48; 2 Chron 6:2.

3 ἤγγικεν γὰρ ἡ βασιλεία τῶν οὐρανῶν (Matt 3:2).

16.3 FORMING THE PERFECT ACTIVE INDICATIVE

1. The perfect active tense is formed from the fourth principal part. As you will recall, the fourth and fifth principal parts are perfect tenses.
   - fourth principal part – perfect *active* tense
   - fifth principal part – perfect middle and *or* passive tense.

     Many thematic verbs will either have a fourth *and* fifth principal part, which are active and passive, respectively. Other verbs will lack a fourth principal part, and the fifth principal part is middle. It is certainly true that some verbs in the GNT have no examples of a fourth principal part, even though they do have a fifth principal part that functions as a passive. For example, παρακαλῶ in 2 Cor 7:13 appears as παρακεκλήμεθα ("we have been comforted"), and οἰκοδομῶ appears in Luke 4:29 as ᾠκοδόμητο ("was built"). Even though the fourth principal parts of these verbs do not occur in the GNT, they do occur elsewhere in Hellenistic literature. Thus, these verbs do not really present exceptions to this rule.
2. If the verb stem begins with a consonant, this initial consonant is reduplicated, with an ε inserted between them. For example, the perfect stem of λυω is λυ- (the same as the present stem). When the first consonant is reduplicated, the stem becomes λελυ-.
3. But if the first consonant is, φ, χ, or θ, this consonant is deaspirated when it is reduplicated to the corresponding unvoiced stop as follows:

φ → π	(e.g., φιλέω → πεφιλ-)
χ → κ	(e.g., χαρίζομαι → κεχαρισ-)
θ → τ	(e.g., θύω → τεθυ-)

4. If the stem begins with an initial vowel, it may lengthen, as in the case of the aorist and imperfect tenses. However, in actual practice, the initial vowel is often left unchanged.
5. Next, the perfect tense formative, κα, is added to the end of the stem (e.g., λελυ- → λελυκα-). A perfect verb formed with κα as a tense consonant is termed a *first* perfect. However, some verbs form a perfect tense with only -α (not -κα). This is known as a *second* perfect tense.
6. Finally, because the perfect tense is a *primary* tense, it takes primary endings (as do the present and future tenses). The α in the tense formative κα appears to have replaced the connecting vowel, except in the third-person singular[4] (reduplication/vowel lengthening + perfect active stem + [κ]α + primary active ending).

[4] Cf. Smyth, 463a.

This can be summarized as follows:

Perfect Active Indicative of λύω

⊕	*Sg.*		
1	λέλυκα[5]	(**le**-li-ka)	(I have set free)
2	λέλυκας	(**le**-li-kas)	(you have set free)
3	λέλυκε(ν)	(**le**-li-ke[n])	(he/she/it has set free)
	Pl.		
1	λελύκαμεν	(le-**li**-ka-men)	(we have set free)
2	λελύκατε	(le-**li**-ka-te)	(you [pl.] have set free)
3	λελύκασι(ν)[6]	(**le**-li-kasi[n])	(they have set free)

Note: The α of the tense formative, κα, is always short, except in the third plural, where the α is long due to compensatory lengthening (but this does not affect the accenting of the antepenult because the ultima is short). The short α allows the antepenult to be accented (e.g., λέλυκα).

16.4 SOME PERFECT ACTIVE FORMS OF PREVIOUSLY LEARNED VERBS

Present	*Perfect*
ἄγω	ἦχα (αγ → ηχ) (2 pf.) (The γ of the stem is aspirated to χ, as often happens with second perfects having stems ending in a labial or velar.)
ἀναβαίνω	ἀναβέβηκα (cf. 2 aor. ἀνέβην)
καταβαίνω	καταβέβηκα (cf. 2 aor. κατέβην)
γινώσκω	ἔγνωκα (cf. 2 aor. ἔγνων)
εὑρίσκω	εὕρηκα
λέγω	εἴρηκα (cf. fut. ἐρῶ, √ ϝρη)
μένω	μεμένηκα
ὁρῶ (-άω)	ἑόρακα / ἑώρακα
πίνω	πέπωκα
πίπτω	πέπτωκα
φέρω	ἐνήνοχα (cf. 2 aor. ἤνεγκα)

[5] I.e., no ending is added.

[6] As you will recall, the third pl. primary ending is -ντι. τ changes to σ, and ν then drops out before σ (-ντι → νσι → σι).

16.5 PERFECT ACTIVE OF CONTRACT VERBS

The perfect tense of contract verbs is easy to form because there are no vocalic contractions. To form the perfect tense of these verbs, reduplicate the initial consonant, or lengthen the intial vowel, and then lengthen the final contract vowel of the verb stem (ε → η, α → η, ο → ω). Next, add the κα tense formative and the perfect endings. Here are some examples:

Pres. act.	*Pf. act.*
ἀγαπῶ (-άω)	ἠγάπηκα
αἰτῶ (-έω)	ᾔτηκα
ἀκολουθῶ (-έω)	ἠκολούθηκα
ἀσθενῶ (-έω)	ἠσθένηκα
λαλῶ (-έω)	λελάληκα
μαρτυρῶ (-έω)	μεμαρτύρηκα
πληρῶ (-όω)	πεπλήρωκα
ποιῶ (-έω)	πεποίηκα
τηρῶ (-έω)	τετήρηκα

Do you know the famous story of Archimedes? When he stepped into the bathtub, he noticed that the more his body sank into the water, the more the water was displaced out of the bathtub. He realized that he could measure the volume of an object by submerging it into water and then collecting and measuring the volume of the displaced water. When he made this discovery, he famously cried out the perfect form of εὑρίσκω: εὕρηκα! εὕρηκα! ("I have found it! I have found it!").

16.6 FORMING THE SECOND PERFECT ACTIVE INDICATIVE

As explained above, some verbs form a perfect without the κ of the first perfect κα tense formative. These are termed *second* perfects. For example, the grammatical form of οἶδα is a second perfect.[7] Similarly, πείθω (**pi**-tho) also forms a second perfect: πέποιθα (**pe**-pi-tha). The perfect of πείθω can mean "I trust" (followed by dat. or ἐν + dat.), in contrast with the present tense ("I persuade," cf. Chapter 10 vocabulary). The verb πέποιθα expresses *stative* aspect and is better translated using the present tense in English (cf. Matt 27:43; Phil 2:24; 2 Thess 3:4), as in the case of οἶδα. Here is the full second perfect active paradigm of πείθω:

[7] In Attic Greek, οἶδα is an athematic verb in some forms (ἴσμεν, ἴστε) from √ ϝιδ (cf. εἶδον). These athematic forms are also found in the GNT (e.g., ἴστε [Jas 1:19; Eph 5:5; Heb 12:17], ἴσασι [Acts 26:4]). The pluperfect form is ᾔδειν, ᾔδεις, etc., but is translated like an imperfect.

Second Perfect Active Indicative of πείθω

	Sg.		
1	πέποιθα	(**pe**-pi-tha)	(I trust)
2	πέποιθας	(**pe**-pi-thas)	(you trust)
3	πέποιθε(ν)	(**pe**-pi-the[n])	(he/she/it trusts)
	Pl.		
1	πεποίθαμεν	(pe-**pi**-tha-men)	(we trust)
2	πεποίθατε	(pe-**pi**-tha-te)	(you [pl.] trust)
3	πεποίθασι(ν)	(pe-**pi**-tha-si[n])	(they trust)

16.7 SECOND PERFECT OF οἶδα ("I KNOW")

The verb οἶδα (**i**-dha) forms a second perfect tense (although it functions as if it were a present tense). As you know, the paradigm is as follows:

Second Perfect Active Indicative of οἶδα

⊕	*Sg.*		
1	οἶδα	(**i**-dha)	(I know)
2	οἶδας	(**i**-dhas)	(you know)
3	οἶδε(ν)	(**i**-dhe[n])	(he/she/it knows)
	Pl.		
1	οἴδαμεν	(**i**-dha-men)	(we know)
2	οἴδατε	(**i**-dha-te)	(you [pl.] know)
3	οἴδασι(ν)	(**i**-dha-si[n])	(they know)

Historical Note

The root of οἶδα originally began with a digamma, √ *ϝιδ-*, √ *ϝοιδ-* , or √ *ϝειδ(ε)-*, comparable to the Latin word *video*. Thus, οἶδα is closely related to the stem of the second aorist verb εἶδον, which is also √ ιδ- (cf. ἴδε, ἰδού). By implication there is a close relationship between "knowing" and "seeing" in the Greek language. The root *ϝιδ-* became the stem οἰδ- in the perfect indicative and εἰδ- in most other tenses and moods, from which the pluperfect, ᾔδειν, is derived.

16.8 PERFECT ACTIVE OF ἔχω

As you will recall, the root of ἔχω ("I have") is √ σ(ε)χ (not √ εχ). As noted above, this root reappeared in its second aorist form, ἔσχον. The perfect form, ἔσχηκα (**e**-skhi-ka), is probably the result of metathesis[8] (i.e., σεχ → σχε → σχη). We can now summarize the four principal parts of ἔχω:

1.	present	ἔχω	(I have)	→ imperfect: εἶχον (I used to have)
2.	future	ἕξω	(I will have)	
3.	second aorist	ἔσχον	(I had)	
4.	perfect	ἔσχηκα	(I have had)	

16.9 FORMATION OF THE PERFECT PASSIVE INDICATIVE

The primary passive endings are used for both the middle and passive forms, as in the case of the present and future tenses. As you know, these are:

	Sg.	*Pl.*
1	-μαι	-μεθα
2	-σαι	-σθε
3	-ται	-νται

In the perfect passive tense, these endings are attached directly to the verb stem *without any connecting vowel or tense consonant* (i.e., reduplication + perfect passive stem + primary passive ending).[9] Thus, the perfect passive of λύω is:

Perfect Passive Indicative of λύω

⊕	*Sg.*		
1	λέλυμαι	(**le**-li-me)	(I have been set free)
2	λέλυσαι	(**le**-li-se)	(you have been set free)
3	λέλυται	(**le**-li-te)	(he/she/it has been set free)
	Pl.		
1	λελύμεθα	(le-**li**-me-tha)	(we have been set free)
2	λέλυσθε	(**le**-lis-the)	(you [pl.] have been set free)
3	λέλυνται	(**le**-lin-de)	(they have been set free)

---

[8] I.e., the interchange of places between two sounds in a word.

[9] The *perfect* passive of ἄγω is:

	Sg.		*Pl.*	
1	ἦγμαι	(**i**-gme)	ἤγμεθα	(**i**-gme-tha)
2	ἦξαι	(**i**-kse)	ἦχθε	(**i**-khthe)
3	ἦκται	(**i**-kte)	(forms a periphrastic pluperfect)	

Notice in this case how the final γ changes depending on the initial consonant of the personal ending. When a verb stem ends in a labial (π, β, φ), velar (κ, γ, χ), or dental (τ, δ, θ) consonant, the consonant undergoes a change in forming the perfect passive. For more information see cf. Smyth, Chapter 409.

16.10 FORMATION OF THE PERFECT MIDDLE INDICATIVE

The perfect middle indicative is formed the same way, with the same endings, as the perfect passive indicative. We will use the perfect middle of ἐγείρω (e-**yi**-ro), namely ἐγήγερμαι, as an example:

	Sg.		
1	ἐγήγερμαι	(e-**yi**-yer-me)	(I have raised)
2	ἐγήγερσαι	(e-**yi**-yer-se)	(you have raised)
3	ἐγήγερται	(e-**yi**-yer-te)	(he/she/it has raised)
	Pl.		
1	ἐγηγέρμεθα	(e-yi-**yer**-me-tha)	(we have raised)
2	ἐγήγερθε[10]	(e-**yi**-yer-the)	(you [pl.] have raised)
3	(forms a periphrastic pluperfect instead)[11]		

16.11 DISTINGUISHING BETWEEN THE PERFECT MIDDLE AND PASSIVE INDICATIVE

Most of what was said about the present passive and middle voice in Chapter 11 can also be applied to the perfect tense:

1. If the lexical form of the fourth principal part is *active* – in other words, it ends in -κα (first perfect), or -α (second perfect) – then it is an *active* verb in the perfect tense, and the fifth principal part is usually a *passive* form.
2. If, on the other hand, no active form is listed in the fourth column of the table of principal parts, then the form listed in the fifth column (i.e., fifth principal part) is usually a *middle* form.[12]

For example, the first five principal parts of πείθω are as follows:

1	2	3	4	5
πείθω,	πείσω,	ἔπεισα,	πέποιθα,	πέπεισμαι

The fourth principal part ends in -α (πέποιθα). Therefore, πείθω forms an active (second) perfect and the fifth principal part, πέπεισμαι, is a *passive* form.

[10] The σ between two consonants drops out: hence, -ρ + σθ → ρθ. In the second pl. pf. mid./pass. of liquid stems λ/ν/ρ + σθ → λθ, νθ, ρθ.

[11] See Section 19.8.

[12] It is certainly true that some verbs have no examples of an active fourth principal part in the GNT, even though they do have a fifth principal part that is passive (cf. Section 16.3).

Now let us look at the principal parts of ἐγείρω ("I raise"):

1	2	3	4	5
ἐγείρω,	ἐγερῶ,	ἤγειρα,	—,	ἐγήγερμαι

According to the table of principal parts, this verb has no fourth principal part. This means that it has no perfect *active* form. Therefore, the fifth principal part, ἐγήγερμαι, is perfect *middle*, not passive. When in doubt, let your lexicon be your guide!

16.12 THE PLUPERFECT TENSE

The pluperfect is the past tense of the perfect. Whereas the perfect tense refers to a state of affairs in the present, the pluperfect describes a state of affairs that is past. The pluperfect is employed less frequently than the perfect tense, except in the case of a few verbs such as οἶδα. Though you are not required to memorize all of the following information, you should develop a basic working knowledge of the pluperfect tense, including the ability to identify and parse pluperfect verbs.

1. The pluperfect active is formed from the same principal part as the perfect active, namely the fourth principal part.
2. As in the case of the perfect, if the stem begins with a consonant, this initial consonant is reduplicated with an ε inserted between them.
3. As in the case of all past tenses in the indicative mood, the pluperfect should also have an initial syllabic augment (ε), but in practice this augment is often missing.
4. The tense formative for the pluperfect is κει. This tense formative is added to the end of the verb stem. These are termed first pluperfects. However, some pluperfects are formed without adding the κ of the tense formative. These are termed second pluperfects.
5. Because it is a past tense, the pluperfect takes *secondary* endings ([augment] + reduplication + perfect active stem + [κ]ει + secondary active endings).

First Pluperfect Active Indicative of λύω

Sg.			
1	(ἐ)λελύκειν	([e]-le-**li**-kin)	(I had set free)[13]
2	(ἐ)λελύκεις	([e]-le-**li**-kis)	(you had set free)
3	(ἐ)λελύκει[14]	([e]-le-**li**-ki)	(he/she/it had set free)

[13] Because the translation "to untie" is awkward here, I have translated this verb as "to set free" instead.

[14] There is no movable ν in the third sg. Otherwise, it would be identical to the first sg.

	Pl.		
1	(ἐ)λελύκειμεν	([e]-le-**li**-ki-men)	(we had set free)
2	(ἐ)λελύκειτε	([e]-le-**li**-ki-te)	(you [pl.] had set free)
3	(ἐ)λελύκεισαν[15]	([e]-le-**li**-ki-san)	(they had set free)

The pluperfect passive also employs secondary endings, with no tense consonant or connecting vowels:

Pluperfect Passive Indicative of λύω

	Sg.		
1	(ἐ)λελύμην	([e]-le-**li**-min)	(I had been set free)
2	(ἐ)λέλυσο	([e]-**le**-li-so)	(you had been set free)
3	(ἐ)λέλυτο	([e]-**le**-li-to)	(he/she/it had been set free)
	Pl.		
1	(ἐ)λελύμεθα	([e]-le-**li**-me-tha)	(we had been set free)
2	(ἐ)λέλυσθε	([e]-**le**-lis-the)	(you [pl.] had been set free)
3	(ἐ)λέλυντο	([e]-**le**-lin-do)	(they had been set free)

16.13 PLUPERFECT OF οἶδα ("I KNOW")

The verb οἶδα forms a *second* pluperfect as its past tense. Because οἶδα is translated in the present tense, the pluperfect form is translated as a simple past tense. The original root of οἶδα was $\sqrt{}_{F}$ ειδ (19.3) (and is closely related to εἶδον → $\sqrt{}_{F}$ ιδ). Thus, the unaugmented stem of the pluperfect stem of οἶδα is ειδ-. When the intial diphthong is lengthened, it becomes ᾔδ-.

Second Pluperfect Active Indicative of οἶδα

	Sg.		
1	ᾔδειν	(**i**-dhin)	(I knew)
2	ᾔδεις	(**i**-dhis)	(you knew)
3	ᾔδει	(**i**-dhi)	(he/she/it knew)
	Pl.		
1	ᾔδειμεν	(**i**-dhi-men)	(we knew)
2	ᾔδειτε	(**i**-dhi-te)	(you [pl.] knew)
3	ᾔδεισαν	(**i**-dhi-san)	(they knew)

[15] -σαν is an alternative third plural secondary ending.

16.14 VOCABULARY TO BE MEMORIZED

1. ἀσθενῶ (-έω) (as-the-**no**), I am sick, ill, weak; 1 aor. ἠσθένησα, pf. act. ἠσθένηκα
2. γεννῶ (-άω) (yen-**no**), I give birth to a child (of women);[16] pass. I am born; fut. γεννήσω (yen-**ni**-so), 1 aor. ἐγέννησα (e-**yen**-ni-sa), pf. act. γεγέννηκα (ye-**yen**-ni-ka), pf. pass. γεγέννημαι (ye-**yen**-ni-me) (Note that the stem has a double ν (γεννα-). This will help you distinguish it from fut. and second aorist forms of γίνομαι, whose stem is γεν-.)
3. γραμματεύς, -έως, ὁ (gram-ma-**tefs**, -**e**-os) a scribe, an expert in the Torah (for paradigm, cf. βασιλεύς, Section 15.2)
4. γράφω (**gra**-fo), I write; fut. γράψω, 1 aor. ἔγραψα, 2 pf. act. γέγραφα, pf. pass. γέγραμμαι
5. ἐκεῖθεν (e-ki-**then**), from there (adv.); cf. ἐκεῖ (the -θεν ending indicates movement away from something)
6. δοῦλος, ὁ (**dhou**-los), a slave, a servant (cf. Section 21.6)

Box 1. δοῦλος

As a juridical term δοῦλος is contrasted with ἐλεύθερος (free). In the Graeco-Roman world, the term δοῦλος specified a slave who was subject to the power of a "master" or "owner" (δεσπότης, *dominus*). In antiquity, slaves had no juridical status. They were usually viewed as objects of possession. A δοῦλος belonged to the οἶκος of his owner. For this reason, a δοῦλος was sometimes called a οἰκέτης (house slave).

The term δοῦλος also has a religious connotation, corresponding to the Hebrew term, עֶבֶד (*eved*) designating a "servant" of a household, or a worshipper of God, or a prophet. Almost half of the occurrences of δοῦλος in the New Testament are found in Paul's letters (i.e., 47 out of 127). In Paul's writings, δοῦλος is used in both ways.

7. μέλλω (**mel**-lo), I am about to (+ infin.), as periphrasis for future, I am going to . . . ; fut. μελλήσω; impf. ἔμελλον and ἤμελλον
8. μηκέτι (mi-**ke**-ti), no longer, no more (with non-ind. moods; cf. οὐκέτι)
9. οὗ (ou), where (adv. of place), derived from the relative pronoun, ὅς (οὗ can also mean "whose")
10. ὄχλος, ὁ (**o**-khlos) a crowd, a throng or mob of common people (cf. "ochlophobia," which means "fear of crowds")
11. παιδίον, τό (pe-**dhi**-on), child, infant (cf. pediatrician, which literally means a "healer of children")

[16] Avoid the archaic English translations, "begat" and "begot." The idea of conceiving a child is also expressed by the verb συλλαμβάνω. Originally, γεννῶ was used of a man's part in the process of procreation and the verb, τίκτω, was used of a woman. But the GNT does not strictly observe this distinction, using the verb γεννῶ of both men and women.

12. παῖς, παιδός, ὁ or ἡ (pes, pe-**dhos**), a boy, a girl, youth (below the age of puberty)[17]
13. παρακαλῶ (-έω) (pa-ra-ka-**lo**), I beg, urge; encourage; request, appeal to; invite; pf. mid. παρακέκλημαι[18] (in MGr, "please, you're welcome")
14. πατρίς, πατρίδος, ἡ (pa-**tris**, pa-**tri**-dhos), homeland, hometown (cf. πατήρ)
15. πορεύομαι (po-**rev**-o-me), I go, proceed; fut. πορεύσομαι, impf. mid. ἐπορευόμην (the aorist form is passive deponent, cf. Section 17.3)[19]
16. πρίν (prin), before (i.e., a marker of one point in time before another)
17. τέρας, -ατος, τό (**te**-ras, -a-tos), an object of wonder, portent, omen; when combined with σημεῖα, it is often translated together as "signs and *wonders*"
18. τότε (**to**-te), then, at that time
19. τιμή, ἡ (ti-**mi**), honor, respect; price, value

Box 2. τιμή

In ancient Mediterranean society, the primary core social values were τιμή ("honor") and its opposite, "shame" (αἰσχύνη). Simply stated, τιμή refers to one's public reputation. Competing for honor and protecting oneself from shame permeated every aspect of public life in the ancient world.

For this reason, the vocabulary of "honor" and "shame" is pervasive in the literature of late antiquity including the GNT. Terms such as "praise" (ἔπαινος), "praiseworthy" (ἐπαινετός), "good/generous" (ἀγαθός), "grace" (χάρις), "generous" (ἐλευθέριος), "shameful" (αἰσχρός), "reputation" (δόξα), "I honor sby" (δοξάζω, τιμῶ, σέβομαι), and "virtue" (ἀρετή), to name but a few, are all related to the concept of τιμή.

16.15 SUPPLEMENTARY INFORMATION

16.15.1 Perfect Active Forms

	1 Perfects
ἀναβαίνω	ἀναβέβηκα
ἀποστέλλω	ἀπέσταλκα
καταβαίνω	καταβέβηκα
μισέω	μεμίσηκα
πίνω	πέπωκα
πίπτω	πέπτωκα
πράσσω	πέπραχα

[17] The gen. pl. of this third declension noun is accented irregularly with an acute on the penult: παίδων (cf. 14.1).

[18] But the pf. pass. form, παρακεκλήμεθα, is attested in 2 Cor 7:13 (cf. Section 16.3, n. 4).

[19] However, the m. acc. pl. pf. mid. ptc., πεπορευμένους, is attested in 1 Pet 4:3.

	2 Perfects
ἀκούω	ἀκήκοα
γίνομαι	γέγονα
γράφω	γέγραφα
ἔρχομαι	ἐλήλυθα
λαμβάνω	εἴληφα
πείθω	πέποιθα

16.15.2 Perfect Middle Forms

δέχομαι	δέδεγμαι
ἐγείρω	ἐγήγερμαι
εὐαγγελίζομαι	εὐηγγέλισμαι
θεάομαι	τεθέαμαι
πορεύομαι	πεπόρευμαι

16.15.3 Perfect Passive Forms

Pres.	*Pf. pass.*
ἀγαπάω	ἠγάπημαι
αἴρω	ἦρμαι
ἀποστέλλω	ἀπέσταλμαι
βαπτίζω	βεβάπτισμαι
γίνομαι	γεγένημαι
γινώσκω	ἔγνωσμαι
γράφω	γέγραμμαι
θεραπεύω	τεθεράπευμαι
κρίνω	κέκριμαι
λαλέω	λελάλημαι
λέγω	εἴρημαι
μισέω	μεμίσημαι
πείθω	πέπεισμαι
πιστεύω	πεπίστευμαι
πληρόω	πεπλήρωμαι
ποιέω	πεποίημαι
πράσσω	πέπραγμαι
σφραγίζω	ἐσφράγισμαι
φανερόω	πεφανέρωμαι
φέρω	ἐνήνεγμαι
φωτίζω	πεφώτισμαι

17.

Aorist Passive and Future Passive Indicative

17.1 AORIST PASSIVE INDICATIVE

The aorist passive voice is the opposite of the aorist active voice: The subject is the *recipient* of the action of the verb (e.g., "he was found," "he was killed"). In a passive construction, the person who performed the action may be expressed by the preposition ὑπό ("by"): for example, "He was found *by* the soldier." This preposition is followed by the genitive case (e.g., ὑπὸ αὐτοῦ, "by him"). By definition, this sixth principal part is the first person singular aorist passive form. The aorist passive tense is formed on the sixth principal part as follows:

1. If the verb stem begins with a consonant, add a syllabic augment (ε) to the beginning of the stem. If the stem begins with a vowel (or double vowel), follow the same rules as the first aorist active.
2. Attach the aorist passive tense formative, θη, to the end of the verb stem. (This θη makes it easy for you to distinguish the aorist passive from the aorist middle form.)
3. Attach the following secondary active secondary endings.

Figure: Relief of horseman brandishing a spear, and funeral banquet with seated woman, and two reclining men (Bagyurdu, central Turkey, *IKonya* 189).

Figure: Relief of two horsemen galloping toward one another, between whom stands a small man (Bozkir, Taurus mountains, *IKonya* 187).

	Sg.	*Pl.*
1	-ν	-μεν
2	-ς	-τε
3	-	-σαν

First Aorist Passive Indicative of λύω

⊕	*Sg.*		*Pl.*	
1	ἐλύθην	(e-**li**-thin)	ἐλύθημεν	(e-**li**-thi-men)
2	ἐλύθης	(e-**li**-this)	ἐλύθητε	(e-**li**-thi-te)
3	ἐλύθη	(e-**li**-thi)	ἐλύθησαν	(e-**li**-thi-san)

Many passive forms are quite predictable and easy to parse. However, the sixth principal parts of many high frequency verbs do undergo minor or major changes. For example:

present		*aorist passive*
καλέω	→	ἐκλήθην[1] (minor change)
λέγω	→	ἐρρέθην[2] (major change, cf. fut. act. ἐρῶ)

Note: The following verbs form aorist passive deponent forms. In other words, it is passive in form, but active in meaning. The three most commonly occurring verbs in the GNT that form aorist passive deponents are ἀποκρίνομαι, φοβέομαι, and πορεύομαι.

Present Middle		*Aorist Passive (deponent)*	
ἀποκρίνομαι	→	ἀπεκρίθην[3]	(I answered)
φοβέομαι	→	ἐφοβήθην	(I feared)
πορεύομαι	→	ἐπορεύθην	(I went)

17.2 AORIST PASSIVE OF VERBS ENDING IN VELARS, DENTALS, AND LABIALS

The stems of verbs ending in velars, dentals, and labials are modified by the addition of -θη as follows:

[1] κλη- shows up in words such as κλῆσις ("calling, vocation"), and the corresponding adjective, κλητός, -ή, -όν ("called").

[2] The root of ἐρῶ was probably ϝερ. Both the second and sixth principal parts are connected to Homeric εἴρω ("I say"). In the case of the aorist passive, the primitive root, ϝερ, seems to have become ϝρε, and the ρ was doubled when the verb is augmented.

[3] As you know, ἀποκρίνομαι forms an aorist *middle* instead, viz. ἀπεκρινάμην.

labials:	π, β, φ + θη	→	φθη-	
	ὁράω	→	ὤφθη-ν[4]	(cf. fut. stem: οπ-)
	λαμβάνω	→	ἐλήμφθη-ν	(cf. 2 aor. ἔλαβον)
velars:	κ, γ, χ + θη	→	χθη-	
	φέρω	→	ἠνέχθη-ν	(cf. 2 aor. ἤνεγκα)
	ἄγω	→	ἤχθη-ν	
dentals:	τ, δ, θ (or ζ) + θη	→	σθη-	
	εὐαγγελίζομαι	→	εὐηγγελίσθη-ν	

In practice, many aorist passive stems cannot be easily predicted. To avoid confusion, it is recommended that you consult a table of principal parts when in doubt.

17.3 THE SECOND AORIST PASSIVE

In the passive voice, the term "second" aorist has a very different meaning than it does in the active voice. In the passive voice, the term "second" aorist means that the θ of the θη passive tense formative is missing. This usage is similar to the so-called second perfect, which has no κ in the tense formative.

Neither the first or second aorist passive has a connecting vowel. In the case of the second aorist passive, the secondary endings are attached to the stem with only η (not θη) as the tense formative. One of the most frequently occurring examples of a second aorist passive is the verb γράφω:

	Sg.	*Pl.*
1	ἐγράφην	ἐγράφημεν
2	ἐγράφης	ἐγράφητε
3	ἐγράφη	ἐγράφησαν

17.4 FUTURE PASSIVE INDICATIVE

The *future* passive is formed on the *same* principal part as the aorist passive, namely the sixth principal part. For this reason, you should never have problems distinguishing a future passive verb from a future middle verb. Following the stem you will find a θη (indicating passive voice), followed by σ (indicating future tense), and the passive endings.

As you know, the future tense does not have an augment. Therefore, to determine the future stem, you must *remove* the syllabic augment from the sixth principal part, or shorten the initial vowel to its original length:

[4] In the third sg., this verb can mean "appeared." Cf. fut. act. ὄψομαι, with οπ- as its stem.

First principal part	*Sixth principal part*	*Future passive form*
διδάσκω	ἐδιδάχθην	→ διδάχθησομαι
ἐγείρω	ἠγέρθην	→ ἐγέρθησομαι

To form the future passive indicative:

1. Attach the tense formative, θησ (remember that σ is the sign of the future).
2. Attach the primary passive endings using ο/ε as a connecting vowel. In other words, add the same endings as employed in the present passive indicative. Thus, the future passive of λύω is:

Future Passive Indicative of λύω

⊕	*Sg.*		
1	λυθήσομαι	(li-**thi**-so-me)	(I will be set free)
2	λυθήσῃ	(li-**thi**-si)	(you will be set free)
3	λυθήσεται	(li-**thi**-se-te)	(he/she/it will be set free)
	Pl.		
1	λυθησόμεθα	(li-thi-**so**-me-θa)	(we will be set free)
2	λυθήσεσθε	(li-**thi**-ses-θe)	(you [pl.] will be set free)
3	λυθήσονται	(li-**thi**-son-de)	(they will be set free)

As noted above, some verbs have unexpected sixth principal parts. For example, the sixth principal part of φέρω is ἠνέχθην (i-**ne**-khthin). In the passive, it can mean to "be moved," or "be driven" by something or someone such as God or the Spirit.

The future passive form is derived from the sixth principal part (not from the future active form, which is οἴσω). Thus, the future passive will be formed on the unaugmented stem, ἐνεχ- , as follows:

Future Passive Indicative of φέρω

	Sg.		
1	ἐνεχθήσομαι	(e- ne-**khthi**-so-me)	(I will have been moved/driven)
2	ἐνεχθήσῃ	(e- ne-**khthi**-si)	(you will have been moved/driven)
3	ἐνεχθήσεται	(e- ne-**khthi**-se-te)	(he/she/it will have been moved/driven)

Pl.

1	ἐνεχθησόμεθα	(e- ne-khthi-**so**-me-θa)	(we will have been moved/driven)
2	ἐνεχθήσεσθε	(e- ne-**khthi**-ses-θe)	(you [pl.] will have been moved/driven)
3	ἐνεχθήσονται	(e- ne-**khthi**-son-de)	(they will have been moved/driven)

17.5 VOCABULARY TO BE MEMORIZED

1. ἔξεστι(ν) (**e**-kse-sti[n]), impers. (third sg.), it is possible, it is permitted, it is lawful (often used this way in the Gospels) (this is a compound form of the third sg. of εἰμί)
2. ἔτος, ἔτους, τό (**e**-tos, **e**-tous), year; it is important to know the plural forms because they occur much more frequently than do the singular forms: ἔτη (nom./acc. pl.), ἐτῶν (gen. pl.), ἔτεσι(ν) (dat. pl.) (for the full third declension paradigm, see ἔθνος, -ους, Section 15.3)
3. εὐθύς, εὐθέως (ef-**this**, ef-**the**-os) (adv.), immediately, at once; "then" (esp. in Mark's gospel)
4. κράβαττος, ὁ (**krav**-va-tos), a stretcher, a poor man's bed/mat
5. ὀκτώ (ok-**to**), eight (cf. "octopus, octagon")
6. πλῆθος, -ους, τό, (**pli**-thos, -ous), a crowd, a quantity
7. φοβοῦμαι (-έομαι) (fo-**vou**-me),[5] I fear, am afraid (of); 1 aor. pass. ἐφοβήθην is deponent. Thus ἐφοβήθη means "he feared," not "he was feared" (cf. "phobia")
8. στοά, -ᾶς, ἡ (sto-**a**, -**as**), shaded porch or portico

Health and Healing

9. ἀσθένεια, ἡ (as-**the**-ni-a),[6] weakness, illness (cf. ἀσθενῶ [-έω])
10. θεραπεύω (the-ra-**pev**-o), I heal, cure; serve; fut. θεραπεύσω, 1 aor. ἐθεράπευσα, pf. mid. τεθεράπευμαι, 1 aor. pass. ἐθεραπεύθην[7] (cf. therapeutic)
11. ξηρός, -ά, -όν (ksi-**ros**, -**a**, -**on**), lit. dry (cf. "xerox," meaning a *dry* photocopy); in the Gospels, this word often means "paralyzed"
12. ὑγιής, -ές (i-yi-**is**, -**es**), whole, sound, healthy (adj. of two terminations) (for the paradigm of this adjective, see ἀληθής, -ές, Section 14.5) (ὑγίεια means "health")
13. χωλός, -ή, -όν (kho-**los**, -**i**, -**on**), lame, unable to walk

[5] φοβέω properly means "to make sby afraid," but in demotic speech it has become φοβίζω.

[6] Contrary to the general rule, abstract α-pure nouns, which are derived from adjectives ending in —ης/-ες, and whose stems end in —ει, have short α in the ending (not long) in the singular nom. and acc. forms (Smyth 219.2 b). This allows the antepenult to be accented: ἀσθένεια, ἀσθενείας, ἀσθενείᾳ, ἀσθένειαν (cf. ἀλήθεια).

[7] Cf. John 5:10; Luke 8:2; Acts 4:14. Here we have example of a pf. verb with both middle and passive forms, and no fourth principal part is attested in the GNT.

17.6 REFERENCE: AORIST PASSIVE FORMS OF COMMONLY OCCURRING GREEK VERBS

1. ἀγαπάω, ἠγαπήθην
2. ἄγω, ἤχθην
3. αἴρω, ἤρθην
4. ἀκούω, ἠκούσθην
5. ἀναγγέλλω, ἀνηγγέλην*
6. ἀποστέλλω, ἀπεστάλην*
7. γεννάω, ἐγεννήθην
8. γίνομαι, ἐγενήθην
9. γινώσκω, ἐγνώσθην
10. γράφω, ἐγράφην*
11. διδάσκω, ἐδιδάχθην
12. δοξάζω, ἐδοξάσθην
13. δύναμαι, ἠδυνήθην
14. ἐγείρω, ἠγέρθην
15. ἐπερωτάω, ἐπηρωτήθην
16. εὐαγγελίζομαι, εὐηγγελίσθην
17. εὑρίσκω, εὑρέθην
18. ζητέω, ἐζητήθην
19. θαυμάζω, ἐθαυμάσθην
20. θεάομαι, ἐθεάθην
21. θέλω, ἠθελήθην
22. θεραπεύω, ἐθεραπεύθην
23. θερίζω, ἐθερίσθην
24. καλέω, ἐκλήθην
25. κηρύσσω, ἐκηρύχθην
26. λαλέω, ἐλαλήθην
27. λαμβάνω, ἐλήμφθην
28. λέγω, ἐρρέθην
29. μαρτυρέω, ἐμαρτυρήθην
30. ὁράω, ὤφθην
31. παρακαλέω, παρεκλήθην
32. πείθω, ἐπείσθην
33. πέμπω, ἐπέμφθην
34. πιστεύω, ἐπιστεύθην
35. πληρόω, ἐπληρώθην
36. πορεύομαι, ἐπορεύθην (pass. dep.)
37. σπείρω, ἐσπάρην*
38. σφραγίζω, ἐσφραγίσθην
39. τηρέω, ἐτηρήθην
40. ὑψόω, ὑψώθην
41. φαίνω, ἐφάνην*
42. φανερόω, ἐφανερώθην
43. φέρω, ἠνέχθην
44. φωτίζω, ἐφωτίσθην
45. χαίρω, ἐχάρην*

* Second aorist passive form (i.e., lacking θ)

18.

Present and Aorist Participles

The use of the participle in the Greek New Testament is widespread. In fact, participles are used much more in Hellenistic Greek than they are in contemporary English. For this reason, participles constitute a very important part of Greek grammar, which must be thoroughly mastered.

The participle is often called a verbal adjective. In other words, a participle has characteristics of both verbs and adjectives. Like a verb, participles have tense (present, aorist, future, perfect)[1] and voice (active, middle, passive). Like adjectives, they have gender (masculine, feminine, neuter), number (singular, plural), and case (nominative, genitive, etc.). Therefore, like the definite article and adjectives, every participle will have twenty-four forms. The participle is negated by μή.

Participles do not belong to the indicative mood or any other mood. Like infinitives, they are an infinite verb form, which is to say they do not require a subject, as do the definite verbs we have learned so far. As such, past-tense participles will never take a syllabic or temporal augment.

18.1 THE PRESENT PARTICIPLE

The present participle is formed from the present-tense stem (i.e., the first principal part). The *aspect* of the present participle is usually *imperfective*, as it is in the present indicative. Remember that the term "aspect" refers to the *kind* of action that is depicted by the verb. The imperfective aspect conceives of the verbal action as being in progress or as unfolding without reference to its completion.

---

1 The use of the future participle is rare in the GNT. Besides its appearance in Acts, there are examples in Matt 27:49 (σώσων), John 6:64 (παραδώσων), Heb 13:17 (ἀποδώσοντες), 1 Pet 3:13 (κακώσων), Luke 22:49 (ἐσόμενον), and 1 Cor 15:37 (γενησόμενον).

Figure: Figure of a husband and wife, with lentoid eyes (probably Isauria, *IKonya* 155).

The active participle declines according to a "3-1-3" pattern.[2] If you know the paradigm for the third declension noun ἄρχων,[3] you should find this paradigm very easy to memorize, at least in the masculine and neuter forms. You should observe how the morpheme -ντ- (preceded by the connecting vowel ο) occurs in most of the cases of the masculine and neuter forms. The feminine active participle follows a first declension (α-impure) pattern.

The rules for accenting participles follow the rules for nouns and adjectives, not verbs. Therefore, the position of the accent in the masculine nominative singular form of each tense will determine where the accent will fall throughout the other forms according to the general rules for the accentuation (cf. Section 2.4).

18.1.1 Present Active Participle of λύω

⊕	*m.*	*fm.*	*nt.*
Sg.			
N	λύων	λύουσα	λῦον[4]
G	λύοντος	λυούσης	λύοντος
D	λύοντι	λυούσῃ	λύοντι
A	λύοντα	λύουσαν	λῦον
Pl.			
N	λύοντες	λύουσαι	λύοντα
G	λυόντων	λυουσῶν[5]	λυόντων
D	λύουσι(ν)	λυούσαις	λύουσι(ν)
A	λύοντας	λυούσας	λύοντα

18.1.2 The Present Passive Participle

The morpheme for the middle participle is -μεν. To this are added the adjectival endings (-ος, -η, -ον, etc). The paradigm is second and first declension (2-1-2) throughout. The feminine active participle follows a first declension (η-pure) pattern:

⊕	*m.*	*fm.*	*nt.*
Sg.			
N	λυόμενος	λυομένη	λυόμενον
G	λυομένου	λυομένης	λυομένου
D	λυομένῳ	λυομένῃ	λυομένῳ
A	λυόμενον	λυομένην	λυόμενον

---

2 I.e., the masculine is third declension, the feminine is first declension, and the neuter is third declension.

3 See Sections 14.1, 26.17.

4 The stem of λυ- is long. Therefore, the accent becomes a circumflex when the ultima is short.

5 In the *active* form, feminine first declension participles behave like feminine first declension nouns, not adjectives. The accent always jumps to the ultima in the feminine genitive plural (whereas the middle

Pl.			
N	λυόμενοι	λυόμεναι	λυόμενα
G	λυομένων	λυομένων	λυομένων
D	λυομένοις	λυομέναις	λυομένοις
A	λυομένους	λυομένας	λυόμενα

18.1.3 Present Middle Participle

As you might expect, the endings of the present passive and present middle participle are identical. Any verb whose first principal part ends in -ομαι is middle, not passive, in the present tense, and can be used for illustration. We will use ἔρχομαι as an example:

⊕	*m.*	*fm.*	*nt.*
Sg.			
N	ἐρχόμενος	ἐρχομένη	ἐρχόμενον
G	ἐρχομένου	ἐρχομένης	ἐρχομένου
D	ἐρχομένῳ	ἐρχομένῃ	ἐρχομένῳ
A	ἐρχόμενον	ἐρχομένην	ἐρχόμενον
Pl.			
N	ἐρχόμενοι	ἐρχόμεναι	ἐρχόμενα
G	ἐρχομένων	ἐρχομένων	ἐρχομένων
D	ἐρχομένοις	ἐρχομέναις	ἐρχομένοις
A	ἐρχομένους	ἐρχομένας	ἐρχόμενα

18.2 PRESENT PARTICIPLE OF εἰμί

The present participle of εἰμί has the same endings as the present active participle. Notice that all forms have a smooth breathing mark (e.g., ὤν, not ὧν). This will help you distinguish the masculine (sg. nom.) participle, ὤν, from the genitive plural relative pronoun, ὧν, and the neuter (sg. nom. and acc.) participle, ὄν, from the masculine singular accusative relative pronoun, ὅν.

⊕	*m.*	*fm.*	*nt.*
Sg.			
N	ὤν	οὖσα	ὄν
G	ὄντος	οὔσης	ὄντος
D	ὄντι	οὔσῃ	ὄντι
A	ὄντα	οὖσαν	ὄν

and passive plural forms follow the pattern of first declension adjectives, with the accent drawn onto the penult, according to the general rules for accents).

Pl.			
N	ὄντες	οὖσαι	ὄντα
G	ὄντων	οὐσῶν	ὄντων
D	οὖσι(ν)	οὔσαις	οὖσι(ν)
A	ὄντας	οὔσας	ὄντα

18.3 FUTURE PARTICIPLE

The future participle is formed from the future-tense stem (second principal part). To form the future participle, simply affix the tense consonant σ to the verb's future active stem and then add the same endings used for the present participle (i.e., future active stem + σ + ο + ντ + third declension ending [m./nt.] or first declension ending [fm.]).

18.3.1 Future Active Participle of λύω

⊕	*m.*	*fm.*	*nt.*
Sg.			
N	λύσων	λύσουσα	λῦσον
G	λύσοντος	λυσούσης	λύσοντος
D	λύσοντι	λυσούσῃ	λύσοντι
A	λύσοντα	λύσουσαν	λῦσον
Pl.			
N	λύσοντες	λύσουσαι	λύσοντα
G	λυσόντων	λυσουσῶν	λυσόντων
D	λύσουσι(ν)	λυσούσαις	λύσουσι(ν)
A	λύσοντας	λυσούσας	λύσοντα

18.3.2 Future Middle Participle

As in the case of the present middle participle, the morpheme for the future middle participle is -μεν. Any verb whose second principal part ends in -ομαι is middle, not passive, in the future tense and can be used as an example. We will use ἔρχομαι again. As you may recall, the future indicative form of ἔρχομαι is ἐλεύσομαι:

⊕	*m.*	*fm.*	*nt.*
Sg.			
N	ἐλευσόμενος	ἐλευσομένη	ἐλευσόμενον
G	ἐλευσομένου	ἐλευσομένης	ἐλευσομένου
D	ἐλευσομένῳ	ἐλευσομένῃ	ἐλευσομένῳ
A	ἐλευσόμενον	ἐλευσομένην	ἐλευσόμενον

Pl.			
N	ἐλευσόμενοι	ἐλευσόμεναι	ἐλευσόμενα
G	ἐλευσομένων	ἐλευσομένων	ἐλευσομένων
D	ἐλευσομένοις	ἐλευσομέναις	ἐλευσομένοις
A	ἐλευσομένους	ἐλευσομένας	ἐλευσόμενα

18.3.3 Future Passive Participle

As you might expect, the endings of the future passive participle are identical to the future middle participle. However, the future passive tense consonant is -θησ (not σ), and the stem for the future passive participle is derived from the sixth principal part, as is the future passive indicative. Depending on the verb, you must either remove the augment from the sixth principal part or shorten the lengthened initial vowel.

⊕	*m.*	*fm.*	*nt.*
Sg.			
N	λυθησόμενος	λυθησομένη	λυθησόμενον
G	λυθησομένου	λυθησομένης	λυθησομένου
D	λυθησομένῳ	λυθησομένῃ	λυθησομένῳ
A	λυθησόμενον	λυθησομένην	λυθησόμενον
Pl.			
N	λυθησόμενοι	λυθησόμεναι	λυθησόμενα
G	λυθησομένων	λυθησομένων	λυθησομένων
D	λυθησομένοις	λυθησομέναις	λυθησομένοις
A	λυθησομένους	λυθησομένας	λυθησόμενα

18.4 FIRST AORIST PARTICIPLE

The aspect of the aorist participle is normally aoristic, as you would expect. The term "aoristic" means that the verbal action is presented as a completed and undifferentiated process.

Verbs that form first aorists in the indicative mood will also form first aorist participles. Like the first aorist active indicative, the first aorist active participle takes -σα as a tense formative. However, the aorist participle does not have an augment (ε). *Only past tenses in the indicative mood have augments.* Therefore, the past tense of the participle (as well as the imperative subjunctive and infinitive) will *not* have a syllabic augment (ε).

The aorist participle is formed from the *un*augmented third principal part. This means it will be necessary for you either to remove the syllabic augment from the indicative aorist form (i.e., third principal part) or shorten the initial vowel to the original, unaugmented vowel (e.g., η → ε / α, ω → ο).

If you know the present active participial endings, the first aorist active participle is very easy to form. In most cases, simply substitute σα in place of -ο- or -ου- as a connecting vowel. The two exceptions are the nominative masculine singular form, λύσας, and the nominative and accusative neuter singular forms, λῦσαν.

The masculine form has a long α in the ending and, therefore, has an acute accent over the penult, whereas the α of the neuter form is short and must carry a circumflex over the penult because the previous υ is long.

18.4.1 First Aorist Active Participle of *λύω*

⊕	*m.*	*fm.*	*nt.*
Sg.			
N	λύσας	λύσασα	λῦσαν
G	λύσαντος	λυσάσης	λύσαντος
D	λύσαντι	λυσάσῃ	λύσαντι
A	λύσαντα	λύσασαν	λῦσαν
Pl.			
N	λύσαντες	λύσασαι	λύσαντα
G	λυσάντων	λυσασῶν	λυσάντων
D	λύσασι(ν)	λυσάσαις	λύσασι(ν)
A	λύσαντας	λυσάσας	λύσαντα

Inflectional Information on Participial Forms of βαίνω

Because many compound forms of -βαίνω occur in the assigned readings in the workbook, some additional explanation is required concerning the inflectional forms of this verb. The aorist participle of compounded forms of βαίνω (e.g., καταβαίνω, ἀναβαίνω) is unexpected, namely -βας, -βαντος, -βαντι, etc.

These forms can be explained as follows. The basic root of βαίνω is √βα. The α of the root undergoes lengthening to βη throughout the most of the principal parts (2. βήσομαι, 3. ἔβην, 4. βέβηκα). However, in the aorist participle (and in some second aorist active imperatival forms), the stem does not lengthen to -η.

Instead, the aorist participial endings are added directly to the root, *without a connecting vowel*, in a similar way as are the participial endings of the athematic verbs. In the nominative masculine singular form, the ντ drops out when σ is added, and the α lengthens in compensation: that is, -βα + ντ + ς → -βας.

18.4.2 First Aorist Middle Participle

If you know the present middle participial endings, the first aorist middle participle is very easy to form. Simply substitute -σα- in place of the -ο- connecting vowel. Any verb whose third principal part ends in -(σ)άμην will form an aorist *middle*, not an aorist active, participle. For example, δέχομαι and (sometimes) ἀποκρίνομαι[6] form aorist middles in the third principal parts (ἐδεξάμην and ἀπεκρινάμην, respectively). We shall use δέχομαι as our example word for the first aorist middle participle. Note how the final velar of the stem, χ, combines with the σα to form ξα in all forms:

⊕	*m.*	*fm.*	*nt.*
Sg.			
N	δεξάμενος	δεξαμένη	δεξάμενον
G	δεξαμένου	δεξαμένης	δεξαμένου
D	δεξαμένῳ	δεξαμένῃ	δεξαμένῳ
A	δεξάμενον	δεξαμένην	δεξάμενον
Pl.			
N	δεξάμενοι	δεξάμεναι	δεξάμενα
G	δεξαμένων	δεξαμένων	δεξαμένων
D	δεξαμένοις	δεξαμέναις	δεξαμένοις
A	δεξαμένους	δεξαμένας	δεξάμενα

18.5 SECOND AORIST ACTIVE PARTICIPLE

Verbs that form second aorists in the indicative mood also form second aorist participles. As in the case of the first aorist participle, the *second* aorist participle does not have an augment (ε). The second aorist participle is also formed from the unaugmented third principal part.

Important!

As you know, in the indicative mood, the second aorist has the same endings as the imperfect tense. *However, in the case of the participle, and all other non-indicative moods, the second aorist has the same endings as the present tense.* Of course, the second aorist employs a different stem than the present participle, namely the same stem as used in the second aorist indicative (i.e., the third principal part).

Our example word is ὁράω. The third principal part of ὁράω is εἶδον. The *un*augmented second aorist stem is ἰδ-.

First principal part ὁρῶ (-άω)
Third principal part εἶδον → √ ἰδ-

Now we can add the same endings used for the present active participle to √ἰδ to form the second aorist active participle. In the case of the second aorist

[6] ἀπεκρινάμην lacks σ because the stem ends in a liquid consonant (ν).

active participle (and the perfect active participle), the accent always remains over the participial endings. This helps us differentiate it from the present participial forms:

⊕	*m.*	*fm.*	*nt.*
Sg.			
N	ἰδών	ἰδοῦσα	ἰδόν
G	ἰδόντος	ἰδούσης	ἰδόντος
D	ἰδόντι	ἰδούσῃ	ἰδόντι
A	ἰδόντα	ἰδοῦσαν	ἰδόν
Pl.			
N	ἰδόντες	ἰδοῦσαι	ἰδόντα
G	ἰδόντων	ἰδουσῶν	ἰδόντων
D	ἰδοῦσι(ν)	ἰδούσαις	ἰδοῦσι(ν)
A	ἰδόντας	ἰδούσας	ἰδόντα

Note: The second aorist participle of γινώσκω is unexpected, namely γνούς, γνόντος, γνόντι, and so on. The ντ of the ending drops out before the sigma in the nominative masculine singular, and the stem vowel lengthens in compensation to γνούς (γνο + ντ + ς → γνο + ς → γνούς).[7]

18.6 SECOND AORIST MIDDLE PARTICIPLE

Given that the verb γίνομαι is middle in the present tense, it is not surprising that it also forms an aorist *middle* in the indicative mood. Moreover, because γίνομαι forms a *second* aorist, in the indicative mood, namely ἐγενόμην, the corresponding participle will also be *second* aorist, with the same stem change (γιν → γεν).

Sg.	*m.*	*fm.*	*nt.*
N	γενόμενος	γενομένη	γενόμενον
G	γενομένου	γενομένης	γενομένου
D	γενομένῳ	γενομένῃ	γενομένῳ
A	γενόμενον	γενομένην	γενόμενον
Pl.			
N	γενόμενοι	γενόμεναι	γενόμενα
G	γενομένων	γενομένων	γενομένων
D	γενομένοις	γενομέναις	γενομένοις
A	γενομένους	γενομένας	γενόμενα

[7] Smyth, 686, 301.

18.7 SUBSTANTIVE AND ATTRIBUTIVE USES OF THE PARTICIPLE

The participle can function as a noun (substantive use) and as an adjective (attributive use). As we shall see in Chapter 19, participles can also function adverbially.

18.7.1 The Substantive Use of the Participle

A participle can function like a noun. Like adjectives, when used with articles, participles are equivalent to nouns: For example, οἱ λέγοντες means "those who are speaking."

In most cases, such substantive participles will be preceded by a definite article: for example, ὁ ἐρχόμενος ("the one who is coming"). These substantive participles are frequently translated with an English relative pronoun (i.e., "the one/he who is . . . ing").

ὁ πιστεύων εἰς τὸν υἱὸν ἔχει ζωὴν αἰώνιον. (John 3:36)

The one who believes in the Son has eternal life.

οὗτός ἐστιν ὁ βαπτίζων ἐν πνεύματι ἁγίῳ. (John 1:33)

. . . this is *the one who baptizes* with the Holy Spirit/Breath (of God).

ἔλεγον οὖν οἱ Ἰουδαῖοι τῷ τεθεραπευμένῳ ... (John 5:10)

Therefore, the Jews said *to the man who was healed* . . .

18.7.2 The Attributive Use of the Participle

An attributive participle functions like an adjective. It can appear in any of the attributive positions (first, second, or third) and must agree with the word it modifies in gender, number, and case. In English, a relative pronoun, "who," "which," "that," may help in the translation. In the examples below, the definite article is bolded and the participle is underlined:

First Attributive Position

ἐλαλοῦμεν **ταῖς** συνελθούσαις γυναιξίν. (Acts 16:13) [article – ptc. - noun]

... we began to speak ***to the*** women *who had gathered.*

Second Attributive Position (more common than first attributive)

πόθεν οὖν ἔχεις **τὸ** ὕδωρ **τὸ** ζῶν; (John 4:11) [article – noun – article - ptc]

From where, then, do you have ***the** living* water?

Ἴδε **ὁ** ἀμνὸς τοῦ θεοῦ **ὁ** αἴρων τὴν ἁμαρτίαν τοῦ κόσμου. (John 1:29)

Behold! ***the*** lamb of God *who takes away* the sin of the world.

Third Attributive Position (especially common when the noun is a proper name)

Σίμων **ὁ** λεγόμενος Πέτρος (Matt 10:2) [noun – article - ptc]

… Simon [being] *called* Peter …

18.8 VOCABULARY TO BE MEMORIZED

1. διδάσκω (dhi-**dha**-sko), I teach; fut. διδάξω, 1 aor. act. ἐδίδαξα, 1 aor. pass. ἐδιδάχθην (cf. διδάσκαλος, and English cognate, "didactic")
2. διδαχή, ἡ (dhi-dha-**khi**), teaching, instruction; cf. the *Didache* is the name of an early Christian treatise (late first/early second century AD).
3. διώκω (dhi-**o**-ko), I pursue; persecute; fut. διώξα, 1 aor. act. ἐδίωξα, 1 aor. pass. ἐδιώχθην
4. δώδεκα (**dho**-dhe-ka), twelve (cf. "dodecaphonic" music, which holds twelve tones in a chromatic scale) (indecl.)
5. εἰσφέρω, (is-**fe**-ro), I lead in, carry in, bring in (cf. principal parts of φέρω)
6. ἐντολή, ἡ (en-do-**li**), commandment, instruction
7. ἐπαγγελία, ἡ (ep-a^{ng}-ge-**li**-a), a promise
8. ἐργάζομαι (er-**ga**-zo-me), I work (for), perform a deed; 1 aor. mid. ἠργασάμην/εἰργασάμην, pf. mid. εἴργασμαι (cf. ἔργον, work, deed) (cf. "erg," a unit of work in physics)
9. ζῳοποιῶ (-έω) (zo-o-pi-**o**), I give life to, make alive; fut. ζῳοποιήσω, 1 aor. ἐζῳοποίησα, aor. pass. ἐζῳοποιήθην (cf. ζωή, ποιῶ)
10. ἴσος, -η, -ον (**i**-sos, -i, -on), same, equal; ἴσα (adv.) equally (an "isosceles" triangle has three sides of equal length)
11. καιρός, ὁ (ke-**ros**), an opportune time, time of harvest, a special occasion, a time of crisis (especially as it concerns the end times), contrasting χρόνος; καιρός is χρόνος, which has been "seized" as an opportunity for doing something.

12. καρδία, ἡ (kar-**dhi**-a), the center of physical, spiritual, and mental life; fig. the "heart" (cf. cardiac): in Greek culture, the σπλάγχνα (intestines) were considered to be the center of the human emotions, not the καρδία (heart). The καρδία was considered to be part of the psychological faculties, along with the διάνοια, πνεῦμα, and ψυχή (see Section 18.9).
13. μεταβαίνω (me-ta-**ve**-no), I leave, move from one place to another; fut. mid. μεταβήσομαι, 2 aor. μετέβην (athematic), pf. μεταβέβηκα, 1 aor. ptc. μεταβάς, μεταβάντος, etc. (cf. ἀναβαίνω, καταβαίνω, and principal parts for βαίνω)
14. μόνος, -η, -ον (**mo**-nos, -i, -on), only, alone (cf. *mono*physite, from μόνος and φύσις [nature], the heterodox Christological doctrine that Christ only had one nature, namely a divine nature, because Jesus' humanity was absorbed by his divinity)
15. ὅμοιως (**o**-mi-os) in the same way, likewise, too (many Greek adverbs end in -ως)
16. πεινῶ (-άω) (pi-**no**), I am hungry; fut. πεινάσω, 1 aor. ἐπείνασα (cf. Section 22.10). Note the position of the stress. It is pronounced pi-**no**. This will help you distinguish this verb from πίνω (**pi**-no), meaning, "I drink."
17. τιμῶ (-άω) (ti-**mo**), I honor; fut. τιμήσω, 1 aor. ἐτίμησα, pf. mid. τετίμημαι (cf. τιμή, δοξάζω see 16.14).
18. φιλῶ (-έω) (fi-**lo**), I love, have deep feeling for; fut. φιλήσω, 1 aor. ἐφίλησα, pf. πεφίληκα (cf. ἀγαπῶ, ἀγάπη). In antiquity, φιλῶ was the most commonly used verb to express love. The verb, ἀγαπῶ, seems to have been adopted by Christians and employed to express distinctly Christian forms of love.
19. ὥσπερ (**o**-sper), just as, even as, like (cf. ὡς)

18.9 "PSYCHOLOGICAL FACULTIES" AS A SEMANTIC DOMAIN[8]

- διάνοια — mind, understanding, intelligence
- καρδία — "heart" as the causative source of a person's psychological life and especially thoughts
- ψυχή — "soul" or "life," as the essence of life in terms of thinking, willing, feeling
- πνεῦμα — spirit, as the non-material, psychological faculty that is potentially sensitive and responsive to God
- συνείδησις — conscience, as the psychological faculty that can distinguish right and wrong
- φρήν — understanding, as the psychological faculty of thoughtful planning, often with implication of being wise and provident.

[8] Louw/Nida, 320 (Chapter 26).

18.10 REFERENCE: NUMBERS (οἱ ἀριθμοί)

	Cardinal Numbers	Ordinal Numbers[9]	Adverbial Numbers
1.	εἷς (m.), μία (fm.), ἕν (nt.)	πρῶτος, -η, -ον	ἅπαξ (once)
2.	δύο, δυσί(ν) (dat.)	δεύτερος, -α, -ον	δίς (twice)
3.	τρεῖς (m., fm.), τρία (nt.)	τρίτος, -η, -ον	τρίς (three times)
4.	τέσσαρες (m., fm.), τέσσαρα (nt.)	τέταρτος, -η, -ον	
5.	πέντε	πέμπτος, -η, -ον	πεντάκις (five times)
6.	ἕξ	ἕκτος, -η, -ον	
7.	ἑπτά	ἕβδομος, -η, -ον	ἑπτάκις (seven times)
8.	ὀκτώ	ὄγδοος, -η, -ον	
9.	ἐννέα	ἕνατος, -η, -ον	
10.	δέκα	δέκατος, -η, -ον	
11.	ἕνδεκα	ἑνδέκατος, -η, -ον	
12.	δώδεκα	δωδέκατος, -η, -ον	
20.	εἴκοσι(ν)	εἰκοστός, -η, -ον	
100.	ἑκατόν	ἑκατοστός, -η, -ον	

9 I.e., first, second, third, etc.

19.

Aorist Passive Participle, Perfect Participle, Adverbial Participles, Genitive Absolute, and Periphrastic Constructions

19.1 FIRST AORIST PASSIVE PARTICIPLE

The aorist passive participle is formed from the sixth principal part, which is to say, on the basis of the aorist passive indicative form. Its endings are very similar to the aorist active endings, with the exception of the nominative masculine and neuter singular forms.

To form the aorist passive participle, simply add to the stem the passive tense formative, -θε, in the masculine and neuter forms and -θει in the feminine forms.[1] Also note that when the consonants -ντ- are deleted in the dative plural (m. and nt.), compensatory lengthening of the vowel occurs:

λυθεντ + σι → λυθε<u>ντ</u>σι → λυθεσι → λυθεῖσι

[1] To be more precise, θεισ in the feminine forms results from additional morphological changes stemming from the addition of the morpheme ντ plus consonantal iota (ι). The σ arises from the combination of τ and consonantal iota; on consonantal iota see Andrew L. Sihler, *New Comparative Greek and Latin Grammar* (Oxford: Oxford University Press, 1995), 187ff (# 191).

Figure: Carved figure of Jonah being eaten by a great fish (Apa, central Turkey, III-IV AD, *IKonya* 212).

First Aorist Passive Participle of λύω

⊕	*m.*	*fm.*	*nt.*
Sg.			
N	λυθείς	λυθεῖσα	λυθέν
G	λυθέντος	λυθείσης	λυθέντος
D	λυθέντι	λυθείσῃ	λυθέντι
A	λυθέντα	λυθεῖσαν	λυθέν
Pl.			
N	λυθέντες	λυθεῖσαι	λυθέντα
G	λυθέντων	λυθεισῶν	λυθέντων
D	λυθεῖσι(ν)	λυθείσαις	λυθεῖσι(ν)
A	λυθέντας	λυθείσας	λυθέντα

The so-called *second* aorist passive participle has no θ. As explained earlier, the term "second" aorist in the passive voice simply means "no θ," nothing else. The most frequently occurring example of the second aorist passive participle in the GNT is γράφω → γραφείς (m. nom.), γραφέντος (m. gen.), γραφεῖσα (fm.), γραφέν (nt.).

19.2 THE PERFECT ACTIVE AND PASSIVE PARTICIPLE

The perfect active participle has many similarities to the present active participle. In fact, by simply removing the ν from the -ντ- of the present participial endings, you will, in many cases, create the perfect participial ending. Note the following:

1. The initial consonant is reduplicated, as it is in the perfect indicative.
2. The distinctive nominative endings for first perfect participles are -κώς, -κυῖα, -κός.[2]
3. κ is characteristic for first perfect active participles. Second perfect participles omit the κ (e.g., γεγραφώς, γεγραφυῖα, γεγραφός).
4. In the perfect active (as in the second aorist active), the accent always remains over the participial endings.

[2] The accent for the fem. gen. pl. follows the pattern for first declension nouns, not adjectives, unlike other passive participles ending in -μένων in the fem. gen. pl.

First Perfect Active Participle of λύω

⊕	*m.*	*fm.*	*nt.*
Sg.			
N	λελυκώς	λελυκυῖα	λελυκός
G	λελυκότος	λελυκυίας	λελυκότος
D	λελυκότι	λελυκυίᾳ	λελυκότι
A	λελυκότα	λελυκυῖαν	λελυκός
Pl.			
N	λελυκότες	λελυκυῖαι	λελυκότα
G	λελυκότων	λελυκυιῶν	λελυκότων
D	λελυκόσι(ν)	λελυκυίαις	λελυκόσι(ν)
A	λελυκότας	λελυκυίας	λελυκότα

Perfect Passive Participle of λέγω *(5th prpt.* εἴρημαι*)*

The perfect passive participle is formed as follows: reduplication/vowel lengthening + perfect passive stem + μεν + adjectival endings, -ος, -η, -ον.

Sg.	*m.*	*fm.*	*nt.*
N	εἰρημένος	εἰρημένη	εἰρημένον
G	εἰρημένου	εἰρημένης	εἰρημένου
D	εἰρημένῳ	εἰρημένῃ	εἰρημένῳ
A	εἰρημένον	εἰρημένην	εἰρημένον
Pl.			
N	εἰρημένοι	εἰρημέναι	εἰρημένα
G	εἰρημένων	εἰρημένων	εἰρημένων
D	εἰρημένοις	εἰρημέναις	εἰρημένοις
A	εἰρημένους	εἰρημένας	εἰρημένα

– The perfect middle perfect participial endings are the same as the perfect passive particle.

19.3 SECOND PERFECT PARTICIPLE OF οἶδα

As noted previously, the original root of οἶδα is √ *ϝιδ-* , √ *ϝοιδ-* , or √ *ϝειδ(ε)-* (Section 16.7).[3] Because οἶδα forms a *second* perfect in the indicative mood, it also forms a second perfect participle:

[3] Thus, the pluperfect stem, when augmented, is ᾔδ- (cf. ᾔδειν).

Sg.	*m.*	*fm.*	*nt.*
	εἰδώς	εἰδυῖα	εἰδός
	εἰδότος	εἰδυίας	εἰδότος
	etc.		

19.4 ADVERBIAL USE OF PARTICIPLES

In a great many cases, participles function adverbially in sentences. In other words, they often answer the question "when?" (temporal), "how?" (means, manner), or "why?" (purpose, cause).

Adverbial participles are grammatically subordinated to the main (controlling) verb of the sentence. This *main* verb will usually be in the indicative mood. In narrative, the relation between the adverbial participle and the main verb is often temporal, specifying the chronological relations between two or more events. However, adverbial participles can also imply other sorts of non-temporal relations.

Here are some of the primary uses of adverbial participles. In each case, the actual meanings of adverbial participles are not determined by the inflection itself. Rather, their meanings must always be inferred from the literary context.

19.5 TEMPORAL ADVERBIAL PARTICIPLES

Many adverbial participles function temporally, which is to say, they specify the time of an action relative to the action of the main verb. Thus, the tense of a temporal participle is always *relative to the tense of the finite verb of the sentence*:

19.5.1 A present temporal adverbial participle denotes an action occurring *at the same time* as the main verb. This *contemporaneous* action can be expressed by using helping words such as "while" or "when" (e.g., "*When the disciples arrived*, Jesus was praying").

19.5.2 An aorist temporal adverbial participle often denotes an action occurring *prior to* the action specified by the main verb. This *antecedent* action can be expressed by using the helping word "after" (e.g., "*After the disciples arrived*, Jesus prayed"). However, *contemporaneous* action is sometimes conveyed when the verb of aorist participle is the *same* as the aorist main verb. In such instances, "when" or "while" may be used as helping words.

19.5.3 A perfect participle, like the perfect indicative, denotes a present state as a result of past actions.

19.6 NON-TEMPORAL USE OF ADVERBIAL PARTICIPLES

Even though adverbial participles often function temporally, especially in narratives, one should not overlook the fact that adverbial participles can have many other meanings, depending on the specific context. Here follow some typical non-temporal uses of adverbial participles:

1. *Causal Participle ("because")*
   The cause of an action or event can be indicated by use of a participle: for example, "*because he wanted* to justify himself, he said to Jesus" (Luke 10:29).
2. *Concessive Participle ("although")*
   A participle can be used to concede or admit a point: for example, "for *although we are walking* in the flesh, we are not fighting according to the flesh" (2 Cor 10:3).
3. *Participle Expressing Means ("by means of")*
   A participle can be employed to specify the manner, or means,[4] by which an action takes place: for example, "*by touching* the ear, he healed him" (Luke 22:51).
4. *Expressing Purpose ("in order to")*
   A participle can specify the purpose of an action:[5] for example, "Elijah is coming *in order to* save him" (Matt 27:49).
5. *Conditional Participle ("if")*
   A participle can also be used to indicate the protasis (i.e., "if" clause, cf. Section 22.6) of a conditional sentence: for example, "*if you keep* yourselves from such things, you will do well" (Acts 15:29).

Because adverbial participles – and indeed *all* participles – are formed using the same endings, the specific meaning of any given participle cannot be determined on the basis of morphology alone. One must always rely on the specific literary context to determine the best translation of a participial phrase.

Needless to say, occasions will arise when the immediate context allows for more than one possibility. For example, Galatians 2:3 is a notorious example of the ambiguity between concessive (although) and causal (because) participles: "But even Titus . . . Ἕλλην ὤν was not compelled to be circumcised." Does Paul mean that "*although* (Titus) was Greek," or "*because* (Titus) was Greek"? In such cases, widening the context further can help resolve the problem.

19.7 THE GENITIVE ABSOLUTE

The *genitive absolute* is a special grammatical construction that has no equivalent in English grammar. If you fail to recognize this grammatical structure in a Greek text,

[4] There are often distinctions between manner and means. Both answer the question "how?", but a participle of manner often cannot be easily preceded by the words "by means of" (e.g., John 20:11, ". . . was standing at the tomb outside weeping . . ."). The participle of manner dramatizes the main verb, whereas a participle of means qualifies, or further defines, the main verb in a more technical sense. This is not to say, that there can never be any overlap between the usage of "manner" and "means" in certain participles.

[5] A future participle is often used in this way.

you will find yourself unable to translate the sentence correctly. Therefore, one must fully master this construction. The genitive absolute has the following features:

1. A genitive participle, often preceded or followed by a noun or pronoun in the genitive case, forming an adverbial phrase.
2. The subject of the participle is *independent* of the subject of the main verb of the sentence.
3. The genitive participle is translated as an adverbial participle (see above): for example, temporal, causal, concessive, and so forth.

Here are some examples:

> ἤδη δὲ αὐτοῦ καταβαίνοντος οἱ δοῦλοι αὐτοῦ ὑπήντησαν αὐτῷ λέγοντες [saying] (John 4:51)
>
> "And *when he was* already *going down*, his slaves met him saying..."
>
> ταῦτα δὲ αὐτῶν λαλούντων αὐτὸς ἔστη ἐν μέσῳ αὐτῶν (Luke 24:36)
>
> "*But while they were speaking these things*, he stood in their midst..."
>
> Καὶ γενομένης ὥρας ἕκτης σκότος ἐγένετο ἐφ᾽ ὅλην τὴν γῆν (Mark 15:33)
>
> "And *when the sixth hour had come*, darkness came upon the whole land..."[6]

19.8 PERIPHRASTIC CONSTRUCTIONS

The term "periphrastic" means a roundabout, or indirect, manner of doing something. In Greek, the so-called periphrastic construction is composed of an auxiliary verb, εἰμί, followed by a participle. In forming a periphrastic construction, no element can come between the auxiliary verb (εἰμί) and the participle, except for terms that complete, or directly modify, the participle itself.

It is often not obvious why Greek authors employed periphrastic constructions. Some scholars have suggested that its use may indicate emphasis. In the case of irregular verbs (and there are many!), periphrastic constructions may have provided a simpler way of forming the perfect and pluperfect tenses, rather than employing the indicative mood. A periphrastic construction may sometimes function as a more emphatic form of the simple verb, or it may draw attention to the participle and its modifiers. Whatever its purpose, the periphrastic construction occurs with great frequency in the New Testament. Three periphrastic tenses are formed with the *present* participle. The perfect, pluperfect, and future perfect periphrastic constructions are formed with the *perfect* participle.

[6] This is an example of the aorist adverbial participle to express contemporaneous action: Both the adverbial participle and the finite main verb are the same verb, and both are in the aorist tense.

present periphrastic	pres. ind. of εἰμί	+	present participle
imperfect periphrastic	impf. ind. of εἰμί	+	present participle
future periphrastic	fut. ind. of εἰμί	+	present participle

perfect periphrastic	pres. ind. of εἰμί	+	perfect participle
pluperfect periphrastic	impf. ind. of εἰμί	+	perfect participle
future perfect periphrastic	fut. ind. of εἰμί	+	perfect participle (rare in GNT)

Here are some examples:

Present Periphrastic (pres. of εἰμί + pres. ptc.)

"… it (the good news) is bearing fruit and increasing … (ἐστίν καρποφούμενον καὶ αὐξανόμενον)" (Col 1:6)

Imperfect Periphrastic (impf. of εἰμί + pres. ptc.)

"only *they were hearing*… (ἀκούοντες ἦσαν)" (Gal 1:23)

Future Periphrastic (fut. of εἰμί + pres. ptc.)

"… and Jerusalem *will be trampled* (ἔσται πατουμένη) upon by the Gentiles" (Luke 21:24b)

Perfect Periphrastic (pres. of εἰμί + perf. ptc.)

"I have been sent ('Απεσταλμένος εἰμί) before him." (John 3:28)

Pluperfect Periphrastic (impf. of εἰμί + perf. ptc.)

"For John *had* not yet *been thrown* (ἦν βεβλημένος) into prison." (John 3:24)

Future Perfect Periphrastic (fut. of εἰμί + perf. ptc.)

"…whatever you bind on earth *will have been bound* (ἔσται δεδεμένον) in heaven and whatever you loose on the earth *will have been loosed* (ἔσται λελυμένον) in heaven." (Matt 16:19)

19.9 VOCABULARY TO BE MEMORIZED

1. ἀνάστασις, -εως, ἡ (a-**na**-sta-sis, -e-os), resurrection
2. διάνοια, ἡ (dhi-**a**-ni-a) mind; understanding, intention, attitude (cf. psychological domain, Section 18.9)
3. δικαιοσύνη, ἡ (dhi-ke-o-**si**-ni), this word means both "justice" and "righteousness"; rather than choose, one might translate it as "justice and righteousness" or as "justice-righteousness," uprightness (cf. adj. δίκαιος, -α, -ον)
4. δικαιῶ (-όω) (dh-ke-**o**), I vindicate, treat as just, justify, cause someone to be released from legal claims; fut. δικαιώσω, 1 aor. ἐδικαίωσα, pf. pass. δεδικαίωμαι, 1 aor. pass. ἐδικαιώθην
5. δοκῶ (-έω) (dh-**ko**), I think, suppose; intrans. I seem; impers., "it seems"; fut. δόξω, 1 aor. ἔδοξα (cf. the heresy known as Docetism, from δοκῶ, which names the heterodox Christological doctrine that Jesus' physical body was an illusion. He only *seemed* to be human.)
6. δοξάζω (dho-**ksa**-zo), I honor, praise (cf. δόξα) ("doxology"); fut. δοξάσω, 1 aor. ἐδόξασα, pf. pass. δεδόξασμαι, 1 aor. pass. ἐδοξάσθην[7]
7. εἰσέρχομαι (i-**ser**-kho-me), I come or go (in or into), enter; fut. εἰσελεύσομαι, 2 aor. εἰσῆλθον, pf. εἰσελήλυθα (cf. principal parts for ἔρχομαι, 25.21)
8. ἐκπορεύομαι (ek-po-**rev**-o-me), I go or come out, come forth; fut. ἐκπορεύσομαι (cf. πορεύομαι)
9. ἐλπίζω (el-**pi**-zo), I hope; fut. ἐλπιῶ,[8] 1 aor. ἤλπισα, pf. ἤλπικα (cf. ἐλπίς)
10. κάθημαι (**ka**-thi-me), I sit, sit down;[9] impf. ἐκαθήμην, fut. καθήσομαι
11. λύχνος, ὁ (**li**-khnos), lamp (made of metal or clay)
12. μνημεῖον, τό (mni-**mi**-on), grave, tomb, monument
13. πόσος, -η, -ον, (**po**-sos, -i, -on), how much, how many; πόσῳ μᾶλλον, how much more?
14. πότερον (**po**-te-ron), whether (adv.)
15. φόβος, ὁ (**fo**-vos), fear, terror (cf. φοβοῦμαι) (cf. "phobia")

---

[7] As noted in Section 16.14 [box 2], the verb, δοξάζω, is closely related to the central social values, τιμή [honor] and αἰσχύνη [shame].

[8] Attic future: ἐλπίζω → ελπιζ + σεω → ελπισεω → ελπιέω → ἐλπιῶ.

[9] This is an athematic verb, like δύναμαι. Its stem is κάθη-.

20.

The Athematic Conjugation (-μι verbs): Part 1 – The Indicative Mood

In previous lessons, most of the verbs we have studied have ended in -ω in the first-person singular. This large family of verbs is called the thematic conjugation because the endings are attached to the verbal stem by means of a *thematic* vowel (e.g., ο/ε in the present tense). It is also called the ω conjugation.

A second major conjugation is called the athematic conjugation because no thematic vowel is used. Athematic verbs are also called -μι verbs because the first-person singular ends with -μι (e.g., εἰμί).

In the history of the Greek language, athematic verbs actually represent an older way of forming verbs. During the period in which the New Testament was being written, they were gradually falling into disuse or being changed into thematic verbs. For this reason, there are fewer athematic verbs in the New Testament than thematic verbs. Nonetheless, it is essential that you have a working knowledge of athematic verbs, owing to their importance.

20.1 STEM CHANGES

Athematic verbs can be classified according to their stem vowel. In this lesson, we will study three of the most important athematic verbs, namely δίδωμι ("I give"), τίθημι ("I put, set"), and ἵστημι ("I set up, stand"). As we shall see, these verbs represent the three possible stem vowels, namely ο, ε, and α. But in each case, the stem vowel of the lexical form has been lengthened. The roots of these verbs are actually √ δο, √ θε, and √ στα, or an inflected compound form of one of these three verbs.

Figure: Plaque picturing a nude male figure with long hair, holding two musical instruments, a plectrum and cithara, with snake and bull's head below (Iconium, *IKonya* 16).

root		*lengthening*		*lexical form*
√ δο	→	δω	→	δίδωμι
√ θε	→	θη	→	τίθημι
√ στα	→	στη	→	ἵστημι

The changing verbal stem is one of many reasons why beginners often find it difficult to identify these verbs. Here is a hint: If you see a verb whose stem consists of δο/δω, θε/θη, στα/στη, first consider the possibility that the verb may be an inflected form of δίδωμι, τίθημι, or ἵστημι, respectively.

20.2 PRESENT VERBAL STEMS OF ATHEMATIC VERBS

If the initial letter of the verbal stem is a consonant, this consonant is reduplicated with ι as a connecting vowel (e.g., √ δο → διδο-). Thus, the lexical form of these verbs *already has* a reduplicated initial consonant. This reduplication, with ι, occurs in the present and imperfect tenses. Having made this general observation, the verbs τίθημι and ἵστημι require special comment.

In the case of τίθημι, the root is √ θε. But the Greek language does not allow the reduplication of an aspirated consonant, such as θ, with another aspirated consonant. In other words, it does not allow θιθε-. The θ (dental) of √ θε is reduplicated with the corresponding *un*aspirated dental, τ. Thus, the present-tense stem of √ θε is τιθε- (not θιθε-).

In the case of ἵστημι, the root √ στα poses another problem. Greek does not allow the reduplication of a sibilant. Thus, initial σ drops off the reduplicated stem, σιστα, and the connecting vowel, ι, is aspirated (by editors) with the addition of a rough breathing mark. Thus, √ στα becomes ἱστα-.

To sum up, after reduplication and the lengthening of the stem vowel, the stems of the *singular* active present forms are as follows:

δο	→	διδω
θε	→	τιθη
στα	→	ἱστη

In the present *plural* forms, the stem vowel is not lengthened. Thus, the present-tense *plural* stems are:

δο	→	διδο
θε	→	τιθε
στα	→	ἱστα

Because the personal ending in the first person singular is -μι, this results in the following lexical forms: δίδωμι, τίθημι, and ἵστημι. The personal endings for the athematic verbs in the present active indicative are as follows:

	Sg.	*Pl.*
1	-μι	-μεν
2	-ς[1]	-τε
3	-σι (from τι)	-ασι(ν) (from ντι)

20.3 PRESENT ACTIVE INDICATIVE OF ATHEMATIC VERBS

If we add the above present active endings to the -μι verbs above, the following paradigms of the present active indicative are formed. Note how the original stem vowel is preserved in the plural forms.

⊕	δίδωμι ("I give")		τίθημι ("I put, set")		ἵστημι ("I set up, stand")	
Sg.						
1	δίδωμι	(**dhi**-dho-mi)	τίθημι	(**ti**-thi-mi)	ἵστημι	(**i**-sti-mi)
2	δίδως	(**dhi**-dhos)	τίθης	(**ti**-this)	ἵστης	(**i**-stis)
3	δίδωσι(ν)	(**dhi**-dho-si[n])	τίθησι(ν)	(**ti**-thi-si[n])	ἵστησι(ν)	(**i**-sti-si[n])
Pl.						
1	δίδομεν	(**dhi**-dho-men)	τίθεμεν	(**ti**-the-men)	ἵσταμεν	(**i**-sta-men)
2	δίδοτε	(**dhi**-dho-te)	τίθετε	(**ti**-the-te)	ἵστατε	(**i**-sta-te)
3	διδόασι(ν)	(dhi-**dho**-a-si[n])	τιθέασι(ν)	(ti-**the**-a-si[n])	ἱστᾶσι(ν)[2]	(i-**sta**-si[n])

The following paradigms are provided to help you see common patterns in the conjugation of athematic verbs. Your challenge is to know how to parse them when you encounter them in the GNT. Observe how the future, perfect (act., mid., and pass.), and aorist passive of athematic verbs, use the same endings as the thematic conjugation.

20.4 PRESENT MIDDLE AND PASSIVE INDICATIVE OF ATHEMATIC VERBS

The endings for the present middle or passive indicative are identical to those of the thematic conjugation.

1 Possibly borrowed from the 2 sg. of secondary active endings.

2 Note how the α of the stem contracts with the α of the ending (ἱστα + ασι → ἱστᾶσι), but does not do so in the case of διδόασι and τιθέασι.

	Sg.	*Pl.*
1	-μαι	-μεθα
2	-σαι	-σθε
3	-ται	-νται

If we apply these middle endings to the verbs above, the following paradigms of the present passive indicative result:

Present Passive Indicative

⊕	δίδωμι	τίθημι	ἵστημι
Sg.			
1	δίδομαι	τίθεμαι	ἵσταμαι
2	δίδοσαι	τίθεσαι	ἵστασαι
3	δίδοται	τίθεται	ἵσταται
Pl.			
1	διδόμεθα	τιθέμεθα	ἱστάμεθα
2	δίδοσθε	τίθεσθε	ἵστασθε
3	δίδονται	τίθενται	ἵστανται

Note: In contrast to thematic verbs, many athematic verbs do have both active and middle forms. This is especially noticeable when these verbs are compounded with prepositions to form other athematic verbs.

20.5 IMPERFECT INDICATIVE OF ATHEMATIC VERBS

The imperfect active indicative is formed as follows: augment + [reduplication] + present stem [short] + modified secondary endings:

20.5.1 Imperfect Active Indicative

	δίδωμι	τίθημι	ἵστημι
Sg.			
1	**ἐδίδουν*** (ἐδίδο-ον)	ἐτίθην	ἵστην
2	**ἐδίδους*** (ἐδίδο-ες)	**ἐτίθεις*** (ἐτίθε-ες)	ἵστης
3	**ἐδίδου*** (ἐδίδο-ε)	**ἐτίθει*** (ἐτίθε-ε)	ἵστη
Pl.			
1	ἐδίδομεν	ἐτίθεμεν	ἵσταμεν
2	ἐδίδοτε	ἐτίθετε	ἵστατε
3	ἐδίδοσαν (or ἐδίδουν)	ἐτίθεσαν (or ἐτίθουν)	ἵστασαν

Note:

- The forms marked by an asterisk (*) are actually thematic forms: These endings are connected to the stem with ο or ε as a connecting vowel.
- The use of -σαν in the third plural forms of the imperfect is unexpected.[3]

20.5.2 Imperfect Passive Indicative

The imperfect passive indicative is formed as follows: augment + [reduplication] + present stem + secondary passive endings:

Sg.

1	ἐδιδόμην	ἐτιθέμην	ἱστάμην
2	ἐδίδοσο	ἐτίθεσο	ἵστασο
3	ἐδίδοτο	ἐτίθετο	ἵστατο

Pl.

1	ἐδιδόμεθα	ἐτιθέμεθα	ἱστάμεθα
2	ἐδίδοσθε	ἐτίθεσθε	ἵστασθε
3	ἐδίδοντο	ἐτίθεντο	ἵσταντο

20.6 FUTURE ACTIVE TENSE OF ATHEMATIC VERBS

The future active tense is formed by lengthening the stem vowel and adding the future tense consonant, σ, followed by the future endings you have already learned. Note that the initial consonant is not reduplicated in the future tense (i.e., the future stem + σ + primary active endings):

⊕	δίδωμι	τίθημι	ἵστημι

Sg.

1	δώσω	θήσω	στήσω
2	δώσεις	θήσεις	στήσεις
3	δώσει	θήσει	στήσει

Pl.

1	δώσομεν	θήσομεν	στήσομεν
2	δώσετε	θήσετε	στήσετε
3	δώσουσι(ν)	θήσουσι(ν)	στήσουσι(ν)

[3] But ἐδίδουν is attested in Mark 3:6, 15:23, and ἐτίθουν is attested in Acts 4:35 and 3:2.

20.7 FIRST AORIST ACTIVE AND PERFECT ACTIVE INDICATIVE OF ATHEMATIC VERBS

In the case of athematic verbs, the tense formative for the *aorist* tense is κα, not σα (with the exception of ἵστημι). The tense formative for the perfect tense is also κα. However, the aorist and perfect tenses are easily distinguished by the reduplication of the initial stem consonant in perfect forms. The aorist tense does *not* reduplicate the first consonant but has an augment instead.

Note: Many grammarians label aorist indicative forms of athematic verbs, as *first* aorists, and aorist *non*-indicative forms of athematic verbs as *second* aorists (though this is not a consistent practice).

The verb ἵστημι is an exception to the above rule. It has *two* aorist forms in the indicative mood a first aorist and a second aorist:

1. ἔστησα is a first aorist, transitive verb that means "I set up, caused to stand." The *transitive* form of ἵστημι uses σα as a tense formative (cf. column (a) below),
2. ἔστην is a second aorist, intransitive verb that means "I stood." The intransitive form employs *no* tense consonant or connecting vowel (cf. column (b) below).

Formation:

- First aorist active: augment + aorist stem + κα/κε (σα/σε for ἵστημι) + secondary active endings
- Second aorist active of ἵστημι: augment + aorist stem + modified secondary active endings
- Perfect active: (reduplication) + perfect stem + κα/κε + primary active endings

⊕	δίδωμι		τίθημι		ἵστημι		
	1 Aorist	*Perfect*	*1 Aorist*	*Perfect*	*1 Aor. (a)*	*2 Aor. (b)*	*Perfect*
Sg.							
1	ἔδωκα	δέδωκα	ἔθηκα	τέθεικα	ἔστησα	ἔστην	ἕστηκα
2	ἔδωκας	δέδωκας	ἔθηκας	τέθεικας	ἔστησας	ἔστης	ἕστηκας
3	ἔδωκε(ν)	δέδωκε(ν)	ἔθηκε(ν)	τέθεικε(ν)	ἔστησε(ν)	ἔστη	ἕστηκε(ν)
Pl.							
1	ἐδώκαμεν	δεδώκαμεν	ἐθήκαμεν	τεθείκαμεν	ἐστήσαμεν	ἔστημεν	ἑστήκαμεν
2	ἐδώκατε	δεδώκατε	ἐθήκατε	τεθείκατε	ἐστήσατε	ἔστητε	ἑστήκατε
3	ἔδωκαν	δεδώκασι(ν)	ἔθηκαν	τεθείκασι(ν)	ἔστησαν	ἔστησαν	ἑστήκασι(ν)

As you know, the perfect tense is also used to signify a present state of being arising from a past action. The verb ἵστημι frequently appears in the perfect tense, ἕστηκα, but is translated in the present tense as "I stand/am standing," because it is a stative verb. The perfect participle of this verb also functions statively (see 21.3). The pluperfect εἱστήκειν is translated in the past tense as "I stood/was standing."

20.8 FIRST AORIST MIDDLE INDICATIVE OF ATHEMATIC VERBS

The first aorist middle indicative of these athematic verbs is formed as follows: augment + aorist middle stem + secondary active endings.

δίδωμι	τίθημι	ἵστημι
ἐδόμην	ἐθέμην	(no middle forms)
ἔδου	ἔθου	
ἔδοτο	ἔθετο	
ἐδόμεθα	ἐθέμεθα	
ἔδοσθε	ἔθεσθε	
ἔδοντο	ἔθεντο	

As noted above, many athematic verbs do have both active and middle forms.

20.9 FIRST AORIST PASSIVE INDICATIVE OF ATHEMATIC VERBS

The first aorist passive indicative of these three athematic verbs is formed as follows: augment + aorist passive stem + θη + secondary active endings.

	δίδωμι	τίθημι	ἵστημι
Sg.			
1	ἐδόθην	ἐτέθην	ἐστάθην
2	ἐδόθης	ἐτέθης	ἐστάθης
3	ἐδόθη	ἐτέθη	ἐστάθη
Pl.			
1	ἐδόθημεν	ἐτέθημεν	ἐστάθημεν
2	ἐδόθητε	ἐτέθητε	ἐστάθητε
3	ἐδόθησαν	ἐτέθησαν	ἐστάθησαν

20.10 VOCABULARY TO BE MEMORIZED

1. ἀνέρχομαι (a-**ner**-kho-me), I go/come up; 2 aor. ἀνῆλθον
2. δαιμόνιον, τό (dhe-**mo**-ni-on), a demon, i.e., a hostile semidivine being with a status between that of humans and of God, an evil spirit. In the ancient Mediterranean, physical and mental illness was often attributed to the work of demons; cf. a fairy (faery, faerie) of Irish culture, which is also a menacing spirit.
3. δίδωμι (**dhi**-dho-mi), I give, grant; fut. δώσω, 1 aor. ἔδωκα, pf. act. δέδωκα, pf. pass. δέδομαι, 1 aor. pass. ἐδόθην

4. εὐχαριστῶ (-έω) (ef-kha-ri-**sto**) I thank, I give thanks; 1 aor. εὐχαρίστησα (or ηὐχαρίστησα), 1 aor. pass. εὐχαριστήθην (cf. "eucharist," the [great] "thanksgiving")[4]
5. θάλασσα, -ης, ἡ, (**tha**-las-sa) sea, lake
6. ἵστημι (**i**-sti-mi), I set up, establish (trans.); I stand (intrans.); fut. στήσω, 1 aor. ἔστησα (trans.), 2 aor. ἔστην (intrans.), pf. act. ἕστηκα, pf. pass. ἕσταμαι, 1 aor. pass. ἐστάθην
7. κατηγορῶ (-έω) (ka-ti-go-**ro**), I bring a legal charge against someone; fut. κατηγορήσω, 1 aor. κατηγόρησα
8. πειράζω (pi-**ra**-zo), I put to the test, tempt; fut. πειράσω, 1 aor. ἐπείρασα, pf. pass. πεπείρασμαι, aor. pass. ἐπειράσθην
9. περισσεύω (pe-ris-**sev**-o), be left over, be more than enough; I increase, I have plenty; fut. περισσεύσω, 1 aor. ἐπερίσσευσα, 1 aor. pass. ἐπερισσεύθην
10. τίθημι (**ti**-thi-mi), I put, set, lay down, give up; fut. θήσω, 1 aor. ἔθηκα, pf. act. τέθεικα, pf. pass. τέθειμαι, aor. pass. ἐτέθην
11. καθίζω (ka-**thi**-zo) intrans. I sit down, stay; trans. cause to sit, set; fut. καθίσω, 1 aor. ἐκάθισα, pf. act. κεκάθικα (cf. κάθημαι)
12. κράζω (**kra**-zo), I call out, cry out, shout; fut. κράξω, 1 aor. ἔκραξα, 2 pf. κέκραγα[5]
13. πάντοτε (**pan**-do-te), always (adv.)
14. πλοῖον, τό (**pli**-on), boat, sometimes specifies a small fishing boat, but other times, a larger, seafaring ship

---

4 In MGr, εὐχαριστῶ means "thank you."

5 Verbs whose present stem ends in -αζ sometimes have a concealed γ in the stem. For example, κράζω is derived from √ κραγ (→ κράξω, ἔκραξα, κέκραγα).

21. The Athematic Conjugation (-μι verbs): Part 2 – δείκνυμι, φημί, and Participles

There are many other athematic-verbs, besides those discussed in the previous lesson. In this lesson we will discuss two other frequently occurring athematic verbs, namely δείκνυμι ("I show, explain") and φημί ("I say"), as well as some non-indicative forms of δίδωμι, τίθημι, and ἵστημι.

21.1 δείκνυμι ("I SHOW, EXPLAIN")

Another relatively common athematic verb in the New Testament is δείκνυμι (**dhi**-kni-mi).[1] This verb is an athematic verb only in the present and imperfect tenses. In the GNT, one finds only the following examples of the present active tense of this verb. In the present tense paradigm, νυ is added to the root, δεικ, to form the present stem, δεικνυ-.

Present Active Indicative
Singular

1 δείκνυμι
2 δεικνύεις[2]
3 δείκνυσι(ν)

The first singular imperfect is ἐδείκνυν.[3] Outside the present and imperfect tenses, δείκνυμι is not athematic, cf. fut. δείξω, 1 aor. ἔδειξα, pf. δέδειχα, 1 aor. pass.

[1] The thematic form, δεικνύω, is already common in Attic Greek. However, μι-verb forms of δείκνυμι are common in the GNT, as are its compound forms.
[2] This is an unexpected form (we would expect δείκνυς).
[3] But 3 pl. impf. form is ἐδείκνυσαν.

Figure: Relief of farmer carrying a long goad, with which he guides a team of oxen pulling a plough (Bozkir, *IKonya* 129).

ἐδείχθην. The verb δείκνυμι inflects as a thematic verb in non-indicative moods, on the verbal root √ δεικ.

21.2 φημί ("I SAY")

The verb φημί (fi-**mi**, √ φα) is an older verb of "saying" that was gradually dying out in the first century AD. Nonetheless, the third-person forms of these verbs occur relatively frequently in the Greek New Testament and should be memorized. As with the other athematic verbs studied in the previous lesson, the root vowel of √ φα lengthens to η in the singular forms of the present and imperfect indicative.[4] φημί is an enclitic verb in the present active indicative (except in second sg.).

Sg.	*Pres.*	*Impf.*
1	φημί	ἔφην
2	φῄς	ἔφης
3	**φησί(ν)**	**ἔφη**[5]
Pl.		
1	φαμέν	ἔφαμεν
2	φατέ	ἔφατε
3	**φασί(ν)**	**ἔφασαν**

The bolded forms are the most commonly occurring forms in the GNT.

21.3 PRESENT AND AORIST ACTIVE PARTICIPLES OF ATHEMATIC VERBS

The participial forms of δίδωμι, τίθημι, and ἵστημι have many similarities to the participles of the thematic verbs. The aorist active participle and the present active participle of these verbs are identical, except for the lack of reduplication of the initial consonant, in the case of the former (or the aspirated vowel in the case of ἵστημι). Of course, the unexpected forms are those in the nominative case, as we have seen before.

Many of the paradigms below are provided for the sake of illustration. It is not expected that you will memorize *every* paradigm, although most of the endings you

4 Future φήσω; 1 aor. ἔφασαν does not occur in GNT.

5 The third singular form, ἔφη, can either be imperfect or 2 aorist. It is not always possible to distinguish between imperfect and aorist forms. Verbs of "saying," such as φημί, often occur in the imperfect tense, especially when introducing a speech of some length (cf. Chapter 12).

should already know. As a learning strategy, try to become familiar with the nominative singular forms, and then try to recognize repeating patterns in the participial endings.

Note also the use of σ in the masculine singular nominative forms.

δίδωμι

	Present Active Participle			*Aorist Active Participle*		
Sg.	*M*	*F*	*N*	*M*	*F*	*N*
N.	διδούς	διδοῦσα	διδόν	δούς	δοῦσα	δόν
G.	διδόντος	διδούσης	διδόντος	δόντος	δούσης	δόντος
D.	διδόντι	διδούσῃ	διδόντι	δόντι	δούσῃ	δόντι
A.	διδόντα	διδοῦσαν	διδόν	δόντα	δοῦσαν	δόν
Pl.						
N.	διδόντες	διδοῦσαι	διδόντα	δόντες	δοῦσαι	δόντα
G.	διδόντων	διδουσῶν	διδόντων	δόντων	δουσῶν	δόντων
D.	διδοῦσι(ν)	διδούσαις	διδοῦσι(ν)	δοῦσι(ν)	δούσαις	δοῦσι(ν)
A.	διδόντας	διδούσας	διδόντα	δόντας	δούσας	δόντα

Note: Except for the reduplication, the aorist forms are identical to the present forms.

τίθημι

	Present Active Participle			*Aorist Active Participle*		
Sg.	*M*	*F*	*N*	*M*	*F*	*N*
N.	τιθείς	τιθεῖσα	τιθέν	θείς	θεῖσα	θέν
G.	τιθέντος	τιθείσης	τιθέντος	θέντος	θείσης	θέντος
D.	τιθέντι	τιθείσῃ	τιθέντι	θέντι	θείσῃ	θέντι
A.	τιθέντα	τιθεῖσαν	τιθέν	θέντα	θεῖσαν	θέν
Pl.						
N.	τιθέντες	τιθεῖσαι	τιθέντα	θέντες	θεῖσαι	θέντα
G.	τιθέντων	τιθεισῶν	τιθέντων	θέντων	θεισῶν	θέντων
D.	τιθεῖσι(ν)	τιθείσαις	τιθεῖσι(ν)	θεῖσι(ν)	θείσαις	θεῖσι(ν)
A.	τιθέντας	τιθείσας	τιθέντα	θέντας	θείσας	θέντα

ἵστημι

	Present Active Participle			Aorist Active Participle		
Sg.	*M*	*F*	*N*	*M*	*F*	*N*
N.	ἱστάς	ἱστᾶσα	ἱστάν	στάς	στᾶσα	στάν
G.	ἱστάντος	ἱστάσης	ἱστάντος	στάντος	στάσης	στάντος
D.	ἱστάντι	ἱστάσῃ	ἱστάντι	στάντι	στάσῃ	στάντι
A.	ἱστάντα	ἱστᾶσαν	ἱστάν	στάντα	στᾶσαν	στάν
Pl.						
N.	ἱστάντες	ἱστᾶσαι	ἱστάντα	στάντες	στᾶσαι	στάντα
G.	ἱστάντων	ἱστασῶν	ἱστάντων	στάντων	στασῶν	στάντων
D.	ἱστᾶσι(ν)	ἱστάσαις	ἱστᾶσι(ν)	στᾶσι(ν)	στάσαις	στᾶσι(ν)
A.	ἱστάντας	ἱστάσας	ἱστάντα	στάντας	στάσας	στάντα

Note: the perfect participle of this verb is relatively common because this is a stative verb. The nominative singular forms of the perfect participle are, ἑστώς, ἑστῶσα, ἑστός.

21.4 PRESENT MIDDLE AND PASSIVE PARTICIPLES OF ATHEMATIC VERBS

The middle and passive athematic participles are easily formed if you know the verbal stem, because the endings are regular second and first declension endings. As in the case of the active participles, these endings are joined to the stem by the morpheme -μεν. The aorist participle lacks reduplication (or, in the case of ἵστημι, the aspiration). The middle and passive participle is formed as follows: (reduplication) + present middle/passive stem + μεν + -ος, -η, -ον.

	Present Middle/Passive	*Aorist Middle/Passive*
δίδωμι	διδόμενος, -η, -ον	δόμενος, -η, -ον
τίθημι	τιθέμενος, -η, -ον	θέμενος, -η, -ον
ἵστημι	ἱστάμενος, -η, -ον	στάμενος, -η, -ον

21.5 VOCABULARY TO BE MEMORIZED

1. ἀγάπη, ἡ (a-**ga**-pi), love (cf. ἀγαπῶ, ἀγαπητός, φιλῶ, φίλος)
2. ἀγρός, ὁ (a-**gros**), field, countryside (cf. θερίζω, θερισμός) ("agriculture")
3. αἷμα, -ατος, τό (**e**-ma, -a-tos), blood (cf. "hematology")
4. ἀποθνῄσκω[6] (a-po-**thni**-sko), I die; fut. ἀποθανοῦμαι, 2 aor. ἀπέθανον
5. ἀπόλλυμι (a-**pol**-li-mi), I destroy, kill; lose, lose out on; fut. ἀπολέσω/ἀπολῶ; this verb can form a first aor. act., ἀπώλεσα, and a second aor. mid., ἀπωλόμην, 2 pf. act. ἀπόλωλα

[6] Some present tense stems have -σκ/-ισκ added to the *present* stem to differentiate it from the future stem (e.g., ἀποθνῄσκω, γινώσκω).

6. γένος, -ους, τό (**ye**-nos, -ous), family, race, nation; offspring, descendants, kind (cf. γεννῶ [-άω])
7. γλῶσσα, -ης, ἡ, (**glos**-sa, -is), tongue (lit.), language (fig.)
8. δείκνυμι (**dhi**-kni-mi), I show, reveal; fut. δείξω, 1 aor. ἔδειξα, 1 aor. pass. ἐδείχθην
9. δύναμις, -εως, ἡ (**dhi**-na-mis, -e-os), power, strength, ability; has the combined meaning of both "potentiality" and "power," act of power (cf. δύναμαι).[7]
10. εἰσπορεύομαι (i-spo-**rev**-o-me), I come/go into
11. ἐμβαίνω (em-**ve**-no), I embark, step in; 2 aor. act. ἐνέβην (athematic; note how ἐμ- changes to ἐν- before an augment), aor. ptc. ἐμβάς (cf. ἀναβαίνω, καταβαίνω, 18.4 [box 1])
12. θυγάτηρ, -τρός, ἡ (thi-**ga**-tir, -**tros**) daughter, a female descendant
13. περιπατῶ (-έω) (pe-ri-pa-**to**), I walk about, go about; I live (fig.)
14. προσέρχομαι (pro-**ser**-kho-me), I come or go to, approach; fut. προσελεύσομαι, 2 aor. προσῆλθον, pf. act. προσελήλυθα
15. πῦρ, -ός, τό (pir, -**ros**) fire (cf. pyromaniac)
16. στάδιοι, -ι-ων (**sta**-dhi-i, -i-on) (m.), stades, furlongs (about 607 feet)
17. φημί (fi-**mi**) (enclitic), I say, I mean, imply; fut. φήσω, impf./2 aor. ἔφη (he said).[8]
18. σπείρω (**spi**-ro), I sow; 1 aor. ἔσπειρα, pf. pass. ἔσπαρμαι (cf. σπέρμα, θερίζω), pf. pass. ἔσπαρμαι (cf. Section 21.7)

21.6 THE HOUSEHOLD (οἰκία, οἶκος) AND KINSHIP AS A SEMANTIC FIELD

▪ ὁ πατήρ (gen. πατρός)	father
▪ ἡ μήτηρ (gen. μητρός)	mother
▪ τὸ τέκνον	child
▪ ὁ or ἡ παῖς (gen. παιδός)	child
▪ ὁ υἱός	son
▪ ἡ θυγάτηρ (gen. θυγατρός)	daughter
▪ ὁ ἀνήρ (gen. ἀνδρός)	husband, man
▪ ἡ γυνή (gen. γυναικός)	wife, woman
▪ ὁ ἀδελφός	brother
▪ ἡ ἀδελφή	sister
▪ ὁ οἰκονόμος	house-steward, manager
▪ ὁ δοῦλος	slave

[7] The term δύναμις is an important technical term in the philosophy of Aristotle. It means "potential," in contrast to ἐνέργεια, i.e., an "action" (cf. Ar. *Eudemian Ethics* II.i.1218b, *Nicomachean Ethics*, I.viii.1098b33). Although δύναμις often means "power" in the GNT, it can also carris the inference of "potential," especially when contrasted with ἐνέργεια.

[8] The 1 aor. form, ἔφησα, does not occur in the GNT.

21.7 "AGRICULTURE" AS A SEMANTIC FIELD: VOCABULARY REVIEW[9]

- ἀγρός — field
- σπείρω — I sow
- σπέρμα, -ατος — seed
- καιρός — time of harvest
- θερίζω — I reap, harvest
- θερισμός — the harvest, a crop
- καρπός — grain, harvest
- γεωργός — a farmer

[9] Cf. Louw/Nida, 516–18 (Chapter 43).

22.

Subjunctive Mood and Conditional Sentences

22.1 MOODS

Greek verbs are found in four so-called *moods*. The term "mood" indicates the relation of the action to reality, as understood by the author. All the verbs studied in the preceding lessons were in the *indicative* mood, with the exception of the Greek participle. The indicative is the most usual mood of everyday discourse and narrative. It is the mood of direct statements, assertions, direct questions, and historical descriptions. We could say that it is the mood of actuality.

The three remaining moods are as follows: the subjunctive, imperative, and optative. (The infinitive and participle are not moods but can be treated as moods for the purposes of parsing.)

Although no absolute distinction can be made between the various moods, the following general comments can be made:

1. *Indicative Mood*: indicates what is real, actual, or certain. However, it is also used in some conditional sentences.
2. *Subjunctive Mood*: affirms the possibility that the verbal idea may come to pass. The degree of possibility, or probability, is indicated by context. It is also used in exhortations of the first-person plural (the *hortatory* subjunctive), in deliberative questions, in conditional sentences, and in some negative commands. The subjunctive has three tenses: present, aorist, and perfect.
3. *Imperative Mood:* is the mood of command or entreaty (cf. Chapter 24). The speaker demands that a verbal idea happen. It is used in commands, exhortations, and prayers.
4. *Optative Mood*: is the mood of wishing and desiring. It is employed only infrequently in the GNT (cf. 22.8).

Figure: Relief ox head wearing a garland (Ephesus).

It is important to remember that *no* distinction is made with respect to time of the verbal action between the present and the aorist tense in the non-indicative moods. Instead, these tenses express only aspect; that is, the present tense expresses imperfective aspect (i.e., an ongoing or repeated action), whereas the aorist expresses only the aoristic aspect. Owing to its lack of specificity, the aorist is the most frequently occurring tense in non-indicative moods.

22.2 FORMATION OF THE PRESENT SUBJUNCTIVE MOOD

Subjunctive verbs employ the following endings, which are attached to the appropriate verbal stems:

	Active		*Middle/Passive*	
	Sg.	*Pl.*	*Sg.*	*Pl.*
1	-ω	-ωμεν	-ωμαι	-ώμεθα
2	-ῃς	-ητε	-ῃ	-ησθε
3	-ῃ	-ωσι(ν)	-ηται	-ωνται

The third sg. active form (-ῃ) and the identical second sg. middle form can be distinguished on the basis of the verb in question (Ask yourself, is it an active or middle verb in a given tense?).

The present subjunctive is easy to form. Simply take the present indicative form and lengthen the connecting vowel. An *iota* (ι) in the personal endings (e.g., -ει, -εις) is written subscript. Because the *present* subjunctive specifies the imperfective aspect, it is used much less frequently than the aorist subjunctive.

You will notice below that some forms of the subjunctive are identical to the indicative mood. In such cases, one must rely on context, or the presence of words such as ἵνα and ἄν, to determine the use of the subjunctive mood.

22.2.1 Present Active Subjunctive of λύω[1]

⊕	*Sg.*	*Pl.*
1	λύω	λύωμεν
2	λύῃς	λύητε
3	λύῃ	λύωσι(ν)

[1] The forms of contract verbs in the subjunctive are predictable: e.g., ποιῶ, ποιῇς, etc.; ἀγαπῶ, ἀγαπᾷς, etc.; πληρῶ, πληροῖς, etc.

Formation of present passive subjunctive: present passive stem + passive subjunctive endings

⊕ *22.2.2 Present Passive Subjunctive of* λύω

1	λύωμαι	λυώμεθα
2	λύῃ	λύησθε
3	λύηται	λύωνται

Formation of present middle subjunctive: by analogy with the present passive subjunctive

⊕ *22.2.3 Present Middle of* ἔρχομαι

1	ἔρχωμαι	ἐρχώμεθα
2	ἔρχῃ	ἔρχησθε
3	ἔρχηται	ἔρχωνται

22.3 FORMATION OF THE AORIST SUBJUNCTIVE MOOD

The aorist subjunctive, with its *aoristic* aspect, occurs far more frequently than does the present subjunctive. As you would expect, the aorist subjunctive has no augment (ε).

22.3.1 The first aorist active subjunctive is easy to form: Simply take the unaugmented first aorist stem and insert σ between the verb stem and the personal endings for the subjunctive:[2]

First Aorist Active Subjunctive of λύω

⊕	*Sg.*	*Pl.*
1	λύσω	λύσωμεν
2	λύσῃς	λύσητε
3	λύσῃ	λύσωσι(ν)

22.3.2 To form the first aorist middle subjunctive, insert σ after the aorist verb stem, and then lengthen the vowel that connects the personal endings, which are the same as the present middle subjunctive endings:

[2] With the exception of οἶδα (εἰδῶ, εἰδῇς, εἰδῇ, etc.), the perfect subjunctive normally is formed periphrastically with the subjunctive of εἰμί and a perfect participle (i.e., λελυκὼς ᾖ, etc.).

First Aorist Middle Subjunctive of δέχομαι

⊕	*Sg.*	*Pl.*
1	δέξωμαι	δεξώμεθα
2	δέξῃ	δέξησθε
3	δέξηται	δέξωνται

–In the example above, the final velar of the verb stem has combined with the sigma of the subjunctive.

22.3.3 To form the first aorist passive subjunctive, take the unaugmented aorist passive stem[3] and insert θε between the verb stem and the personal ending, with the expected contractions (i.e., [unaugmented] aorist passive stem + θε + active subjunctive endings):

First Aorist Passive Subjunctive of λύω

⊕	*Sg.*	*Pl.*
1	λυθῶ	λυθῶμεν
2	λυθῇς	λυθῆτε
3	λυθῇ	λυθῶσι(ν)

22.3.4 Second Aorist Active Subjunctive

As you know, outside of the indicative mood, the second aorist has the same endings as the present tense. Therefore, to form the *second* aorist subjunctive

1. Take the stem of the third principal part;
2. Remove the augment or shorten the initial vowel to its original length;
3. Add the present subjunctive endings to the verb stem.

For example, the third principal part of ἐσθίω is ἔφαγον. The second aorist stem is φαγ-. By adding the present subjunctive endings, the following paradigm is formed:

Second Aorist Active Subjunctive of ἐσθίω

	Sg.	*Pl.*
1	φάγω	φάγωμεν
2	φάγῃς	φάγητε
3	φάγῃ	φάγωσι(ν)

The *second* aorist passive subjunctive has the same endings as the first aorist passive (see above), but it lacks the θ (e.g., γραφῶ, γραφῇς, γραφῇ, etc.).

[3] The stem can change from the present tense to the aorist passive tense: e.g., λέγω, ἐρρέθην; ὁρῶ, ὤφθην.

22.4 SUBJUNCTIVE FORMS OF OTHER COMMON VERBS

It is not expected that you will memorize all the paradigms below. The remaining paradigms are provided to help you recognize common patterns in the subjunctive endings. Your challenge is to learn how to identify and parse these verbs when you encounter them in the GNT.

As you know, the verbs εἰμί ("I am"), οἶδα ("I know"), and γινώσκω ("I know") occur with great frequency. The subjunctive forms of εἰμί are identical to the subjunctive endings themselves, with the exception of the placement of the accent. The subjunctive forms of εἰμί, οἶδα, and γινώσκω are as follows:

⊕	εἰμί (√ εσ)	οἶδα (√ ειδ)[4]	γινώσκω (√ γνο)
Sg.			
1	ὦ	εἰδῶ	γνῶ
2	ᾖς	εἰδῇς	γνῷς
3	ᾖ	εἰδῇ	γνῷ or γνοῖ[5]
Pl.			
1	ὦμεν	εἰδῶμεν	γνῶμεν
2	ἦτε	εἰδῆτε	γνῶτε
3	ὦσι(ν)	εἰδῶσι(ν)	γνῶσι(ν)

Remember that in the case of γινώσκω, the initial consonant of the root (√ γνο) was reduplicated and vowel lengthened to form the present stem, γιγνώσκω (Attic), which became γινώσκω in Hellenistic Greek (cf. 10.4.2).

22.5 ACTIVE SUBJUNCTIVE OF ATHEMATIC VERBS

	δίδωμι (√ δο)		τίθημι (√ θε)		ἵστημι (√ στα)	
Sg.	*Pres.*	*Aor.*	*Pres.*	*Aor.*	*Pres.*	*Aor.*
1	διδῶ	δῶ	τιθῶ	θῶ	ἱστῶ	στῶ
2	διδῷς	δῷς	τιθῇς	θῇς	ἱστῇς	στῇς
3	διδῷ	δῷ	τιθῇ	θῇ	ἱστῇ	στῇ
Pl.						
1	διδῶμεν	δῶμεν	τιθῶμεν	θῶμεν	ἱστῶμεν	στῶμεν
2	διδῶτε	δῶτε	τιθῆτε	θῆτε	ἱστῆτε	στῆτε
3	διδῶσι(ν)	δῶσι(ν)	τιθῶσι(ν)	θῶσι(ν)	ἱστῶσι(ν)	στῶσι(ν)

[4] Remember, the root of οἶδα originally began with a digamma, √ ϝιδ-, √ ϝοιδ-, or √ ϝειδ(ε)-.

[5] γνοι is attested in Mark 5:43, 9:30; Luke 19:15.

22.6 THE USE OF THE SUBJUNCTIVE IN CONDITIONAL SENTENCES

A conditional (or "hypothetical") sentence contains two clauses:

1. Protasis: a dependent "if" clause that expresses a condition;
2. Apodosis: the main clause that expresses a consequence of the fulfillment of the condition.

For example: "*If* he commands, I will obey."

(protasis) (apodosis)

There are three kinds of conditional sentences in Hellenistic Greek:

22.6.1 Real or Simple Condition (εἰ + any tense and mood)

This class of conditional sentence makes a logical connection between the protasis and the apodosis: "*if* this is true, *then* that is also true." In other words, the conditional particle, εἰ ("if") in the protasis is followed by a supposition of a fact, followed by the indicative in the apodosis. The condition and its consequences are simply stated, without reference to whether the condition is in fact fulfilled.

The protasis is not always assumed to be true; it may be put forward hypothetically for the sake of argument. The apodosis can also employ the imperative mood. For example:

Protasis: "If (i.e., assuming) you are the Son of God (εἰ υἱὸς εἶ τοῦ θεοῦ)"
Apodosis: "throw yourself down (βάλε σεαυτὸν κάτω)." (Matt 4:7).

22.6.2 Future Condition Expressing a Possibility or Uncertainty (ἐάν + subjunctive, verb in apodosis in any tense and mood)

In the protasis, the conditional particle, ἐάν ("if") is followed by a verb (in the subjunctive mood) expressing the supposition of a possibility or uncertainty. In other words, the situation is *undetermined*. The indicative or imperative follows in the apodosis: for example, "*If* you have the confidence of a grain of mustard seed (ἐὰν ἔχητε πίστιν ὡς κόκκον σινάπεως), then you will say to this mountain … (ἐρεῖτε τῷ ὄρει τούτῳ …)" (Matt 17:20).

22.6.3 Contrary to Fact Statement (εἰ + verb in past tense indicative mood … ἄν + verb in imperfect or aorist indicative)

This class of conditional statement poses a hypothetical condition, which is presumed to be false: "*If* this were the case (and it isn't), *then* that this would also be true too (but its not)."

By way of example in English, take the sentence, "If I knew you were coming [which I didn't], I would have baked a cake [so I didn't]." In negative statements, the negative particle in the protasis ("if" clause) almost always uses μή, whereas οὐ is used in the apodosis.

- Imperfect tense: for example, "*If* you believed Moses, you *would* believe in me (εἰ γὰρ ἐπιστεύετε Μωϋσεῖ, ἐπιστεύετε ἂν ἐμοί)" (John 5:46).
- Aorist tense: for example, "for *if they had* known, they *would not have* crucified the Lord of glory (εἰ γὰρ ἔγνωσαν, οὐκ ἂν τὸν κύριον τῆς δόξης ἐσταύρωσαν)" (1 Cor 2:8). Similarly, in the following case, the pluperfect of οἶδα is used. Since οἶδα is translated as a present tense ("I know"), the pluperfect is translated as a past tense: "If you *had known* the gift of God, ... you would have asked him, and he *would have* given you living water" (εἰ ᾔδεις τὴν δωρεὰν τοῦ θεοῦ... σὺ ἂν ᾔτησας αὐτὸν καὶ ἔδωκεν ἂν σοι ὕδωρ ζῶν [John 4:10]).

22.7 OTHER USES OF THE SUBJUNCTIVE MOOD

Somerset Maugham once quipped of the English subjunctive mood that it "is in its death throes, and the best thing to do is to put it out of its misery as soon as possible." In contrast to the use of the subjunctive mood in modern English, the use of the subjunctive in Hellenistic Greek was quite robust and is an essential part of Greek grammar. In practice, you will often use the helping words "may," "might," or "should" to express the subjunctive. The subjunctive mood is negated by μή.

22.7.1 Hortatory Subjunctive

Used to express an imperative in the first-person plural: for example, "let us have (ἔχωμεν) peace with God" (Rom 5:1 in Codex Vaticanus). Here is a prayer from the Greek Orthodox liturgy that employs the hortatory subjunctive:

Leader	Εὐχαριστήσωμεν τῷ κυρίῳ	(*Let us give thanks* to the Lord!)
People	Ἄξιον καὶ δίκαιον.	(It is worthy and just [to thank the Lord].)

22.7.2 Prohibitions

A negative command or prohibition can be expressed in the aorist subjunctive with μή: for example, "Do not think that... (μὴ νομίσητε)" (Matt 5:17). We will return to this topic when we consider the imperative mood (chap. 24).

22.7.3 Emphatic Future Negation

The aorist subjunctive, preceded by οὐ μή, expresses a very strong denial: for example, "…unless your righteousness exceeds that of the scribes and Pharisees, you *will never* enter (οὐ μὴ εἰσέλθητε) the kingdom of God" (Matt 5:20).[6] Sometimes the future indicative tense follows οὐ μη instead of the subjunctive (owing to the affinity between the future tense and subjunctive mood).

22.7.4 To Express Deliberation or Doubt

The subjunctive is also used in questions to express deliberation or doubt: for example, "What *should* we do (τί ποιῶμεν)?" (John 6:28).

22.7.5 Purpose

The idea of purpose ("in order that") can be expressed with ἵνα (or ὅπως) followed by the subjunctive mood: "*in order that* (ἵνα) through his poverty you might become rich (πλουτήσητε)" (2 Cor 8:9).[7]

22.7.6 Explanation

The so-called *epexegetic* ἵνα (or *explanatory* ἵνα), followed by the subjunctive, is often used in John and Paul to explain the content, motive, or manner of an action: for example, "This is the work of God, that you might believe (ἵνα πιστεύητε) in him whom he sent" (John 6:29).

22.8 REFERENCE: OPTATIVE MOOD

The optative is the mood of wishing and desiring. It often requires the English helping word "may." Though this mood was very important in Attic Greek, it was used much less frequently in the Hellenistic period. During the period in which the GNT was being written, the functions of the optative mood were largely taken over by the subjunctive mood. Nonetheless, the fact that there are sixty-eight examples of the use of the optative mood in the GNT (23 pres., 45 aor.) means that this subject cannot be ignored by more advanced students.

---

[6] While this usage is rare in papyri, it is very frequent in LXX, which has probably influenced the Greek of the NT. Perhaps it is used to make the text sound like the LXX.

[7] Occasionally ἵνα is followed by the future indicative instead of the subjunctive (e.g., Gal 2:4; 4:17). There is an affinity between the future and the subjunctive, both in origin and in sense, because both concern an expectation that is not a realized fact.

Present Act.	*1 Aorist Act.*
λύ-οιμι	λύσαιμι
λύ-οις	λύσαις, or -ειας
λύ-οι	λύσαι, or -ειε(ν)
λύ-οιμεν	λύσαιμεν
λύ-οιτε	λύσαιτε
λύ-οιεν	λύσαιεν, or -ειαν
Present Passive	*1 Aorist Middle*
λυοίμην	λυσαίμην
λύοιο	λύσαιο
λύοιτο	λύσαιτο
λυοίμεθα	λυσαίμεθα
λύοισθε	λύσαισθε
λύοιντο	λύσαιντο

22.9 VOCABULARY TO BE MEMORIZED

1. ἀνίστημι (a-**ni**-sti-mi), trans. (in fut. and 1 aor. act.): I raise (the dead), I appoint (prophets), I help get up; intrans. (in 2 aor. and all mid. forms): I rise, stand up; fut. ἀναστήσω, 1 aor. ἀνέστησα, 2 aor. ἀνέστην (cf. ἀνάστασις)
2. ἀνοίγω (a-**ni**-go), I open; fut. ἀνοίξω, 1 aor. ἀνέῳξα/ἤνοιξα/ἠνέῳξα,[8] 2 pf. ἀνέῳγα, pf. pass. ἀνέῳγμαι/ηνέῳγμαι, 1 aor. pass. ἀνεῴχθην/ἠνοίχθην/ἠνεῴχθην, 2 aor. ἠνοίγην
3. βάλλω (**val**-lo),[9] I throw, throw down; fut. βαλῶ, 2 aor. ἔβαλον, pf. βέβληκα, pf. pass. βέβλημαι, aor. pass. ἐβλήθην
4. ἐκβάλλω (ek-**val**-lo), I drive out, expel; fut. ἐκβαλῶ, 2 aor. ἐξέβαλον, pf. ἐκβέβληκα, aor. pass. ἐξεβλήθην
5. Ἕλλην, -ηνος, ὁ (**el**-lin, -inos), a Greek (or Gentile); Ἑλληνίς, -ίδος, ἡ, a Greek (or Gentile) woman
6. ἐλπίς, -ίδος, ἡ (el-**pis**, -**i**-dhos), hope (cf. ἐλπίζω)
7. ἔξω (**e**-kso), (with gen.) out of, outside (do not confuse ἔξω with ἕξω, which is the future of ἔχω)
8. ἔπειτα (**e**-pi-ta), adv. then, next
9. ἔσχατος, -η, -ον (**e**-skha-tos, -i, -on), last (cf. "eschatology")

[8] The Greeks were not sure whether or not the αν- syllable of ἀνοίγω was a prepositional prefix. This created doubts about how to augment this verb. As a result, many past forms of this verb are augmented two or three times: e.g., ἀνέῳξα is augmented twice and ἠνέῳξα is augmented three times.

[9] Present-tense stems that end in double consonants are often derived from roots with single consonants (e.g., √ βαλ → βάλλω).

10. κηρύσσω (ki-**ris**-so), I proclaim; 1 aor. ἐκήρυξα, 1 aor. pass. ἐκηρύχθην[10]
11. παραδίδωμι (pa-ra-**dhi**-dho-mi), I hand over; fut. παραδώσω, 1 aor. παρέδωκα, pf. παραδέδωκα, pf. pass. παραδέδομαι, 1 aor. pass. παρεδόθην
12. τρώγω (**tro**-go), lit. I eat noisily, I eat; in MGr, τρώγω is the usual verb used to express the idea of "eating." In the Gospel of John, this verb seems to be used (instead of ἐσθίω) in order to express the idea of the real eating of physical food, as opposed to some sort of spiritualized eating, perhaps in refutation of Docetists or proto-gnostics.
13. ψεύστης, -ου, ὁ (**psef**-stis), a liar

22.10 "EATING AND DRINKING" AS SEMANTIC DOMAIN

▪ ἐσθίω	I eat
▪ τρώγω	I eat
▪ πεινῶ	I hunger
▪ ἄρτος	bread, loaf, food
▪ βρῶμα	food
▪ πίνω	I drink
▪ ὕδωρ (gen. -ατος)	water
▪ οἶνος	wine
▪ διακονῶ [-έω]	I serve, wait on sby at table
▪ διάκονος	a waiter of tables

[10] This verb has a hidden velar, κ, in the verbal root √ κηρυγ that causes morphological changes in the principal parts.

23.

The Infinitive

Infinitives are verbal nouns. Like verbs, they have tense and voice, and can take subjects and objects. When an article is used with an infinitive, it turns the infinitive into a noun (e.g., τὸ λέγειν, "the speech"). Thus, infinitives can function like substantives (although they do not decline). When an infinitive functions as a neuter substantive, it is often qualified by a neuter article. The subject of an infinitive, when expressed, is always in the *accusative* case (not the nominative case).

23.1 BASIC FACTS ABOUT INFINITIVES

1. Infinitives are formed in five tenses – present, aorist, future, perfect (and, less frequently, future perfect) – and three voices (active, middle, passive), but they have no person or number.
2. Infinitives are negated by μή.
3. You are already familiar with the tense indicators. As you shall see, these tense indicators are also used with the infinitive:
   - future active -σ
   - first aorist active -σα
   - first aorist passive -θη
   - first perfect active -κε
4. The *second* aorist infinitive has the same endings as the present infinitive, but the stem and accent change.
5. The tense of the infinitive indicates the *aspect* of the action, not the time of action. Most infinitives you encounter will be in the aorist tense. This tense has

Figure: Christian metrical funerary inscription (Dagdere, central Turkey, *IKonya* 205).

an aoristic aspect. It expresses the simple (or summary) occurrence of a verbal action. The present infinitive expresses the ongoing or repeated occurrence of a verbal action (i.e., imperfective aspect), and the perfect infinitive expresses a completed action with continuing results (perfective aspect).

23.2 FORMING THE INFINITIVE

	Present	*1 aorist*	*2 aorist*	*Future*	*Perfect*
active	-ειν	-σαι	-εῖν	-σειν	-κέναι[1]
middle	-εσθαι	-σασθαι	-έσθαι	-σεσθαι	-σθαι
passive	-εσθαι	-θῆναι	-ῆναι	-θήσεσθαι	-σθαι

Some Examples

	Present	*1 aorist*	*2 aorist*	*Future*	*Perfect*
active	λύειν	λῦσαι	λαβεῖν	λύσειν	λελυκέναι
middle	ἔρχεσθαι	δέξασθαι	γενέσθαι	γενήσεσθαι	βεβαπτίσθαι
passive	λύεσθαι	λυθῆναι	γραφῆναι	λυθήσεσθαι	λελῦσθαι

Box 1. Infinitives: Additional Information

1. The present active infinitives of ε-contract verbs are regular (e.g., ποιεῖν), but the infinitive forms of α-contract and ο-contract verbs are irregular:
   - ἀγαπάω → ἀγαπα- + ειν = ἀγαπᾶν (not ἀγαπᾷν)
   - πληρόω → πληρο- + ειν = πληροῦν (not πληροῖν)
2. The infinitive of εἰμί is εἶναι.
3. The infinitive of οἶδα is εἰδέναι.
4. As you would expect, the σ of the -σα tense formative of the aorist and future tenses is deleted when forming an infinitive of liquid verbs: for example, μεῖναι (not μεῖνσαι), βάλεσθαι (not βάλσεσθαι).

[1] -εναι (2 pf.).

Box 2. Accenting Infinitives

1. Present and future infinitives: all voices have a recessive accent.
2. First aorist *active* infinitives are accented on the penult.
3. Second aorist active infinitives are accented with a circumflex on the ultima.
4. Aorist passive infinitives are accented with a circumflex on the penult.
5. 1 aorist middle infinitives are accented with a recessive accent.
6. 2 aorist middle infinitives are accented with an acute on the penult.
7. Perfect active, middle, and passive infinitives are accented with an acute or circumflex on the penult.

23.3 REFERENCE: INFINITIVES OF ATHEMATIC VERBS

The present and aorist active infinitives of athematic verbs use the ending -ναι. (This ending is also used for the perfect active infinitive of the thematic verbs.) The middle and passive present forms use the -σθαι ending, which was introduced above:

	δίδωμι		τίθημι	
	Present	*Aorist*	*Present*	*Aorist*
active	διδόναι	δοῦναι	τιθέναι	θεῖναι
passive	δίδοσθαι	δοθῆναι	τίθεσθαι	τεθῆναι

	ἵστημι	
	Present	*Aorist*
active	ἱστάναι	στῆναι
passive	ἵστασθαι	σταθῆναι

Note: Some of the above infinitival forms only occur in the GNT as compound verbs.

23.4 USES OF THE INFINITIVE

23.4.1 Subject of Impersonal Verbs

Some Greek verbs are called *impersonal* verbs. These include δεῖ ("it is necessary")[2] and ἔξεστιν ("it is possible/lawful"). These verbs are followed by the infinitive. For example:

> ἔξεστιν τοῖς σάββασιν θεραπεῦσαι; (Matt 12:10)
> "Is it lawful *to heal* on the Sabbath?"

[2] Impf. ἔδει, subj. δέῃ, ptc. δέον, δέοντος, etc.

Some impersonal verbs take the accusative form of nouns and personal pronouns. For example: δεῖ με + infin. ("it is necessary *for me* to do such and such a thing"); that is, "I must do such and such a thing."

23.4.2 Complementary Infinitive

Infinitives often follow verbs of "being able," "wishing," "wanting," "knowing how," "trying," "seeking," "asking," "allowing," and so forth. English has this same usage (e.g., "I want *to go* to the bookstore."). For example:

καὶ τίς δύναται σωθῆναι; (Mark 10:26)
"... and who is able *to be saved*?"

εἴ τις θέλει πρῶτος εἶναι, ἔσται πάντων ἔσχατος (Mark 9:35)
"... if anyone wishes *to be* first, he will be last of all."

23.4.3 Infinitive of Purpose

An infinitive without an article can be used to express purpose. For example:

ἤλθομεν προσκυνῆσαι αὐτῷ (Matt 2:2)
"... we have come *(in order) to worship* him."

Ἄνθρωποι δύο ἀνέβησαν εἰς τὸ ἱερὸν προσεύξασθαι (Luke 18:10)
"Two men went up to the Temple *(in order) to pray...*"

23.4.4 Articular Infinitive Expressing Purpose

When an infinitive is preceded by a genitive neuter article, it may also express purpose. When an infinitive is preceded by an article (always neuter), it is termed an *articular infinitive*. If the infinitive has an explicit subject, it will be in the accusative case. If there is an object, it will also be in the accusative case.

σκοτισθήτωσαν οἱ ὀφθαλμοὶ αὐτῶν τοῦ μὴ βλέπειν (Rom 11:10)
"Let their eyes be darkened *in order that they might not see.*"

The prepositions εἰς or πρός followed by the articular infinitive (with the neuter article in accusative case) also express purpose:

εἰς + accusative article + infinitive → "in order to/that"
πρός + accusative article + infinitive → "in order to/that"

Example:

Διὰ τοῦτο [salvation is] ἐκ πίστεως,... εἰς τὸ εἶναι βεβαίαν [sure] τὴν ἐπαγγελίαν[3] παντὶ τῷ σπέρματι... (Rom 4:16–17)

"Therefore, [salvation is] on the basis of faith,... in order that the promise might be dependable to every descendant..."

23.4.5 Articular Infinitive of Time

The articular infinitive in conjunction with various prepositions can express the time of an action:

πρό	+	genitive neuter article + infinitive	→	"before"	(antecedent time)
ἐν	+	dative neuter article + infinitive	→	"when/while"	(simultaneous time)
μετά	+	accusative neuter article + infinitive	→	"after"	(subsequent time)

Less commonly,

ἕως + genitive article + infinitive → "until"

Example:

ἀλλὰ μετὰ τὸ ἐγερθῆναί με προάξω ὑμᾶς εἰς τὴν Γαλιλαίαν (Mark 14:28)
"But *after I am raised*, I will go before you to Galilee."

23.4.6 Articular Infinitive of Cause

διά + *accusative* neuter article + infinitive → "because"

Examples:

καὶ διὰ τὸ μὴ ἔχειν ῥίζαν ἐξηράνθη (Mark 4:6)
"and *because it had no root* it dried up."

αὐτὸς δὲ Ἰησοῦς οὐκ ἐπίστευεν αὐτὸν αὐτοῖς διὰ τὸ αὐτὸν γινώσκειν πάντας... (John 2:24)
"However, Jesus himself did not entrust himself to them *because he knew* them all..."

---

[3] τὴν ἐπαγγελίαν is the subject of the infinitive.

23.5 ὥστε WITH INFINITIVE TO EXPRESS RESULT

When ὥστε is followed by an infinitive, the infinitive expresses the result of an action ("so that"):

Example:

> ἡ πίστις ὑμῶν ἡ πρὸς τὸν θεὸν ἐξελήλυθεν, ὥστε μὴ χρείαν ἔχειν ἡμᾶς λαλεῖν τι. (1 Thess 1:8)
>
> "Your confidence toward God has gone out, *so that we have no need* to say anything."

23.6 REFERENCE: OTHER USES OF THE INFINITVE

23.6.1 Indirect Discourse

Verbs of saying, reporting, and proclaiming (e.g., λέγω, ἀπαγγέλλω), as well as verbs of knowing (e.g., γίνωσκω, ἀγνοέω), are often followed by the infinitive (e.g., "he said *that*...," "I know *that*..."). Infinitives used in indirect discourse can indicate relative time because they assume the role of an indicative verb.

In the case of verbs of saying, the tense of the infinitive should be the same tense as the tense of the indicative verb used by the speaker of the direct discourse. This infinitive will appear without a definite article.

Example:

> ὁ λέγων ἐν αὐτῷ μένειν..." (1 John 2:6)
>
> "The one who says *that he abides* in him..."
>
> οἵτινες λέγουσιν ἀνάστασιν μὴ εἶναι..." (Mark 12:18)
>
> "... those who say *that there is* no resurrection..."

23.6.2 Appositional Infinitive

The infinitive can also be used to explain nouns and adjectives.

Example:

> Τοῦτο γάρ ἐστιν θέλημα τοῦ θεονλ, ὁ ἁγιασμὸς ὑμῶν, ἀπέχεσθαι ὑμᾶς ἀπὸ τῆς πορνείας." (1 Thess 4:3)

"For this is the will of God, your sanctification, *namely that you abstain* from prohibited sexual acts."

(The infinitive ἀπέχεσθαι is in apposition to the noun ἁγιασμός.)

θρησκεία καθαρὰ...αὕτη ἐστίν, ἐπισκέπτεσθαι ὀρφανοὺς καὶ χήρας (James 1:27)
"This is pure religion, *namely to visit* orphans and widows."

(The infin. ἐπισκέπτεσθαι is in apposition to θρηκεία καθαρά.)

23.7 VOCABULARY TO BE MEMORIZED

1. ἀποκτείνω, (a-po-**kti**-no), I kill, put to death; fut. ἀποκτενῶ, 1 aor. ἀπέκτεινα, 1 aor. pass. ἀπεκτάνθην (cf. ἀποθνῄσκω)
2. πάρειμι (**pa**-ri-mi), I am present, am here (cf. παρουσία, lit. "presence," but also a technical term for Christ's seconding "coming"); fut. παρέσομαι
3. πλήρης, -ες (**pli**-ris, -es), full, complete (declines like ἀληθής, -ές, cf. Section 14.5)[4]
4. σκληρός, -ά, -όν (skli-**ros**, -**a**, -**on**), hard, difficult (cf. arterial sclerosis, i.e., "hardening of the arteries")
5. σῴζω (**so**-zo),[5] I save, rescue, deliver; fut. σώσω, 1 aor. ἔσωσα, pf. act. σέσωκα, pf. pass. σέσῳσμαι/σέσωμαι, 1 aor. pass. ἐσώθην (cf. σωτήρ, σωτηρία)
6. ὠφελῶ (-έω) (o-fe-**lo**), I gain, profit, be of value; fut. ὠφελήσω, 1 aor. ὠφέλησα, 1 aor. pass. ὠφελήθην

[4] But apparently indeclinable in John 1:14 and Acts 6:5, where the adjectival case does not agree with the noun it modifies.

[5] Among the possible stems for this verb are σω- and σωι-.

24.

Imperative Mood

The imperative is the mood of making commands, as it is in English. The imperative has three tenses: present, aorist, and perfect.[1] Unlike English, Hellenistic Greek also has a *third*-person imperative, which means something like, "let him/them do such and such a thing." Do you recall Marie Antoinette's famous alleged retort: When she was informed that the peasants in the city of Paris had no bread to eat, she responded, "Then *let them* eat cake!" This is the third-person imperative.

24.1 THE USE OF THE IMPERATIVE TO EXPRESS COMMANDS

As you know, the aorist subjunctive mood with μή is used for strong prohibitions or negative commandments (e.g., "Thou shalt not ..."). The imperative is normally used for weaker prohibitions, as well as for commands and orders.

There is no distinction between the present and the aorist tenses in non-indicative moods with respect to time (i.e., past, present, future). The present tense is used to express imperfective *aspect* (i.e., an ongoing or repeated action), whereas the aorist tense expresses the aoristic aspect (the verbal action is presented as a completed and undifferentiated process). For this reason most imperatives you encounter will be in the aorist tense because its aspect lacks the greater specificity of the aspect of the present tense.

1. Generally speaking, the *present* imperative is reserved for general or repeatable instructions. This includes commands that should be practiced as a way of life. For example:

[1] There is also a perfect imperative. It occurs only four times in the GNT.

Figure: Statue of a lion (ancient Ephesus).

λογίζεσθε ἑαυτοὺς εἶναι νεκροὺς μὲν τῇ ἁμαρτίᾳ.
"… *reckon* yourselves to be dead to sin …" (Rom 6:11)

2. The aorist imperative is generally employed for *specific* directions or commands. For example:

   ἀσπάσασθε Ἀπελλῆν τὸν δόκιμον ἐν Χριστῷ.
   "*Greet* Apelles, the approved in Christ." (Rom 16:10)

24.2 FORMING THE IMPERATIVE

1. In the case of the first aorist imperative, the second-person singular active ending is -σον. A good example of this is the "Kyrie" of the Eucharist, which uses the imperative form of the verb ἐλεέω ("I have mercy"):

   Κύριε ἐλέησον, Χριστὲ ἐλέησον, Κύριε ἐλέησον.
   "Lord have mercy, Christ have mercy, Lord have mercy."

2. The second person singular, first aorist *middle* imperative ending is -σαι. Because it is identical to the aorist active *infinitive* ending, care must be taken so as not to mistake one for the other in a given context. The second-person singular ending in the present middle and passive ending is -ου. Likewise, this could be mistaken for the second-person imperfect middle indicative, except for the fact that the imperfect indicative also has an augment.
3. The second-person *plural* endings (-ετε, -εσθε, -σατε, -σασθε) of the active and middle imperative, as well as the second pl. present passive, are identical to the indicative forms. The context will help you decide whether the form is indicative or imperative.

Active Imperative

	Present	*1 aorist*	*2 aorist*
Sg.			
2	λῦε	λῦσον	λάβε
3	λυέτω	λνσάτω	λαβέτω
Pl.			
2	λύετε	λύσατε	λάβετε
3	λυέτωσαν	λυσάτωσαν	λαβέτωσαν

Passive Imperative

Sg.			
2	λύου	λύθητι	γράφητι
3	λυέσθω	λυθήτω	γραφήτω

Pl.

2	λύεσθε	λύθητε	γράφητε
3	λυέσθωσαν	λυθήτωσαν	γραφήτωσαν

Middle Imperative

Sg.

2	ἔρχου	λῦσαι	γενοῦ
3	ἐρχέσθω	λυσάσθω	γενέσθω

Pl.

2	ἔρχεσθε	λύσασθε	γένεσθε
3	ἐρχέσθωσαν	λυσάσθωσαν	γενέσθωσαν

It is not expected that you will memorize all the paradigms in this lesson. They are provided to help you see common patterns and for your future reference.

Box 1. Reference: Imperative Forms of Other Important Verbs

	εἰμί (pres.)	γινώσκω (2 aor.)	οἶδα (pf.)
Sg.			
2	ἴσθι	γνῶθι	ἴσθι
3	ἔστω	γνώτω	ἴστω
Pl.			
2	ἔστε	γνῶτε	ἴστε
3	ἔστωσαν	γνώτωσαν	ἴστωσαν

Box 2. Reference: Active Imperative Forms of Athematic Verbs

	δίδωμι		τίθημι		ἵστημι	
Sg.	*Pres.*	*2 Aor.*	*Pres.*	*2 Aor.*	*Pres.*	*2 Aor.*
2	δίδου	δός	τίθει	θές	ἵστη	στῆθι
3	διδότω	δότω	τιθέτω	θέτω	ἱστάτω	στήτω
Pl.						
2	δίδοτε	δότε	τίθετε	θέτε	ἵστατε	στῆτε
3	διδότωσαν	δότωσαν	τιθέτωσαν	θέτωσαν	ἱστάτωσαν	στήτωσαν

24.3 SUMMARY: EXPRESSIONS OF PROHIBITION

A negative command is called a *prohibition*. Prohibitions may be expressed in the following ways:

1. οὐ with future indicative to express general commands, especially when quoting the LXX (e.g., οὐκ ἐκπειράσεις, "You shall not tempt…" [Matt 4:7, Luke 4:12]; οὐκ…ζήσεται… "One shall not live…" [Matt 4:4; Luke 4:4]).
2. μή followed by present imperative, prohibiting a continuous action.
3. μή followed by aorist imperative, prohibiting an undefined action.
4. μή followed by aorist subjunctive. This is a stronger prohibition. This construction is used for general commandments and to forbid an action from occurring (e.g., μὴ θαυμάσῃς, "Do not be amazed" [John 3:7]).
5. οὐ μή followed by aorist subjunctive: This construction is known as *emphatic future negation* ("you shall never…").[2]

24.4 VOCABULARY TO BE MEMORIZED

1. ἁγιάζω (a-yi-**a**-zo), I set apart as sacred to God; regard as sacred, treat as holy, reverence (cf. ἅγιος, -α, -ον); 1 aor. ἁγίασα, pf. pass. ἁγίασμαι, 1 aor. pass. ἁγιάσθην
2. ἀφίημι (a-**fi**-i-mi), I let go, send away, leave (John 4:28); release from legal or moral obligation, forgive, allow; fut. ἀφήσω, 1 aor. ἀφῆκα, pf. pass. ἀφέωμαι, 1 aor. pass. ἀφέθην
3. ὀφείλημα, -ατος, τό (o-**fi**-li-ma, -a-tos), a debt (cf. ὀφείλω, "I owe")
4. ὀφειλέτης, ὁ (o-fi-**le**-tis), one who is under obligation, a debtor
5. πειρασμός, ὁ (pi-ra-**smos**), a temptation (to sin), a test or trial (to learn the character of sthg)
6. πλανῶ (-άω) (pla-**no**), I lead astray; pass. I go astray, am misled; fut. πλανήσω, 1 aor. ἐπλάνησα, pf. pass. πεπλάνημαι (sometimes in act. sense in GNT), 1 aor. pass. ἐπλανήθην

---

[2] See Section 22.7.3.

Appendix 1.

Principal Parts of the Greek Verb

This is a list of principal parts of many of the irregular verbs that occur in the GNT. Principal parts that do not occur in the New Testament (either in a simple or compound form) are represented by a dash (–). All the forms are given in the first-person singular, indicative mood. Note that compound forms are given only in special cases. It is advisable to learn the principal parts both orally and in written form.

1. ἀγαπάω, ἀγαπήσω, ἠγάπησα, ἠγάπηκα, ἠγάπημαι, ἠγαπήθην
2. ἄγω, ἄξω, ἤγαγον/ἦξα, ἦχα, ἦγμαι, ἤχθην
3. αἱρέω, αἱρήσομαι, εἱλόμην εἱλάμην (cf. 2 aor. infin. ἑλεῖν)
4. αἴρω, ἀρῶ, ἦρα, ἦρκα, ἦρμαι, ἤρθην
5. ἀκούω, ἀκούσω/ἀκούσομαι, ἤκουσα, ἀκήκοα, –, ἠκούσθην
6. ἀνοίγω, ἀνοίξω, ἀνέῳξα/ἤνοιξα/ἠνέῳξα, ἀνέῳγα, ἀνέῳγμαι/ηνέῳγμαι/ἤνοιγμαι, ἀνεῴχθην/ἠνοίχθην/ἠνεῴχθην
7. ἀποθνῄσκω, ἀποθανοῦμαι, ἀπέθανον, –, –, –
8. ἀπόλλυμι, ἀπολέσω/ἀπολῶ, ἀπώλεσα/ἀπωλόμην, –, ἀπόλωλα
9. ἀποστέλλω, ἀποστελῶ, ἀπέστειλα, ἀπέσταλκα, ἀπέσταλμαι, ἀπεστάλην
10. ἀφίημι, ἀφήσω, ἀφῆκα, ἀφεῖκα, ἀφεῖμαι, ἀφέθην
11. βαίνω, βήσομαι, ἔβην, βέβηκα, –, –
12. βάλλω, βαλῶ, ἔβαλον/ἔβαλα, βέβληκα, βέβλημαι, ἐβλήθην
13. γίνομαι, γενήσομαι, ἐγενόμην, γέγονα, γεγένημαι, ἐγενήθην
14. γινώσκω, γνώσομαι, ἔγνων, ἔγνωκα, ἔγνωσμαι, ἐγνώσθην
15. γράφω, γράψω, ἔγραψα, γέγραφα, γέγραμμαι, ἐγράφην
16. δείκνυμι, δείξω, ἔδειξα, –, –, ἐδείχθην
17. δέχομαι, δέξομαι, ἐδεξάμην, –, δέδεγμαι, ἐδέχθην
18. διδάσκω, διδάξω, ἐδίδαξα, –, –, ἐδιδάχθην
19. δίδωμι, δώσω, ἔδωκα, δέδωκα, δέδομαι, ἐδόθην

20. ἐγείρω, ἐγερῶ, ἤγειρα, –, ἐγήγερμαι, ἠγέρθην
21. ἔρχομαι, ἐλεύσομαι, ἦλθον, ἐλήλυθα
22. ἐσθίω, φάγομαι, ἔφαγον, –, –, –
23. εὑρίσκω, εὑρήσω, εὗρον, εὕρηκα, –, εὑρέθην
24. ἔχω, ἕξω, ἔσχον, ἔσχηκα, –, –
25. ζάω (√ζη), ζήσω/ζήσομαι, ἔζησα, –, –, –
26. ἵστημι, στήσω, ἔστησα/ἔστην, ἕστηκα, ἕσταμαι, ἐστάθην
27. καλέω, καλέσω, ἐκάλεσα, κέκληκα, κέκλημαι, ἐκλήθην
28. κηρύσσω, κηρύξω, –, ἐκήρυξα, –, κεκήρυγμαι, ἐκηρύχθην
29. κρίνω, κρινῶ, ἔκρινα, κέκρικα, κέκριμαι, ἐκρίθην
30. λαμβάνω, λήμψομαι, ἔλαβον, εἴληφα, εἴλημμαι, ἐλήμφθην
31. λέγω/φημί, ἐρῶ, εἶπον, εἴρηκα, εἴρημαι, ἐρρέθην/ἐρρήθην
32. μένω, μενῶ, ἔμείνα, μεμένηκα, –, –
33. οἶδα (pf.), εἰδήσω (fut.), ᾔδειν (plpf.)
34. ὁράω, ὄψομαι, εἶδον, ἑόρακα/ἑώρακα, –, ὤφθην
35. πάσχω, –, ἔπαθον, πέπονθα, –, –
36. πείθω, πείσω, ἔπεισα, πέποιθα, πέπεισμαι, ἐπείσθην
37. πέμπω, πέμψω, ἔπεμψα, –, –, ἐπέμφθην
38. πίμπλημι, –, ἐπλησα, –, –, ἐπλήσθην
39. πίνω, πίομαι, ἔπιον, πέπωκα, –, ἐπόθην
40. πίπτω, πεσοῦμαι, ἔπεσον/ἔπεσα, πέπτωκα, –, –
41. σῴζω, σώσω, ἔσωσα, σέσωκα, σέσῳσμαι/σέσωμαι, ἐσώθην
42. τάσσω, τάξομαι, ἔταξα, τέταχα, τέταγμαι, ἐτάχθην
43. τίκτω, τέξομαι, ἔτεκον, –,–, ἐτέχθην
44. τίθημι, θήσω, ἔθηκα, τέθεικα, τέθειμαι, ἐτέθην
45. τρέφω, –, ἔθρεψα, –, τέθραμμαι, ἐτράφην
46. τυγχάνω, τεύξομαι, ἔτυχον, τέτευχα, –, –
47. φέρω, οἴσω, ἤνεγκα, ἐνήνοχα, ἐνήνεγμαι, ἠνέχθην

Appendix 2.

Summary of Paradigms

VERBS

NOUNS

ADJECTIVES

18 "2-1-2" Type Adjectives, ἀγαθός
19 Heteroclite "2-1-2" Type Adjectives, πολύς, μέγας
20 "3-1-3" Type Adjectives, πᾶς, οὐδείς
21 Third Declension Adjectives of Two Terminations, ἀληθής
22 Comparative Adjectives of Two Terminations, μείζων

PRONOUNS

23 Personal Pronouns, ἐγώ, σύ, αὐτός
24 Demonstrative Pronouns, οὗτος, ἐκεῖνος
25 Relative Pronouns, ὅς, ἥ, ὅ
26 Reflexive Pronouns, ἐμαυτοῦ, σεαυτοῦ, ἑαυτοῦ
27 Reciprocal Pronoun – ἀλλήλων
28 The Indefinite Pronoun, τις, τι
29 The Interrogative Pronoun, τίς, τί

1. THEMATIC VERBS – ACTIVE, λύω

Indicative

Pres.	*Impf.*	*Fut.*	*1 Aor.*	*Pf.*	*Plpf.*
(a)	(b)	(c)	(d)	(e)	(f)
λύω	ἔλυον	λύσω	ἔλυσα	λέλυκα	(ἐ)λελύκειν
λύεις	ἔλυες	λύσεις	ἔλυσας	λέλυκας	(ἐ)λελύκεις
λύει	ἔλυε(ν)	λύσει	ἔλυσε(ν)	λέλυκε(ν)	(ἐ)λελύκει
λύομεν	ἐλύομεν	λύσομεν	ἐλύσαμεν	λελύκαμεν	(ἐ)λελύκειμεν
λύετε	ἐλύετε	λύσετε	ἐλύσατε	λελύκατε	(ἐ)λελύκειτε
λύουσι(ν)	ἔλυον	λύσουσι(ν)	ἔλυσαν	λελύκασι(ν)	(ἐ)λελύκεισαν

Subjunctive

(a)	(b)
λύω	λύσω
λύῃς	λύσῃς
λύῃ	λύσῃ
λύωμεν	λύσωμεν
λύητε	λύσητε
λύωσι(ν)	λύσωσι(ν)

Pres. *Impf.* *Fut.* *1 Aor.* *Pf.* *Plpf.*

Optative

(a)	(b)
λύοιμι	λύσαιμι
λύοις	λύσαις, or -ειας
λύοι	λύσαι, or -ειε(ν)
λύοιμεν	λύσαιμεν
λύοιτε	λύσαιτε
λύοιεν	λύσαιεν, or -ειαν

Imperative

(a)	(b)
λῦε	λῦσον
λυέτω	λυσάτω
λύετε	λύσατε
λυέτωσαν, or -όντων	λυσάτωσαν, or -σάντων

Infinitive

(a)	(b)	(c)	(d)
λύειν	λύσειν	λῦσαι	λελυκέναι

Participle

(a)	(b)	(c)	(d)
λύων[1]	λύσων[2]	λύσας[3]	λελυκώς[4]
λύοντος	λύσοντος	λύσαντος	λελυκότος
λύοντι	λύσοντι	λύσαντι	λελυκότι
λύοντα	λύσοντα	λύσαντα	λελυκότα
λύοντες	λύσοντες	λύσαντες	λελυκότες
λυόντων	λυσόντων	λυσάντων	λελυκότων
λύουσι(ν)	λύσουσι(ν)	λύσασι(ν)	λελυκόσι(ν)
λύοντας	λύσοντας	λύσαντας	λελυκότας

1 λύων, λύουσα, λῦον.
2 λύσων, λύσουσα, λῦσον.
3 λύσας, λύσασα, λῦσαν.
4 λελυκώς, λελυκυῖα, λελυκός.

2. THEMATIC VERBS – MIDDLE, λύω

Pres.	*Impf.*	*Fut.*	*1 Aor.*	*Pf.*	*Plpf.*
Indicative					
(a)	(b)	(c)	(d)	(e)	(f)
λύομαι	ἐλυόμην	λύσομαι	ἐλυσάμην	λέλυμαι	(ἐ)λελύμην
λύῃ	ἐλύου	λύσῃ	ἐλύσω	λέλυσαι	(ἐ)λέλυσο
λύεται	ἐλύετο	λύσεται	ἐλύσατο	λέλυται	(ἐ)λέλυτο
λυόμεθα	ἐλυόμεθα	λυσόμεθα	ἐλυσάμεθα	λέλύμεθα	(ἐ)λελύμεθα
λύεσθε	ἐλύεσθε	λύσεσθε	ἐλύσασθε	λέλυσθε	(ἐ)λέλυσθε
λύονται	ἐλύοντο	λύσονται	ἐλύσαντο	λέλυνται	(ἐ)λέλυντο

Subjunctive

(a)	(b)
λύωμαι	λύσωμαι
λύῃ	λύσῃ
λύηται	λύσηται
λυώμεθα	λυσώμεθα
λύησθε	λύσησθε
λύωνται	λύσωνται

Optative

(a)	(b)
λυοίμην	λυσαίμην
λύοιο	λύσαιο
λύοιτο	λύσαιτο
λυοίμεθα	λυσαίμεθα
λύοισθε	λύσαισθε
λύοιντο	λύσαιντο

Imperative

(a)	(b)
λύου	λῦσαι
λυέσθω	λυσάσθω
λύεσθε	λύσασθε
λυέσθωσαν, or -έσθων	λυσάσθωσαν or –σάσθων

Pres.	*Impf.*	*Fut.*	*1 Aor.*	*Pf.*	*Plpf.*

Infinitive

(a)	(b)	(c)	(d)
λύεσθαι	λύσεσθαι	λύσασθαι	λελῦσθαι

Participle

(a)	(b)	(c)	(d)
λυόμενος[5]	λυσόμενος[6]	λυσάμενος[7]	λελυμένος[8]
λυομένου	λυσομένου	λυσαμένου	λελυμένου
λυομένῳ	λυσομένῳ	λυσαμένῳ	λελυμένῳ
λυόμενον	λυσόμενον	λυσάμενον	λελυμένον
λυόμενοι	λυσόμενοι	λυσάμενοι	λελυμένοι
λυομένων	λυσομένων	λυσαμένων	λελυμένων
λυομένοις	λυσομένοις	λυσαμένοις	λελυμένοις
λυομένους	λυσομένους	λυσαμένους	λελυμένους

3. THEMATIC VERBS – PASSIVE INDICATIVE, λύω

Pres.	*Impf.*	*Fut.*	*1 Aor.*	*Pf.*	*Plpf.*

Indicative

(a)	(b)	(c)	(d)	(e)	(f)
λύομαι	ἐλυόμην	λυθήσομαι	ἐλύθην	λέλυμαι	(ἐ)λελύμην
λύῃ	ἐλύου	λυθήσῃ	ἐλύθης	λέλυσαι	(ἐ)λέλυσο
λύεται	ἐλύετο	λυθήσεται	ἐλύθη	λέλυται	(ἐ)λέλυτο
λυόμεθα	ἐλυόμεθα	λυθησόμεθα	ἐλύθημεν	λελύμεθα	(ἐ)λελύμεθα
λύεσθε	ἐλύεσθε	λυθήσεσθε	ἐλύθητε	λέλυσθε	(ἐ)λέλυσθε
λύονται	ἐλύοντο	λυθήσονται	ἐλύθησαν	λέλυνται	(ἐ)λέλυντο

Subjunctive

(a)	(b)
λύωμαι	λυθῶ
λύῃ	λυθῇς
λύηται	λυθῇ
λυώμεθα	λυθῶμεν
λύησθε	λυθῆτε
λύωνται	λυθῶσι(ν)

5 λυόμενος, λυομένη, λυόμενον.
6 λυσόμενος, λυσομένη, λυσόμενον.
7 λυσάμενος, λυσαμένη, λυσάνμενον.
8 λελυμένος, λελυμένη, λελυμένον.

Pres. *Impf.* *Fut.* *1 Aor.* *Pf.* *Plpf.*

Optative

(a)	(b)
λυοίμην	λυθείην
λύοιο	λυθείης
λύοιτο	λύθείη
λυοίμεθα	λυθεῖμεν, or θείημεν
λύοισθε	λυθεῖτε, or θείητε
λύοιντο	λυθεῖεν, or -θείησαν

Imperative

(a)	(b)
λύου	λῦσαι
λυέσθω	λυσάσθω
λύεσθε	λύσασθε
λυέσθωσαν, or -έσθων	λυσάσθωσαν, or -σάσθων

Infinitive

(a)	(b)	(c)
λύεσθαι	λυθήσεσθαι	λυθῆναι

Participle

	(a)	(b)	(c)	(d)
N	λυόμενος[9]	λυθησόμενος[10]	λυθείς[11]	λελυμένος[12]
G	λυομένου	λυθησομένου	λυθέντος	λελυμένου
D	λυομένῳ	λυθησομένῳ	λυθέντι	λελυμένῳ
A	λυόμενον	λυθησόμενον	λυθέντα	λελυμένον
N	λυόμενοι	λυθησόμενοι	λυθέντες	λελυμένοι
G	λυομένων	λυθησομένων	λυθέντων	λελυμένων
D	λυομένοις	λυθησομένοις	λυθεῖσι(ν)	λελυμένοις
A	λυομένους	λυθησομένους	λυθέντας	λελυμένους

9 λυόμενος, λυομένη, λυόμενον.
10 λυθησόμενος, λυθησομένη, λυθησόμενον.
11 λυθείς, λυθεῖσα, λυθέν.
12 λελυμένος, λελυμένη, λελυμένον.

4. CONTRACT VERBS, ποιῶ, ἀγαπῶ, πληρῶ

Present Active

Present Active Indicative

(a)	(b)	(c)	(d)
ποιῶ	ἀγαπῶ	πληρῶ	ζῶ
ποιεῖς	ἀγαπᾷς	πληροῖς	ζῇς
ποιεῖ	ἀγαπᾷ	πληροῖ	ζῇ
ποιοῦμεν	ἀγαπῶμεν	πληροῦμεν	ζῶμεν
ποιεῖτε	ἀγαπᾶτε	πληροῦτε	ζῆτε
ποιοῦσι(ν)	ἀγαπῶσι(ν)	πληροῦσι(ν)	ζῶσι(ν)

Imperfect Active Indicative

(a)	(b)	(c)	(d)
ἐποίουν	ἠγάπων	ἐπλήρουν	ἔζων
ἐποίεις	ἠγάπας	ἐπλήρους	ἔζης
ἐποίει	ἠγάπα	ἐπλήρου	ἔζη
ἐποιοῦμεν	ἠγαπῶμεν	ἐπληροῦμεν	ἐζῶμεν
ἐποιεῖτε	ἠγαπᾶτε	ἐπληροῦτε	ἐζῆτε
ἐποίουν	ἠγάπων	ἐπλήρουν	ἔζων

Present Active Imperative

(a)	(b)	(c)	(d)
ποίει	ἀγάπα	πλήρου	ζῆ
ποιείτω	ἀγαπάτω	πληρούτω	ζήτω
ποιεῖτε	ἀγαπᾶτε	πληροῦτε	ζῆτε
ποιείτωσαν	ἀγαπάτωσαν	πληρούτωσαν	ζώντων

Present Active Subjunctive

(a)	(b)	(c)	(d)
ποιῶ	ἀγαπῶ	πληρῶ	ζῶ
ποιῇς	ἀγαπᾷς	πληροῖς	ζῇς
ποιῇ	ἀγαπᾷ	πληροῖ	ζῇ
ποιῶμεν	ἀγαπῶμεν	πληρῶμεν	ζῶμεν
ποιῆτε	ἀγαπᾶτε	πληρῶτε	ζῆτε
ποιῶσι(ν)	ἀγαπῶσι(ν)	πληρῶσι(ν)	ζῶσι(ν)

Present Active Infinitive

(a)	(b)	(c)	(d)
ποιεῖν	ἀγαπᾶν	πληροῦν	ζῆν

Present Active Participle

	(a)	(b)	(c)	(d)
m.	ποιῶν	ἀγαπῶν	πληρῶν	ζῶν
fm.	ποιοῦσα	ἀγαπῶσα	πληροῦσα	ζῶσα
nt.	ποιοῦν	ἀγαπῶν	πληροῦν	ζῶν

Present Passive

Present Passive Indicative

(a)	(b)	(c)
ποιοῦμαι	ἀγαπῶμαι	πληροῦμαι
ποιῇ or -εῖ	ἀγαπᾶσαι[13]	πληροῖ
ποιεῖται	ἀγαπᾶται	πληροῦται
ποιούμεθα	ἀγαπώμεθα	πληρούμεθα
ποιεῖσθε	ἀγαπᾶσθε	πληροῦσθε
ποιοῦνται	ἀγαπῶνται	πληροῦνται

Imperfect Passive Indicative

(a)	(b)	(c)
ἐποιούμην	ἠγαπώμην	ἐπληρούμην
ἐποιοῦ	ἠγαπῶ	ἐπληροῦ
ἐποιεῖτο	ἠγαπᾶτο	ἐπληροῦτο
ἐποιούμεθα	ἠγαπώμεθα	ἐπληρούμεθα
ἐποιεῖσθε	ἠγαπᾶσθε	ἐπληροῦσθε
ἐποιοῦνται	ἠγαπῶντο	ἐπληροῦντο

Present Passive Imperative

(a)	(b)	(c)
ποιοῦ	ἀγαπῶ	πληροῦ
ποιείσθω	ἀγαπάσθω	πληρούσθω
ποιεῖσθε	ἀγαπᾶσθε	πληροῦσθε
ποιείσθωσαν	ἀγαπάσθωσαν	πληρούσθωσαν

---

[13] Cf. Section 11.9.

Present Passive Subjunctive

(a)	(b)	(c)
ποιῶμαι	ἀγαπῶμαι	πληρῶμαι
ποιῇ	ἀγαπᾷ	πληροῖ
ποιῆται	ἀγαπᾶται	πληρῶται
ποιώμεθα	ἀγαπώμεθα	πληρώμεθα
ποιῆσθε	ἀγαπᾶσθε	πληρῶσθε
ποιῶνται	ἀγαπῶνται	πληρῶνται

Present Passive Infinitive

(a)	(b)	(c)
ποιεῖσθαι	ἀγαπᾶσθαι	πληροῦσθαι

Present Middle Contract Verbs, δέομαι, χρῶμαι, διαβεβαιοῦμαι

Present Middle Indicative

δέομαι[14]	χρῶμαι	διαβεβαιοῦμαι
δέῃ	χρᾶσαι[15]	διαβεβαιοῖ
δεῖται	χρᾶται	διαβεβαιοῦται
δεόμεθα	χρώμεθα	διαβεβαιούμεθα
δεῖσθε	χρᾶσθε	διαβεβαιοῦσθε
δέονται	χρῶνται	διαβεβαιοῦνται

Imperfect Middle Indicative of Contract Verbs

ἐδεόμην	ἐχρώμην	διαβεβαιούμην
ἐδέου	ἐχρῶ	διαβεβαιοῦ
ἐδεῖτο	ἐχρᾶτο	διαβεβαιοῦτο
ἐδεόμεθα	ἐχρώμεθα	διαβεβαιούμεθα
ἐδεῖσθε	ἐχρᾶσθε	διαβεβαιοῦσθε
ἐδέοντο	ἐχρῶντο	διαβεβαιοῦντο

Present Middle Imperative of Contract Verbs

δέου	χρῶ	διαβεβαιοῦ
δείσθω	χράσθω	διαβεβαιούσθω
δεῖσθε	χρᾶσθε	διαβεβαιοῦσθε
δείσθωσαν	χράσθωσαν	διαβεβαιούσθωσαν

[14] This verb is unusual because ε + ο do not contract as do other ε-contract verbs. The root is √ δεε.

[15] Cf. Section 11.9.

5. THEMATIC VERBS – οἶδα (ϝιδ, ϝειδ, ϝοιδ)

Active Indicative

(a)	(b)	(c)
Pf.	*Pfpf.*	*Fut.*
οἶδα	ᾔδειν	εἰδήσω, εἴσομαι
οἶσας, οἶσθα	ᾔδεις	etc.
οἶδε(ν)	ᾔδει	
οἴδαμεν, ἴσμεν	ᾔδειμεν	
οἴδατε, ἴστε	ᾔδειτε	
οἴδασι(ν), ἴδαδιν	ᾔδεισαν	

Perfect Active Subjunctive Perfect Active Imperative

εἰδῶ	
εἰδῇς	ἴσθι
εἰδῇ	ἴστω
εἰδῶμεν	
εἰδῆτε	ἴστε
εἰδῶσι(ν)	ἴστωσαν

Perfect Active Infinitive

εἰδέναι

Perfect Active Participle

m.	*fm.*	*nt.*
εἰδώς	εἰδυῖα	εἰδός
εἰδότος	εἰδυίας	εἰδότος
etc.		

6. THEMATIC VERBS – γινώσκω

Active Indicative

(a)	(b)[16]	(c)	(d)	(e)	(f)
Pres.	*2 Aor.*	*Fut.*	*Pf.*	*Plpf.*	*Impf.*
γινώσκω	ἔγνων	γνώσομαι	ἔγνωκα	ἐγνώκειν	ἐγινώσκον
γινώσκεις	ἔγνως				
γινώκει	ἔγνω				

[16] γινώσκω is athematic in the 2 aorist.

γινώσκομεν	ἔγνωμεν
γινώσκετε	ἔγνωτε
γινώσκουσι(ν)	ἔγνωσαν

Aorist Active Optative

γνοίην
γνοίης
γνοίη
γνοῖμεν or γνοίημεν
γνοῖτε or γνοίητε
γνοῖεν or γνοίησαν

Aorist Active Subjunctive

γνῶ
γνῷς
γνῷ or γνοῖ

γνῶμεν
γνῶτε
γνῶσι(ν)

Aorist Active Infinitive

γνῶναι

Aorist Active Imperative

26.6.6 2 Aorist Active Participle

γνῶθι	N	γνούς	γνοῦσα	γνόν
γνώτω	G	γνόντος		
	D	γνόντι		
γνῶτε	A	γνόντα		
γνώτωσαν		etc.		

7. ATHEMATIC VERBS: δύναμαι and κάθημαι

Present Middle Indicative

(a)	(b)
δύναμαι	κάθημαι
δύνασαι or δύνῃ	κάθῃ
δύναται	κάθηται
δυνάμεθα	καθήμεθα
δύνασθε	κάθησθε
δύνανται	κάθηνται

8. ATHEMATIC VERBS – ACTIVE INDICATIVE

Present Active Indicative

(a)	(b)	(c)
δίδωμι	τίθημι	ἵστημι
δίδως	τίθης	ἵστης
δίδωσι(ν)	τίθησι(ν)	ἵστησι(ν)
δίδομεν	τίθεμεν	ἵσταμεν
δίδοτε	τίθετε	ἵστατε
διδόασι(ν)	τιθέασι(ν)	ἱστᾶσι(ν)[17]

Imperfect Active Indicative

(a)	(b)	(c)
ἐδίδουν	ἐτίθην	ἵστην
ἐδίδους	ἐτίθεις	ἵστης
ἐδίδου	ἐτίθει	ἵστη
ἐδίδομεν	ἐτίθεμεν	ἵσταμεν
ἐδίδοτε	ἐτίθετε	ἵστατε
ἐδίδοσαν	ἐτίθεσαν	ἵστασαν

Future Active Indicative

(a)	(b)	(c)
δώσω	θήσω	στήσω
δώσεις	θήσεις	στήσεις
δώσει	θήσει	στήσει
δώσομεν	θήσομεν	στήσομεν
δώσετε	θήσετε	στήσετε
δώσουσι(ν)	θήσουσι(ν)	στήσουσι(ν)

Aorist Active Indicative

		transitive	*intransitive*
(a)	(b)	(c)	(d)
ἔδωκα	ἔθηκα	ἔστησα[18]	ἔστην[19]
ἔδωκας	ἔθηκας	ἔστησας	ἔστης
ἔδωκε(ν)	ἔθηκε(ν)	ἔστησε(ν)	ἔστη
ἐδώκαμεν	ἐθήκαμεν	ἐστήσαμεν	ἔστημεν
ἐδώκατε	ἐθήκατε	ἐστήσατε	ἔστητε
ἔδωκαν	ἔθηκαν	ἔστησαν	ἔστησαν

[17] Note how the α of the stem contracts with the α of the ending.
[18] Transitive use: "I set up, I caused to stand."
[19] Intransitive form: "I stood."

Perfect Active Indicative

(a)	(b)	(c)
δέδωκα	τέθεικα	ἕστηκα
δέδωκας	τέθεικας	ἕστηκας
δέδωκε(ν)	τέθεικε(ν)	ἕστηκε(ν)
δεδώκαμεν	τεθείκαμεν	ἑστήκαμεν
δεδώκατε	τεθείκατε	ἑστήκατε
δεδώκασι(ν)	τεθείκασι(ν)	ἑστήκασι(ν)

9. ATHEMATIC VERBS – ACTIVE INDICATIVE, δείκνυμι, φημί

26.9.1	*26.9.2*	
Pres.	*Pres.*	*Impf.*
δείκνυμι, δεικνύω	φημί	ἔφην
δεικνύεις	φῄς	ἔφης
δείκνυσι(ν)	φησί(ν)	ἔφη (and 2 aor.)
δείκνυμεν	φαμέν	ἔφαμεν
δείκνυτε	φατέ	ἔφατε
δεικνύασι(ν)	φασί(ν)	ἔφασαν

10. ATHEMATIC VERBS – MIDDLE INDICATIVE, δίδωμι, τίθημι, ἵστημι

Present Middle Indicative

(a)	(b)	(c)
δίδομαι	τίθεμαι	ἵσταμαι
δίδοσαι	τίθεσαι	ἵστασαι
δίδοται	τίθεται	ἵσταται
διδόμεθα	τιθέμεθα	ἱστάμεθα
δίδοσθε	τίθεσθε	ἵστασθε
δίδονται	τίθενται	ἵστανται

Imperfect Middle Indicative

(a)	(b)	(c)
ἐδιδόμην	ἐτιθέμην	ἱστάμην
ἐδίδοσο	ἐτίθεσο	ἵστασο
ἐδίδοτο	ἐτίθετο	ἵστατο
ἐδιδόμεθα	ἐτιθέμεθα	ἱστάμεθα
ἐδίδοσθε	ἐτίθεσθε	ἵστασθε
ἐδίδοντο	ἐτίθεντο	ἵσταντο

Future Middle Indicative

(a)	(b)	(c)
δώσομαι	θήσομαι	στήσομαι
δώσῃ	θήσῃ	στήσῃ
δώσεται	θήσεται	στήσεται
δωσόμεθα	θησόμεθα	στησόμεθα
δώσεσθε	θήσεσθε	στήσεσθε
δώσονται	θήσονται	στήσονται

Aorist Middle Indicative

(a)	(b)	
ἐδόμην	ἐθέμην	(no middle forms)
ἔδου	ἔθου	
ἔδοτο	ἔθετο	
ἐδόμεθα	ἐθέμεθα	
ἔδοσθε	ἔθεσθε	
ἔδοντο	ἔθεντο	

Perfect Middle Indicative

(a)	(b)	(c)
δέδομαι	τέθειμαι	ἕσταμαι
δέδοσαι	τέθεισαι	ἕστασαι
δέδοται	τέθειται	ἕσταται
δεδόμεθα	τεθείμεθα	ἑστάμεθα
δέδοσθε	τεθείσθε	ἕστασθε
δέδονται	τεθείνται	ἕστανται

11. ATHEMATIC VERBS – PASSIVE INDICATIVE

Present Passive Indicative

(a)	(b)	(c)
δίδομαι	τίθεμαι	ἵσταμαι
δίδοσαι	τίθεσαι	ἵστασαι
δίδοται	τίθεται	ἵσταται
διδόμεθα	τιθέμεθα	ἱστάμεθα
δίδοσθε	τίθεσθε	ἵστασθε
δίδονται	τίθενται	ἵστανται

Imperfect Passive Indicative

(a)	(b)	(c)
ἐδιδόμην	ἐτιθέμην	ἱστάμην
ἐδίδοσο	ἐτίθεσο	ἵστασο
ἐδίδοτο	ἐτίθετο	ἵστατο
ἐδιδόμεθα	ἐτιθέμεθα	ἱστάμεθα
ἐδίδοσθε	ἐτίθεσθε	ἵστασθε
ἐδίδοντο	ἐτίθεντο	ἵσταντο

Future Passive Indicative

(a)	(b)	(c)
δοθήσομαι	τεθήσομαι	σταθήσομαι
δοθήσῃ	τεθήσῃ	σταθήσῃ
δοθήσεται	τεθήσεται	σταθήσεται
δοθησόμεθα	τεθησόμεθα	σταθησόμεθα
δοθήσεσθε	τεθήσεσθε	σταθήσεσθε
δοθήσονται	τεθήσονται	σταθήσονται

Aorist Passive Indicative

(a)	(b)	(c)
ἐδόθην	ἐτέθην	ἐστάθην
ἐδόθης	ἐτέθης	ἐστάθης
ἐδόθη	ἐτέθην	ἐστάθη
ἐδόθημεν	ἐτέθημεν	ἐστάθημεν
ἔδόθητε	ἐτέθητε	ἐστάθητε
ἔδόθησαν	ἐτέθησαν	ἐστάθησαν

Perfect Passive Indicative

(a)	(b)	
δέδομαι	τέθειμαι	ἕσταμαι
δέδοσαι	τέθεισαι	ἕστασαι
δέδοται	τέθειται	ἕσταται
δεδόμεθα	τεθείμεθα	ἑστάμεθα
δέδοσθε	τέθεισθε	ἕστασθε
δέδονται	τέθεινται	ἕστανται

12. ATHEMATIC VERBS – NON-INDICATIVE MOODS

δίδωμι (√ δο) τίθημι (√ θε) ἵστημι (√ στα)

Subjunctive – Active

(a)	(b)	(c)	(d)	(e)	(f)
Pres.	*Aor.*	*Pres.*	*Aor.*	*Pres.*	*Aor.*
διδῶ	δῶ	τιθῶ	θῶ	ἱστῶ	στῶ
διδῷς	δῷς	τιθῇς	θῇς	ἱστῇς	στῇς
διδῷ	δῷ	τιθῇ	θῇ	ἱστῇ	στῇ
διδῶμεν	δῶμεν	τιθῶμεν	θῶμεν	ἱστῶμεν	στῶμεν
διδῶτε	δῶτε	τιθῆτε	θῆτε	ἱστῆτε	στῆτε
διδῶσι(ν)	δῶσι(ν)	τιθῶσι(ν)	θῶσι(ν)	ἱστῶσι(ν)	στῶσι(ν)

Imperative – Active

(a)	(b)	(c)	(d)	(e)	(f)
Pres.	*Aor.*	*Pres.*	*Aor.*	*Pres.*	*Aor.*
δίδου	δός	τίθει	θές	ἵστη	στῆθι
διδότω	δότω	τιθέτω	θέτω	ἱστάτω	στήτω
δίδοτε	δότε	τίθετε	θέτε	ἵστατε	στῆτε
διδότωσαν	δότωσαν	τιθέτωσαν	θέτωσαν	ἱστάτωσαν	στήτωσαν

Infinitive of Athematic Verbs

Active Infinitive

(a)	(b)	(c)	(d)	(e)	(f)
Pres.	*2 Aor.*	*Pres.*	*2 Aor.*	*Pres.*	*2 Aor.*
διδόναι	δοῦναι	τιθέναι	θεῖναι	ἱστάναι[20]	στῆσαι/στῆναι

Middle Infinitive

(a)	(b)	(c)	(d)	(e)	(f)
δίδοσθαι	δόσθαι	τίθεσθαι	θέσθαι	ἵστασθαι	στήσασθαι

[20] ἱστάνειν is also attested.

Passive Infinitive

(a)	(b)	(c)	(d)	(e)	(f)
δίδοσθαι	δοθῆναι	τίθεσθαι	τεθῆναι	ἵστασθαι	σταθῆναι

Participle- Active of Athematic Verbs

(a)	(b)	(c)	(d)	(e)	(f)
Pres.	*Aor.*	*Pres.*	*Aor.*	*Pres.*	*Aor.*
διδούς[21]	δούς[22]	τιθείς[23]	θείς[24]	ἱστάς[25]	στάς[26]
διδόντος	δόντος	τιθέντος	θέντος	ἱστάντος	στάντος
διδόντι	δόντι	τιθέντι	θέντι	ἱστάντι	στάντι
διδόντα	δόντα	τιθέντα	θέντα	ἱστάντα	στάντα
διδόντες	δόντες	τιθέντες	θέντες	ἱστάντες	στάντες
διδόντων	δόντων	τιθέντων	θέντων	ἱστάντων	στάντων
διδοῦσι(ν)	δοῦσι(ν)	τιθεῖσι(ν)	θεῖσι(ν)	ἱστᾶσι(ν)	στᾶσι(ν)
διδόντας	δόντας	τιθέντας	θέντας	ἱστάντας	στάντας

Pres. Middle and Passive and Aor. Middle Participle

(a)	(b)	(c)	(d)	(e)	(f)
Pres.[27]	*Aor.*[28]	*Pres.*[29]	*Aor.*	*Pres.*[30]	*Aor.*
διδόμενος	δόμενος	τιθέμενος	θέμενος[31]	ἱστάμενος	στάμενος[32]

Aor. Passive Participle

m.	δοθείς	τεθείς	σταθείς
fm.	δοθεῖσα	τεθεῖσα	σταθεῖσα
nt.	δοθέν	τεθέν	σταθέν

[21] διδούς, διδοῦσα, διδόν.
[22] δούς, δοῦσα, δόν.
[23] τιθείς, τιθεῖσα, τιθέν.
[24] θείς, θεῖσα, θέν.
[25] ἱστάς, ἱστᾶσα, ἱστάν; for pf. ptc. of this verb see 21.3.
[26] στάς στᾶσα, στάν.
[27] διδόμενος, -η, -ον.
[28] δόμενος, -η, -ον.
[29] τιθέμενος, -η, -ον.
[30] ἱστάμενος, -η, -ον.
[31] θέμενος, -η, -ον.
[32] στάμενος, -η, -ον.

13. ATHEMATIC VERBS: εἰμί

Indicative

(a) *Pres.*	(b) *Impf.*	(c) *Fut.*
εἰμί	ἤμην	ἔσομαι
εἶ	ἦς	ἔσῃ
ἐστί(ν)	ἦν	ἔσται
ἐσμέν	ἦμεν[33]	ἐσόμεθα
ἐστέ	ἦτε	ἔσεσθε
εἰσί(ν)	ἦσαν	ἔσονται

Present Subjunctive

ὦ
ᾖς
ᾖ

ὦμεν
ἦτε
ὦσι(ν)

Imperative of εἰμί

ἴσθι
ἔστω (also ἤτω)

ἔστε
ἔστωσαν or ἔστων

Infinitive

εἶναι

Participle of εἰμί

	m.	*fm.*	*nt.*
N	ὤν	οὖσα	ὄν
G	ὄντος	οὔσης	ὄντος
D	ὄντι	οὔσῃ	ὄντι
A	ὄντα	οὖσαν	ὄν

[33] Alternative form: ἤμεθα.

	m.	*fm.*	*nt.*
N	ὄντες	οὖσαι	ὄντα
G	ὄντων	ουσῶν	ὄντων
D	οὖσι(ν)	οὔσαις	οὖσι(ν)
A	ὄντας	οὔσας	ὄντα

NOUNS

14. The Definite Article

	Singular			*Plural*		
	m.	*fm.*	*nt.*	*m.*	*fm.*	*nt.*
N	ὁ	ἡ	τό	οἱ	αἱ	τά
G	τοῦ	τῆς	τοῦ	τῶν	τῶν	τῶν
D	τῷ	τῇ	τῷ	τοῖς	ταῖς	τοῖς
A	τόν	τήν	τό	τούς	τάς	τά
V	ὦ	ὦ	ὦ	ὦ	ὦ	ὦ

15. Nouns - First Declension

	(a) *η-Pure*		(b) *α-Pure*		(c) *α-Impure*		(d) *masc. of first decl.*	
N	φωνή	φωναί	ἐκκλησία	ἐκκλησίαι	δόξα	δόξαι	μαθητής	μαθηταί
G	φωνῆς	φωνῶν	ἐκκλησίας	ἐκκλησιῶν	δόξης	δοξῶν	μαθητοῦ	μαθητῶν
D	φωνῇ	φωναῖς	ἐκκλησίᾳ	ἐκκλησίαις	δόξῃ	δόξαις	μαθητῇ	μαθηταῖς
A	φωνήν	φωνάς	ἐκκλησίαν	ἐκκλησίας	δόξαν	δόξας	μαθητήν	μαθητάς
V	φωνή	φωνάι	ἐκκλησία	ἐκκλησίαι	δόξα	δόξαι	μαθητά	μαθητάι

16. Nouns – Second Declension

	(a) *m.*		(b) *nt.*	
N	κόσμος	κόσμοι	τέκνον	τέκνα
G	κόσμου	κόσμων	τέκνου	τέκνων
D	κόσμῳ	κόσμοις	τέκνῳ	τέκνοις
A	κόσμον	κόσμους	τέκνον	τέκνα
V	κόσμε	κόσμοι	τέκνον	τέκνα

17. Nouns – Third Declension

	(a) *dental*	(b) *dental*	(c) *dental*	(d) *dental*	(e) *velar*	(f) *liquid*	(g) *liquid*
N	ἄρχων	νύξ	φῶς	ἐλπίς	σάρξ	ἀνήρ	πατήρ
G	ἄρχοντος	νυκτός	φωτός	ἐλπίδος	σαρκός	ἀνδρός	πατρός
D	ἄρχοντι	νυκτί	φωτί	ἐλπίδι	σαρκί	ἀνδρί	πατρί
A	ἄρχοντα	νύκτα	φῶς	ἐλπίδα	σάρκα	ἄνδρα	πατέρα
V	ἄρχων	νύξ	φῶς	ἐλπίς	σάρξ	ἄνερ	πάτερ
N	ἄρχοντες	νύκτες	φῶτα	ἐλπίδες	σάρκες	ἄνδρες	πατέρες
G	ἀρχόντων	νυκτῶν	φώτων	ἐλπίδων	σαρκῶν	ἀνδρῶν	πατέρων
D	ἄρχουσι(ν)	νυξί(ν)	φωσι(ν)	ἐλπίσι(ν)	σαρξί(ν)	ἀνδράσι(ν)	πατράσι(ν)
A	ἄρχοντας	νύκτας	φῶτα	ἐλπίδας	σάρκες	ἄνδρας	πατέρας
V	ἄρχοντες	νύκτες	φῶτα	ἐλπίδες	σάρκες	ἄνδρες	πατέρες

	(i) -μα	(j) -ε/ευ	(k) -ο/ου
N	ὄνομα	βασιλεύς	ἔθνος
G	ὀνόματος	βασιλέως	ἔθνους
D	ὀνόματι	βασιλεῖ	ἔθνει
A	ὄνομα	βασιλέα	ἔθνος
V	ὄνομα	βασιλεῦ	ἔθνος
N	ὀνόματα	βασιλεῖς	ἔθνη
G	ὀνομάτων	βασιλέων	ἐθνῶν
D	ὀνόμασι(ν)	βασιλεῦσι(ν)	ἔθνεσι(ν)
A	ὀνόματα	βασιλεῖς	ἔθνη
V	ὀνόματα	βασιλεῖς	ἔθνη

ADJECTIVES

18. "2-1-2" Type Adjectives, ἀγαθός

	Singular			*Plural*		
	m.	*fm.*	*nt.*	*m.*	*fm.*	*nt.*
N	ἀγαθός	ἀγαθή	ἀγαθόν	ἀγαθοί	ἀγαθαί	ἀγαθά
G	ἀγαθοῦ	ἀγαθῆς	ἀγαθοῦ	ἀγαθῶν	ἀγαθῶν	ἀγαθῶν
D	ἀγαθῷ	ἀγαθῇ	ἀγαθῷ	ἀγαθοῖς	ἀγαθαῖς	ἀγαθοῖς
A	ἀγαθόν	ἀγαθήν	ἀγαθόν	ἀγαθούς	ἀγαθάς	ἀγαθά
V	ἀγαθέ	ἀγαθή	ἀγαθόν	ἀγαθοί	ἀγαθαί	ἀγαθά

19. Heteroclite "2-1-2" Type Adjectives

a) πολύς, πολλή, πολύ

	Singular			*Plural*		
	m.	*fm.*	*nt.*	*m.*	*fm.*	*nt.*
N	πολύς	πολλή	πολύ	πολλοί	πολλαί	πολλά
G	πολλοῦ	πολλῆς	πολλοῦ	πολλῶν	πολλῶν	πολλῶν
D	πολλῷ	πολλῇ	πολλῷ	πολλοῖς	πολλαῖς	πολλοῖς
A	πολύν	πολλήν	πολύ	πολλούς	πολλάς	πολλά

b) μέγας, μεγάλη, μέγα

	m.	*fm.*	*nt.*	*m.*	*fm.*	*nt.*
N	μέγας	μεγάλη	μέγα	μεγάλοι	μεγάλαι	μεγάλα
G	μεγάλου	μεγάλης	μεγάλου	μεγάλων	μεγάλων	μεγάλων
D	μεγάλῳ	μεγάλῃ	μεγάλῳ	μεγάλοις	μεγάλαις	μεγάλοις
A	μέγαν	μεγάλην	μέγα	μεγάλους	μεγάλας	μεγάλα

20. "3-1-3" Type Adjectives

a) πᾶς, πᾶσα, πᾶν

N	πᾶς	πᾶσα	πᾶν	πάντες	πᾶσαι	πάντα
G	παντός	πάσης	παντός	πάντων	πασῶν	πάντων
D	παντί	πάσῃ	παντί	πᾶσι(ν)	πάσαις	πᾶσι(ν)
A	πάντα	πᾶσαν	πᾶν	πάντας	πάσας	πάντα

b) οὐδείς, οὐδεμία, οὐδέν

N	οὐδείς	οὐδεμία	οὐδέν
G	οὐδενός	οὐδεμιᾶς	οὐδενός
D	οὐδενί	οὐδεμιᾷ	οὐδενί
A	οὐδένα	οὐδεμίαν	οὐδέν

21. Third Declension Adjective of Two Terminations, ἀληθής

	Singular		*Plural*	
	m./fm.	*nt.*	*m./fm.*	*nt.*
N	ἀληθής	ἀληθές	ἀληθεῖς	ἀληθῆ
G	ἀληθοῦς	ἀληθοῦς	ἀληθῶν	ἀληθῶν
D	ἀληθεῖ	ἀληθεῖ	ἀληθέσι(ν)	ἀληθέσι(ν)
A	ἀληθῆ	ἀληθές	ἀληθεῖς	ἀληθῆ
V	ἀληθές	ἀληθές	ἀληθεῖς	ἀληθῆ

22. Comparative Adjective of Two Terminations, μείζων

	Singular		*Plural*	
	m./fm.	*nt.*	*m./fm.*	*nt.*
N	μείζων	μεῖζον	μείζονες, μείζους	μείζονα, μείζω
G	μείζονος	μείζονος	μειζόνων	μειζόνων
D	μείζονι	μείζονι	μείζοσι(ν)	μείζοσι(ν)
A	μείζονα, μείζω	μεῖζον	μείζονας, μείζους	μείζονα, μείζω
V	μεῖζον	μεῖζον	μείζονες, μείζους	μείζονα, μείζω

PRONOUNS

23. Personal Pronouns, ἐγώ, σύ, αὐτός

	(a) *First Person*		(b) *Second Person*	
	Sg.	*Pl.*	*Sg.*	*Pl.*
N	ἐγώ	ἡμεῖς	σύ	ὑμεῖς
G	ἐμοῦ, μου	ἡμῶν	σοῦ, σου	ὑμῶν
D	ἐμοί, μοι	ἡμῖν	σοί, σοι	ὑμῖν
A	ἐμέ, με	ἡμᾶς	σέ, σε	ὑμᾶς

(c)
Third Person

	Singular			*Plural*		
	m.	*fm.*	*nt.*	*m.*	*fm.*	*nt.*
N	αὐτός	αὐτή	αὐτό	αὐτοί	αὐταί	αὐτά
G	αὐτοῦ	αὐτῆς	αὐτοῦ	αὐτῶν	αὐτῶν	αὐτῶν
D	αὐτῷ	αὐτῇ	αὐτῷ	αὐτοῖς	αὐταῖς	αὐτοῖς
A	αὐτόν	αὐτήν	αὐτό	αὐτούς	αὐτάς	αὐτά

24. Demonstrative Pronouns, οὗτος, ἐκεῖνος

a) οὗτος, αὕτη, τοῦτο (**"this"**)

	Singular			*Plural*		
	m.	*fm.*	*nt.*	*m.*	*fm.*	*nt.*
N	οὗτος	αὕτη	τοῦτο	οὗτοι	αὗται	ταῦτα
G	τούτου	ταύτης	τούτου	τούτων	τούτων	τούτων
D	τούτῳ	ταύτῃ	τούτῳ	τούτοις	ταύταις	τούτοις
A	τοῦτον	ταύτην	τοῦτο	τούτους	ταύτας	ταῦτα

b) ἐκεῖνος, ἐκείνη ἐκεῖνο (**"that"**)

	Singular			*Plural*		
	m.	*fm.*	*nt.*	*m.*	*fm.*	*nt.*
N	ἐκεῖνος	ἐκείνη	ἐκεῖνο	ἐκεῖνοι	ἐκεῖναι	ἐκεῖνα
G	ἐκείνου	ἐκείνης	ἐκείνου	ἐκείνων	ἐκείνων	ἐκείνων
D	ἐκείνῳ	ἐκείνῃ	ἐκείνῳ	ἐκείνοις	ἐκείναις	ἐκείνοις
A	ἐκεῖνον	ἐκείνην	ἐκεῖνο	ἐκείνους	ἐκείνας	ἐκεῖνα

25. Relative Pronouns, ὅς, ἥ, ὅ

	Singular			*Plural*		
	m.	*fm.*	*nt.*	*m.*	*fm.*	*nt.*
N	ὅς	ἥ	ὅ	οἵ	αἵ	ἅ
G	οὗ	ἧς	οὗ	ὧν	ὧν	ὧν
D	ᾧ	ᾗ	ᾧ	οἷς	αἷς	οἷς
A	ὅν	ἥν	ὅ	οὕς	ἅς	ἅ

26. Reflexive Pronouns – ἐμαυτοῦ, σεαυτοῦ, ἑαυτοῦ

	Singular			*Plural*		
	m.	*fm.*	*nt.*	*m.*	*fm.*	*nt.*
a) *First-Person Reflexive Pronoun*						
G	ἐμαυτοῦ	ἐμαυτῆς		ἑαυτῶν	ἑαυτῶν	
D	ἐμαυτῷ	ἐμαυτῇ		ἑαυτοῖς	ἑαυταῖς	
A	ἐμαυτόν	ἐμαυτήν		ἑαυτούς	ἑαυτάς	
b) *Second-Person Reflexive Pronoun*						
G	σεαυτοῦ	σεαυτῆς		ἑαυτῶν	ἑαυτῶν	
D	σεαυτῷ	σεαυτῇ		ἑαυτοῖς	ἑαυταῖς	
A	σεαυτόν	σεαυτήν		ἑαυτούς	ἑαυτάς	
c) *Third-Person Reflexive Pronoun*						
G	ἑαυτοῦ	ἑαυτῆς	ἑαυτοῦ	ἑαυτῶν	ἑαυτῶν	ἑαυτῶν
D	ἑαυτῷ	ἑαυτῇ	ἑαυτῷ	ἑαυτοῖς	ἑαυταῖς	ἑαυτοῖς
A	ἑαυτόν	ἑαυτήν	ἑαυτό	ἑαυτούς	ἑαυτάς	ἑαυτά

27. Reciprocal Pronoun – ἀλλήλων

G	ἀλλήλων
D	ἀλλήλοις
A	ἀλλήλους

28. The Indefinite Pronoun, τις, τι

	m./fm. Enclitic		*nt.* Enclitic	
Sg.				
N	τις		τι	
G	τινος	(τινός)	τινος	(τινός)
D	τινι	(τινί)	τινι	(τινί)
A	τινα	(τινά)	τι	
Pl.				
N	τινες	(τινές)	τινα	(τινά)
G	τινων	(τινῶν)	τινων	(τινῶν)
D	τισι(ν)	(τισί, τισίν)	τισι(ν)	(τισί, τισίν)
A	τινας	(τινάς)	τινα	(τινά)

29. The Interrogative Pronoun, τίς, τί

	m./fm.	*nt.*
N	τίς	τί
G	τίνος	τίνος
D	τίνι	τίνι
A	τίνα	τί
N	τίνες	τίνα
G	τίνων	τίνων
D	τίσι(ν)	τίσι(ν)
A	τίνας	τίνα

Summary of Vocabulary to Be Memorized

(bracketed numbers refer to chapter numbers)

1. ἀγαθός, -ή, -όν (7)
2. ἀγαπάω (4)
3. ἀγάπη (21)
4. ἀγαπητός, ή, όν (4)
5. ἄγγελος (1)
6. ἁγιάζω (24)
7. ἅγιος, -α, -ον (8)
8. ἀγρός (21)
9. ἄγω (10)
10. ἀδελφή (6)
11. ἀδελφός (6)
12. αἷμα, -ατος (21)
13. αἴρω (9)
14. αἰτέω (4)
15. αἰώνιος, -ον (10)
16. ἀκούω (2)
17. ἀλήθεια (6)
18. ἀληθής, -ές (14)
19. ἀληθινός, -ή, -όν (6)
20. ἀληθῶς (8)
21. ἀλλά (2)
22. ἀλλήλων (8)
23. ἄλλος, -η, -ο (14)
24. ἁμαρτία (6)
25. ἀμήν (1)
26. ἀμνός (5)
27. ἄν (8)
28. ἀνά (2)
29. ἀναβαίνω (11)
30. ἀναγγέλλω (12)
31. ἀνάστασις (19)
32. ἀνέρχομαι (20)

33. ἀνήρ, ἀνδρός (14)
34. ἄνθρωπος (5)
35. ἀνίστημι (22)
36. ἀνοίγω (22)
37. ἄνωθεν (10)
38. ἄξιος, -α, -ον (7)
39. ἅπας, ἅπασα, ἅπαν (15)
40. ἀπεκρίθη (6)
41. ἀπέρχομαι (13)
42. ἀπό, ἀπ᾽, ἀφ᾽ (8)
43. ἀποθνῄσκω (21)
44. ἀποκρίνομαι (11)
45. ἀποκτείνω (23)
46. ἀπόλλυμι (21)
47. ἀποστέλλω (10)
48. ἀπόστολος (1)
49. ἄρτι (2)
50. ἄρτος (13)
51. ἀρχή (6)
52. ἄρχω, ἄρχομαι (11)
53. ἄρχων, ἄρχοντος (14)
54. ἀσθένεια (17)
55. ἀσθενέω (16)
56. ἀσπάζομαι (11)
57. αὐτός, -ή, -ό (8)
58. ἀφίημι (24)
59. βάλλω (22)
60. βαπτίζω (3)
61. βασιλεία (10, 14)
62. βασιλεύς, -εως (15)
63. βλέπω (3)
64. Γαλιλαία (1)
65. γάμος (9)
66. γάρ (3)
67. γεννάω (16)
68. γένος, -ους (21)
69. γῆ (11)
70. γυνή, γυναικός (9, 14)
71. γίνομαι (11)
72. γινώσκω (8)
73. γλῶσσα (21)
74. γραμματεύς, -έως (16)

75. γραφή (10)
76. γράφω (16)
77. δαιμόνιον (20)
78. δέ (2)
79. δεῖ (10)
80. δείκνυμι (21)
81. δεῦτε (14)
82. δεύτερος, -α, -ον (10)
83. δέχομαι (12)
84. δηνάριον (13)
85. δία, δι'(3)
86. διὰ τοῦτο (6)
87. διάκονος (9)
88. διάνοια (19)
89. διδάσκαλος (3)
90. διδάσκω (18)
91. διδαχή (18)
92. δίδωμι (20)
93. διέρχομαι (13)
94. δίκαιος, -α, -ον (7)
95. δικαιοσύνη (19)
96. δικαιόω (19)
97. διψῶ (-άω) (12)
98. διώκω (18)
99. δοκέω (19)
100. δόξα (6)
101. δοξάζω (19)
102. δοῦλος (16)
103. δύναμαι (11)
104. δύναμις, -εως (21)
105. δύο, δυσί(ν) (15)
106. δώδεκα (18)
107. δωρεά (12)
108. ἐάν (10)
109. ἐὰν μή (10)
110. ἑαυτοῦ, -ῆς, -οῦ (8)
111. ἐγγύς (2)
112. ἐγείρω (3)
113. ἐγώ (6)
114. ἔθνος, -νους (15)
115. εἰ (7)
116. εἶδεν (3)

117. εἰμί (3)
118. εἶπεν, -ον, -αν (7)
119. εἰρήνη (13)
120. εἰς (6)
121. εἷς, μία, ἕν (15)
122. εἰσέρχομαι (19)
123. εἰσπορεύομαι (21)
124. εἰσφέρω (18)
125. ἐκ, ἐξ (6)
126. ἕκαστος, -η, -ον (7)
127. ἐκβάλλω (22)
128. ἐκεῖ (3)
129. ἐκεῖθεν (16)
130. ἐκεῖνος, -η, -ο (7)
131. ἐκκλησία (6)
132. ἐκπορεύομαι (19)
133. Ἕλλην, -ηνος (22)
134. ἐλπίζω (19)
135. ἐλπίς, ἐλπίδος (22)
136. ἐμαυτοῦ, -ῆς (8)
137. ἐμβαίνω (21)
138. ἐμός, -ή, -όν (7)
139. ἐν (6)
140. ἐνθάδε (12)
141. ἐντολή (18)
142. ἐνώπιον (12)
143. ἕξ (2)
144. ἐξέρχομαι (13)
145. ἔξεστι(ν) (17)
146. ἐξουσία (6)
147. ἔξω (22)
148. ἑορτή (10)
149. ἐπαγγελία (18)
150. ἐπαίρω (13)
151. ἐπάνω (12)
152. ἐπαύριον (5)
153. ἔπειτα (22)
154. ἐπί, ἐπ᾽, ἐφ᾽ (8)
155. ἐργάζομαι (18)
156. ἔργον (5)
157. ἔρημος, -ον (7)
158. ἔρχομαι (11)

159. ἐρωτάω (13)
160. ἐσθίω (13)
161. ἔσχατος, -η, -ον (22)
162. ἕτερος, -α, -ον (14)
163. ἔτι (14)
164. ἔτος, ἔτους (17)
165. εὐαγγέλιον (12)
166. εὐαγγελίζομαι (13)
167. εὐθέως, εὐθύς (17)
168. εὑρίσκω (3)
169. εὐχαριστέω (20)
170. ἔχω (3)
171. ἕως (9)
172. ζάω (4)
173. ζῆλος (9)
174. ζητέω (12)
175. ζωή (6)
176. ζῳοποιέω (18)
177. ἤ (2)
178. ἤδη (9)
179. ἥκω (9)
180. Ἠλίας (7)
181. ἡμεῖς (8)
182. ἡμέρα (8)
183. ἡμέτερος, -α, -ον (7)
184. ἦν (6)
185. θάλασσα, -ης (20)
186. θάνατος (5)
187. θαυμάζω (13)
188. θεάομαι (12)
189. θέλημα, -ατος (15)
190. θέλω (4)
191. θεός (1)
192. θεραπεύω (17)
193. θερίζω (13)
194. θερισμός (13)
195. θεωρέω (5)
196. θυγάτηρ, -τρός (21)
197. ἴδε, ἴδου, ἰδού, ἴδετε (5)
198. ἴδιος, -α, -ον (6)
199. ἱερόν (9)
200. Ἱεροσόλυμα (1)

201. Ἰησοῦς (1)
202. ἵνα (5)
203. Ἰορδάνης (1)
204. Ἰουδαία (1)
205. Ἰουδαῖος, -α, -ον (7)
206. ἴσος, -η, -ον (18)
207. Ἰσραήλ (1)
208. Ἰσραηλίτης (8)
209. ἵστημι (20)
210. Ἰωάννης (1)
211. κἀγώ (3)
212. κάθημαι (19)
213. καθίζω (20)
214. καθώς (7)
215. καί (2)
216. καιρός (18)
217. καλέω (4)
218. καλός, -ή, -όν (9)
219. καρδία (18)
220. καρπός (13)
221. κατά (2)
222. καταβαίνω (11)
223. κατηγορέω (20)
224. κηρύσσω (22)
225. κόσμος (1)
226. κράβαττος (17)
227. κράζω (20)
228. κρίνω (10)
229. κρίσις (10)
230. κύριος (5)
231. λαλέω (4)
232. λαμβάνω (10)
233. λέγω (4)
234. λόγος (2)
235. λύχνος (19)
236. λύω (2)
237. μᾶλλον (11)
238. μαθητής (6)
239. μαρτυρέω (4)
240. μαρτυρία (4)
241. μέγας, μεγάλη, μέγα (7)
242. μείζων, -ον (15)

243. μέλλω (16)
244. μέν (3)
245. μένω (3)
246. μέσος, -η, -ον (7)
247. Μεσσίας (1)
248. μετά (2)
249. μεταβαίνω (18)
250. μή (9)
251. μηδείς, μηδεμία, μηδέν (15)
252. μηκέτι (16)
253. μήτηρ, -τρός (14)
254. μήτι (13)
255. μισέω (11)
256. μνημεῖον (19)
257. μόνος, -η, -ον (18)
258. Μωϋσῆς (14)
259. ναός (9)
260. νεκρός, -ά, -όν (9)
261. νόμος (5)
262. νῦν (9)
263. νύξ, νυκτός (14)
264. ξηρός, -ά, -όν (17)
265. ὁδός (6)
266. οἶδα (9)
267. οἰκία (9)
268. οἶκος (9)
269. οἶνος (9)
270. ὀκτώ (17)
271. ὅμοιως (18)
272. ὁμολογέω (4)
273. ὄνομα, -ατος (15)
274. ὀπίσω (5)
275. ὅπου (5)
276. ὁρῶ (-άω) (4)
277. ὀργή (11)
278. ὄρος, -ους, τό (14)
279. ὅς, ἥ, ὅ (8)
280. ὅσος, -η, -ον (13)
281. ὅστις, ἥτις, ὅτι (15)
282. ὅταν (9)
283. ὅτε (4)
284. ὅτι (4)

285. οὗ (16)
286. οὐ, οὐκ, οὐχ (3)
287. οὐδέ (6)
288. οὐδείς, οὐδεμία, οὐδέν (15)
289. οὐκέτι (13)
290. οὖν (2)
291. οὔπω (9)
292. οὐρανός (5)
293. οὔτε (2)
294. οὗτος, αὕτη, τοῦτο (7)
295. οὕτω, οὕτως (9)
296. οὐχί (4)
297. ὀφειλέτης (24)
298. ὀφείλημα, -ατος (24)
299. ὄχλος (16)
300. παιδίον (16)
301. παῖς, παιδός (16)
302. πάλιν (12)
303. πάντοτε (20)
304. παρά (6)
305. παραδίδωμι (22)
306. παρακαλῶ (-έω) (16)
307. πάρειμι (23)
308. πᾶς, πᾶσα, πᾶν (15)
309. πάσχα (9)
310. πατήρ, -τρός (14)
311. πατρίς, -ίδος (16)
312. Παῦλος (1)
313. πείθω (10)
314. πεινάω (18)
315. πειράζω (20)
316. πειρασμός (24)
317. πέμπω (3)
318. πέντε (12)
319. πέραν (4)
320. περί (6)
321. περιπατέω (21)
322. περισσεύω (20)
323. Πέτρος (1)
324. Πιλᾶτος (1)
325. πίνω (12)
326. πίπτω (10)

327. πιστεύω (2)
328. πίστις, -εως (14)
329. πιστός, -ή, -όν (7)
330. πηγή (12)
331. πλανάω (24)
332. πλείων, -ον (15)
333. πλῆθος, -ους (17)
334. πλήρης -ες (23)
335. πληρῶ (-όω) (4)
336. πλησίον (12)
337. πλοῖον (20)
338. πνεῦμα, -ατος (8)
339. πνέω (10)
340. πόθεν (9)
341. ποῖος, ποία, ποῖον (7)
342. ποιῶ (-έω) (4)
343. πόλις, -εως (14)
344. πολύς, πολλή, πολύ (7)
345. πονηρός, -ά, -όν (11)
346. πορεύομαι (16)
347. πόσος, -η, -ον (19)
348. πότερον (19)
349. ποῦ (8)
350. πράσσω (13)
351. πρίν (16)
352. πρό (8)
353. πρός (6)
354. προσέρχομαι (21)
355. προσεύχομαι (12)
356. προσκυνέω (4)
357. προφήτης (2)
358. πρῶτος, -η, -ον (7)
359. πῦρ, -ός (21)
360. πῶς (10)
361. ῥαββί (1)
362. ῥῆμα, -ατος (12)
363. σάββατον (5)
364. σάρξ, σαρκός (14)
365. σεαυτοῦ, -ῆς (8)
366. σημεῖον (9)
367. Σίμων, -ωνος (3)
368. σκληρός, -ά, -όν (23)

369. σκοτία (6)
370. σκότος, -ους (15)
371. σός, -ή, -όν (7)
372. σπείρω (21)
373. σπέρμα, -ατος (15)
374. στάδιοι, -ων (21)
375. στοά (17)
376. σύ (8)
377. σύν (11)
378. συνάγω (13)
379. συναγωγή (2)
380. σφραγίζω (11)
381. σῴζω (23)
382. σῶμα, -ατος (15)
383. σωτήρ, -ῆρος (14)
384. σωτηρία (14)
385. τέ (2)
386. τέκνον (5)
387. τέρας, τέρατος (16)
388. τέσσαρες, τέσσαρα (15)
389. τηρέω (4)
390. τίθημι (20)
391. τιμάω (18)
392. τιμή (16)
393. τίς, τί (15)
394. τις, τι (15)
395. τοιοῦτος, -αύτη, -οῦτο(ν) (12)
396. τόπος (5)
397. τότε (16)
398. τρεῖς, τρία (15)
399. τρίτος, -η, -ον (9)
400. τρώγω (22)
401. ὑγιής, ές (17)
402. ὕδωρ, -δατος (14)
403. υἱός (3)
404. ὑμεῖς (8)
405. ὑμέτερος, -α, -ον (7)
406. ὑπάγω (10)
407. ὑπέρ (11)
408. ὑπό, ὑπ', ὑφ' (8)
409. ὑψόω (11)
410. φαίνω (3)

411. φανερόω (4)
412. Φαρισαῖος (3)
413. φέρω (10)
414. φημί (21)
415. φιλέω (18)
416. φίλος (11)
417. φόβος (19)
418. φοβέομαι (17)
419. φυλακή (11)
420. φωνέω (4)
421. φωνή (6)
422. φῶς, -τός (4)
423. φωτίζω (3)
424. χαίρω (12)
425. χαρά (12)
426. χάρις, -ιτος (14)
427. χριστός, Χριστός (2)
428. χρόνος (3)
429. χωλός, -ή, -όν (17)
430. χώρα (13)
431. χωρίς (4)
432. ψεύστης (22)
433. ψυχή (13)
434. ὥρα (8)
435. ὡς (4)
436. ὥσπερ (18)
437. ὥστε (11)
438. ὠφελέω (23)

Subject Index

Index of Greek Words Discussed

Lexicon of Greek Words in Texts for Translation

A

ἀγαθός, -ή, -όν, good, beneficial, generous, useful (cf. 7.1, 26.18)

ἀγάπη, love

ἀγαπητός, -ή, -όν, beloved, dear(est)

ἀγαπῶ (-άω), I love (cf. 25.1, 26.4)

ἄγγελος, messenger, a heavenly messenger, angel

ἁγιάζω, I set apart as sacred to God, treat as holy, reverence

ἅγιος, -α, -ον, set apart for God, consecrated, holy

ἀγρός, field, farm, countryside

ἄγω, I lead, bring, go (cf. 25.2, 16.9, n. 9)

ἀδελφή, sister

ἀδελφός, brother; in plural, "brothers and sisters"

ἀδικία, wrongdoing, injustice

αἷμα, -ατος, blood

Αινών, Aenon, town in the Jordon valley, 8 miles south of Schythopolis

αἴρω, I take, take up, take away (cf. 25.4)

αἰτῶ (-έω), I ask, request, require

αἰώνιος, -ον, eternal, unending, everlasting

ἀκολουθῶ (-έω), I follow, accompany

ἀκούω, I hear, listen to (cf. 25.5)

ἀλήθεια, truth

ἀληθής (m. and fm.), -ές (nt.), true, truthful (cf. 14.5)

ἀληθινός, -ή, -όν, true, trustworthy, genuine

ἀληθῶς, truly

ἀλλά, ἀλλ', but (much stronger than δέ)

ἀλλήλων, one another, each other (cf. 26.27)

ἄλλος, -η, -ο, another, other

ἁμαρτία, sin, sinfulness; sin offering

ἀμήν, amen, truly, indeed

ἀμνός, lamb

ἄν (an), particle indicating contingency

ἀνά, each, each one, apiece (prep.)

ἀναβαίνω, I go up, ascend (cf. 25.11, 18.4.1)

ἀναγγέλλω, I tell, proclaim, report

ἀνάκειμαι, I am seated at table, to be seated to eat as a dinner guest

ἀναχορῶ (-έω), I withdraw, go away

ἄνεμος, wind

ἀνάστασις, -εως, resurrection

'Ανδρέας, Andrew

ἀνέρχομαι, I go/come up

ἀνήρ, ἀνδρός, man, husband (cf. 14.3)

ἄνθρωπος, a human being of either sex, person, a man

ἀνίστημι, trans. (in fut. and 1 aor. act.) I raise (the dead), I appoint (prophets), I help get up; intrans. (in 2 aor. and all mid. forms) I rise, stand up

ἀνοίγω, I open; restore, heal (of sight and hearing) (cf. 25.6)

ἄντλημα, -ατος, bucket

ἄνωθεν, from above, again

ἄξιος, -α, -ον, worthy, deserving

ἅπας, ἅπασα, ἅπαν, intensive form of πᾶς, πᾶσα, πᾶν

ἀπεκρίθη, he answered (see ἀποκρίνομαι)

ἀπέρχομαι, I depart, go away

ἀπό, ἀπ', ἀφ', (w. gen.) from, away from

ἀποθνῄσκω, I die, face death (cf. 25.7)

ἀποκρίνομαι, I answer, reply

ἀποκτείνω, I kill, put to death, murder

ἀπόλλυμι, I destroy, kill, lose; lose out on, mid. perish (cf. 25.8)
ἀπολύω, I release, set free; mid. leave
ἀποστέλλω, I send (cf. 25.9)
ἀπόστολος, an emissary, apostle, one who is sent to fulfill a task
ἀριθμός, number, total
ἄρτι, now, just now
ἄρτος, bread, loaf, food
ἀρχή, beginning, first
ἄρχομαι, I begin
ἄρχω, act. I rule, govern
ἄρχων, -οντος, ruler, official, authority (cf. 26.17)
ἀσθένεια, weakness, illness
ἀσθενῶ (-έω), I am sick, ill, am weak
ἀσπάζομαι, I greet, say goodbye
αὐτός, αὐτή, αὐτό, he, she, it; himself, herself, itself; same (cf. 8.3–4)
ἀφίημι, I cancel, forgive, allow, let go, send away; release from legal or moral obligation (cf. 25.10)

Β
βαθύς, -εῖα, -ύ, deep
βάλλω, I throw, throw down
βαπτίζω, I baptize; I dip or plunge into water
βασιλεία, kingdom, empire, rule, reign
βασιλεύς, king (cf. 15.2)
Βηθανία, -ας, Bethany
Βηθζαθά, Bethzatha, a pool in northeast Jerusalem
Βηθσαϊδά, Bethsaida
βλέπω, I see, look on/at
βραχύς, -εῖα, -ύ, a little, short; βραχύ τι, a little, a small amount (John 6:7)
βρῶμα, food
βρῶσις, eating, a meal

Γ
Γαλιλαία, Galilee
Γαλιλαῖος, -α, -ον a Galilean
γάμος, wedding, wedding banquet
γάρ, for (post-positive), since, then
γεμίζω, I fill
γεννῶ (-άω), I give birth to a child (of woman); be a father of (of a man); pass. I am born
γένος, -ους, τό, family, race, nation; offspring, descendants, kind (cf. 15.3)
γῆ, the earth, land
γίνομαι, I become, I am, it happens (cf. 25.13)
γινώσκω, I know, learn (cf. 25.14, 26.6)
γλῶσσα, tongue, language
γογγύζω, I complain, grumble, mutter
γραμματεύς, -έως, scribe, expert in the Jewish law (cf. 15.2)
γραφή, passage of Scripture (sg.), Hebrew Scriptures (pl.)
γράφω, I write (cf. 25.15)
γυνή, γυναικός woman, wife

Δ
δαιμόνιον, demon, evil spirit, a god
Δαυίδ, David
δέ, but, and (post-positive); it usually implies some sort of weak contrast, but can also be used w. explanatory force meaning "indeed," "and moreover"
δεῖ (w. acc.), (impersonal verb), it is necessary, should
δείκνυμι, I show, reveal (cf. 25.16, 21.1, 26.9)
δεξιός, -ά, -όν, right (opposite left)
δεῦτε, come!
δεύτερος, -α, -ον, second
δέχομαι, I receive, accept (cf. 25.17)
δηνάριον, δηνάρια (pl.), denarius, denaria
διά, (1) (w. gen.) through, by means of; (2) (w. acc.) because of, on account of; διὰ τοῦτο, therefore
διάβολος, devil
διάκονος, household steward, waiter, servant
διάνοια, mind, understanding, intention, attitude
διδάσκαλος, teacher
διδάσκω, I teach (cf. 25.18)

διδαχή, teaching, instruction
δίδωμι, I give, grant (cf. 25.19, 26.8, 10, 11, 12)
διέρχομαι, I go or pass through
δίκαιος, -α, ον, ethically just, fair, righteous (cf. 7.1)
δικαιοσύνη, justice, uprightness
δικαιῶ (-όω), I vindicate, treat as just, cause someone to be released from legal claims, justify
διψῶ (-άω), I am thirsty
διώκω, I persecute, pursue
δοκῶ (-έω), I think, suppose; intrans. I seem; impers. it seems
δόξα, fame, honor, glory, reputation
δοξάζω, I honor, praise
δοῦλος, slave
δύναμαι, I can, am able (cf. 11.10)
δύναμις, -εως, power, potentiality, act of power
δύο, δυσί(ν), two (cf. 15.9)
δώδεκα, twelve
δωρεά, gift

E

ἐάν, if, even if; ἐὰν μή, unless, except
ἑαυτοῦ, ἑαυτῆς, reflexive pronoun, himself, herself, itself; possessive pronoun, his, hers, etc. (cf. 26.26)
ἐγγύς, near, close to
ἐγείρω, I rise up, get up, wake up; I raise up (the dead) (cf. 25.20)
ἐγώ, I (cf. 8.1)
ἔθνος, ἔθνους (nt.), nation, pl. Gentiles (cf. 15.3, 26.17)
εἰ, if, whether
εἶδεν, εἶδον, he saw, they saw
εἶδος, -ους, nt., visible form, outward appearance
εἴκοσι, twenty
εἰμί, I am (cf. 26.13)
εἶπεν, he/she said, εἶπον, they said, εἶπαν, they said (cf. 10.3)
εἰρήνη, peace
εἰς w. acc., into, to, as; for (expressing the goal of an action)
εἷς, μία, ἕν, one (cf. 15.9)
εἰσέρχομαι, I come/go in or into, enter
εἰσπορεύομαι, I go/come in, enter
εἰσφέρω, I lead in, carry in, bring in
εἴτε, if, whether, εἴτε … εἴτε …, whether … or …
ἐκ, ἐξ, (w. gen.) from, out of
ἕκαστος, -η, -ον, each, every
ἐκβάλλω, I drive out, expel
ἐκεῖ, there, in that place
ἐκεῖθεν, from there (adv.)
ἐκεῖνος, -η, -ο, that (cf. 7.5)
ἐλεύθερος, -α, -ον, free; as noun, freeman, freewoman
ἐκκλησία, an assembly of people, a congregation
ἐκπορεύομαι, I go or come out, come forth
Ἕλλην -ηνος, a Greek, non-Jew, Gentile
Ἑλληνίς, -ίδος, a Greek or Gentile woman
ἐλπίζω, I hope
ἐλπίς, ἐλπίδος, hope (cf. 14.2)
ἐμαυτοῦ, -ῆς, myself, my own (cf. 26.26)
ἐμβαίνω, I embark, step in (a boat) (cf. 18.4.1, App. 1.11)
ἐμός, -ή, -όν, my, mine
ἐν, (w. dat.) in, among, with; when, while, during
ἐνθάδε, here, into this place
ἐνώπιον (w. gen.) before, in the presence of
ἐντολή, commandment, instruction
ἕξ, six
ἐξέρχομαι, I come or go out or forth, get out
ἔξεστι(ν), impers. it is permitted or lawful, it is possible
ἐξουσία, authority
ἔξω, (w. gen.) out of, outside
ἑορτή, festival, feast
ἐπαγγελία, a promise
ἐπαίρω, I raise, lift up
ἐπάνω, (w. gen.), on, over, above
ἐπαύριον, adv. the next day
ἔπειτα, adv. then, next

ἐπερωτῶ (-άω), I ask for, I question
ἐπί, ἐπ', ἐφ', (1) (w. gen.) on, upon; (2) (w. dat.) on, on the basis of; (3) (w. acc.) on, around
ἑπτά, seven
ἐργάζομαι, I work (for), perform a deed
ἔρημος, -ον, deserted; as noun, a wilderness, desert
ἔργον, work, deed, task
ἔρχομαι, I come, I go (cf. 25.21)
ἐρωτῶ (-άω), I ask (sby a question), request, beseech sby concerning sthg
ἐσθίω, I eat (cf. 25.22)
ἔσχατος, -η, -ον, last, final; lowest
ἕτερος, -α, -ον, another, different, one of two
ἔτι, still, yet (adv.)
ἕτοιμος, -η, -ον, ready, prepared
ἔτος, ἔτους (nt.), ἔτη (pl.) year
εὐαγγέλιον, a joyful announcement, good news
εὐαγγελίζομαι, I announce good news
εὐθύς, εὐθέως, immediately, at once
εὑρίσκω, I find, discover (cf. 25.23)
εὐχαριστῶ (-έω), I thank, give thanks
ἔχω, trans. I have, hold; intrans. I am (cf. 25.24, 16.8)
ἕως, (1) conj. until (w. any tense); while (w. pres. ind. only); (2) prep. w. gen. to, until, as far as

Z

ζῶ (-άω), I live, am alive (cf. 4.8, n. 10, App. 1.25)
ζῆλος, zeal, jealousy
ζητῶ (-έω), I seek, look for
ζωή, life
ζῳοποιῶ (-έω), I give life to, make alive

H

ἤ, or, than
ἤδη, now, already
ἥκω, I have come, am present
Ἠλίας, -οῦ, Elijah
ἥλιος, sun
ἡμεῖς, we (cf. 8.1)
ἡμέρα, day
ἡμέτερος, -α, -ον, our
ἦν, he/she/it was
Ἠσαΐας, Isaiah

Θ

θάλασσα, -ης, sea, lake
θάνατος, death
θαυμάζω, intrans. I marvel, wonder, am amazed; trans. I marvel or wonder at, admire
θεάομαι, I see, look at, watch, observe
θέλημα, -ατος, will, desire
θέλω, I will, am willing, wish, want, desire
θεραπεύω, I heal, cure, serve
θερίζω, I reap, harvest, gather
θερισμός, harvest, crop
θεός, God, god
θεωρῶ (-έω), I see, watch, observe, perceive
θυγάτηρ, -τρός, daughter, female descendant
θύρα, door (of a house), gate
θρόνος, throne
θύω, I sacrifice, slaughter

I

ἴδε, ἴδου, ἰδού, ἴδετε, look! see! listen!
ἴδιος, -α, -ον, one's own, belonging to one, personal
ἱερόν, temple, temple precincts
Ἱεροσόλυμα, τά and ἡ, Jerusalem (indecl.)
Ἰησοῦς, Jesus (cf. 5.14)
ἱμάτιον, garment, clothing, cloak (of outer garments)
ἵνα, in order that, that (explaining sthg), so that (where ὥστε is excepted)
Ἰορδάνης, Jordan river
Ἰουδαία, Judaea
Ἰουδαῖος, -α, ον, Jewish/Judean (adj.); Jew/Judean (noun)
Ἰσκαριώτης and Ἰσκαριώθ, Iscariot
ἴσος, -η, -ον, equal, same; ἴσα (adv.) equally

Ἰσραήλ, Israel
Ἰσραηλίτης, -ου, Israelite
ἵστημι, trans. I set, establish; intrans. I stand (cf. 25.26, 26.8, 10–12)
Ἰωάννης, John
Ἰωσήφ, Joseph

K

κἀγώ, and I, but I, I also
κάθημαι, I sit, sit down (cf. 26.7)
καθίζω, intrans. I sit down, stay; trans. cause to sit, set
καθώς, just as, as
καί, and; also, even (adv.)
καιρός, an opportune time, time of harvest, a season, a time of crisis (especially as it concerns the end times)
κἀκεῖνος = καὶ ἐκείνος, "and that man," "and he"
κακός, -ή, -όν, bad, evil, dangerous
καλῶ (-έω), I call, name, invite, summon (cf. 25.27)
καλός, -ή, -όν, good, useful, praiseworthy, excellent, fine
καλῶς, well, rightly, correctly
Κανά, Cana
καρδία, the center of physical, spiritual, and mental life; fig. heart
καρπός, grain, harvest; result; gain
κατά, (1) acc. according to; (2) gen. against, down from
καταβαίνω, I go down, descend (cf. 18.4.1, App. 1.11)
κατηγορῶ (-έω), I bring a legal charge against someone
Καφαρναούμ, Capernaum
κεφαλή, head
κηρύσσω, I proclaim (cf. 25.28)
Κηφᾶς, -ᾶ, Cephas, Aramaic equivalent of Greek name Πέτρος
κοπιῶ (-άω), I work, work hard, labor
κόσμος, the world (as a place of human habitation)
κράβαττος, stretcher, a poor man's bed/mat
κράζω, I call out, cry out, shout
κρατῶ (-έω), I hold, take, take hold of
κρίνω, I judge, decide, determine (cf. 25.29)
κρίσις, -εως (f.), judgment, condemnation
κρυπτός, -ήν, -όν, secret, hidden, private
κύριος, earthly master or lord; Lord, as title of God and Christ

Λ

λαλῶ (-έω), I speak, say
λαλία, what is said, accent, manner of speech
λαμβάνω, I take, take hold of, receive (cf. 25.30)
λαός, people, nation
λέγω, I say, speak, tell (cf. 25.31)
λίθος, stone, precious stone
λόγος, a statement, a saying, an utterance, a message, reply, story, speech; very rarely "divine Wisdom"
λοιπός, -ή, -όν, rest, remaining, other
λύχνος, lamp
λύω, I loose, untie, set free, destroy; do away w., abolish (cf. 26.1–3)

M

μακάριος, -α, -ον, blessed, fortunate, happy
μαθητεύω, trans. I make disciples; intrans. I am a disciple
μαθητής, -οῦ, a disciple, a follower (cf. 6.7)
μᾶλλον, more, rather; μᾶλλον ... ἤ, more/rather ... than
μαρτυρῶ (-έω), I bear witness, testify
μαρτυρία, testimony, evidence
μάρτυς, -υρος, witness
μέγας, μεγάλη, μέγα, large, great (cf. 7.4)
μείζων, -ον, (comp. of μέγας) greater; sometimes = superl. greatest (cf. 15.8)
μέλλω, I am about to, am going to, intend to
μέν, particle indicating contrast, emphasis or continuation; indeed
μέντοι, however

μένω, I remain, stay (cf. 25.32)
μέσος, -η, -ον, middle, in the middle
Μεσσίας, -ου, Messiah
μετά, (1) (w. gen.) w., among; (2) (w. acc.) after, behind
μεταβαίνω, I leave, move fr. one place to another, go (cf. 18.4.1, App. 1.11)
μή, not (often used w. non-indicative verbs)
μηδέ, nor, and not, not even (w. non-indicative moods); also used to negate questions expecting the answer "no"
μηδείς, μηδεμία, μηδέν, no one, nothing, no (w. non-ind. moods)
μηκέτι, no longer, no more (w. non-ind. moods)
μήτηρ, -τρός, mother
μήτι, used in questions to indicate negative answer expected
μικρός, -ά, -ον, little, small, of little importance
μισῶ (-έω), I hate, despise, disregard
μίσθος, pay, wages; reward
μνημεῖον, grave, tomb, monument
μόνος, -η, -ον, only, alone
Μωϋσῆς, -έως, Moses

N

Ναζαρέτ, Nazareth
Ναθαναήλ, Nathanael
ναός, temple, inner part of temple, including Jewish temple, sanctuary
νεκρός, -ά, -όν, dead, lifeless; pl. the dead
Νικόδημος, Nicodemus
νοῦς, νοός (m.), mind, intellect, understanding, attitude
νύμφη, bride
νυμφίος, bridegroom
νῦν, now, at the present
νύξ, νυκτός (f.), night (cf. 14.2)
νόμος, law, the Torah

Ξ

ξηρός, -ά, όν, dry; paralyzed

O

ὁδός, ἡ, way, road, journey
οἶδα, I know, understand, perceive (cf. 25.33, 9.7, 16.7, 16.13, 19.3, 26.5)
οἶκος, house, household
οἰκία, house, household
οἶνος, wine
ὄκτω, eight
ὅλος, -η, -ον, whole, all
ὅμοιως, in the same way, likewise, too
ὁμολογῶ (-έω), I confess, admit, declare
ὄνομα, -ατος, name (cf. 15.1)
ὀπίσω, w. gen., after, behind
ὅπου, where (non-interrogative)
ὅπως, that, in order that
ὁρῶ (-άω), I see (cf. 25.34)
ὀργή, anger, wrath
ὄρος, -ους, τό, mountain, hill
ὅς, ἥ, ὅ, who, which, what (cf. 26.25)
ὅσος, -η, -ον, as much/many as, as great as, all
ὅστις, ἥτις, ὅτι, who, which, whoever, whichever
ὅταν, when, whenever
ὅτε, when, while
ὅτι, that, because (cf. 5.8)
οὗ, where, to which
οὗ, gen. of relative pronoun ὅ meaning "whose"
οὐ, οὐκ, οὐχ, not, no
οὐδέ, not even, and not, nor; οὐδέ… οὐδέ… neither… nor…
οὐδείς, οὐδεμία, οὐδέν, no one, nothing, no (cf. 15.4.2)
οὐκέτι, no longer, no more (w. ind. mood)
οὖν, then (temporal), therefore (in a discourse or line of argument)
οὔπω, not yet
οὐρανός, sky, heaven, circumlocation for the divine name
οὐτέ, not, nor; οὐτέ… οὐτέ…, neither… nor…
οὗτος, αὕτη, τοῦτο, this (cf. 7.5)
οὕτω, οὕτως, (1) adv. in this way, thus, so; (2) adj. such; (3) as follows

οὐχί, not, not so, no indeed; also occurs in questions expecting a positive answer
ὀφειλέτης, -ου, one who is under obligation, a debtor
ὀφείλημα, -ατος, debt
ὀφείλω, I owe, ought to, be obligated
ὀφθαλμός, eye
ὄχλος, crowd, a throng or mob of common people
ὀψία, evening

Π

παιδάριον, a child, youth
παιδίον, child, infant
παῖς, -δός (m. and f.), boy, girl, youth
πάλιν, again, once more, furthermore
πάντοτε, always (adv.)
παρά, 1) (w. gen.) from, by; 2) (w. dat.) in the presence of; 3) (w. acc.) beside, along
παραδίδωμι, I hand over
παρακαλῶ (-έω), I invite, beg, urge, encourage; request, appeal to
πάρειμι, I am present, am here
παρρησία, openness, boldness, confidence
πᾶς, πᾶσα, πᾶν, (1) without the article each, every (pl. all); (2) w. the article entire, whole, all; (3) everyone, all things (cf. 15.4.1)
πάσχα, Passover (festival), Passover meal, Passover lamb
πατήρ, -τρός, father (cf. 14.3)
πατρίς, -ίδος (f.), homeland, hometown
Παῦλος, Paul
πείθω, I persuade, convince; pf act. and pass. trust, have confidence in (cf. 16.6, 25.36)
πεινῶ (-άω), I hunger, am hungry
πειράζω, I put to the test, tempt
πειρασμός, a period/process of testing, a trial, a test
πέμπω, I send, appoint (cf. 25.37)
πέντε, five
πέραν (w. gen.) beyond, on the other side, across to (the other side)
περί (1) (w. gen.) about, concerning; (2) (w. acc.) around, near
περιπατῶ (-έω), I walk about, go about, I live
περισσεύω, be left over, be more than enough; I increase, have plenty
περιτέμνω, I circumcise
περιτομή, circumcision
Πέτρος, Peter
Πιλᾶτος, Pilate
πίμπλημι, I fill, fulfill, end (cf. 25.38)
πίνω, I drink (cf. 25.39)
πίπτω, I fall, fall down (cf. 25.40)
πιστεύω, I entrust myself to, I believe (in), I have confidence in
πίστις, -εως, confidence, faithfulness, belief, faith; cf. the adjective, πιστός, -ή, -όν
πιστός, ή, όν, trustworthy, faithful
πηγή, spring of water, well
πλανῶ (-άω), I lead astray, mislead; pass. I go astray, am misled, mistaken
πλείων, -ον, (comp. of πολύς) more, many; the most
πλῆθος, -ους (n.) crowd, quantity
πλήρης, -ες, full, complete
πληρῶ (-όω), I fill, fulfill (cf. 26.4)
πλησίον, (w. gen.) near; ὁ πλησίον, neighbor
πλοιάριον, small boat
πλοῖον, boat, ship
πνεῦμα, breath, human spirit, one's inner self, a ghost, Spirit/Breath (of God), a wind
πνῶ (-έω), I blow (of wind)
πόθεν, from where? where? (interrogative)
ποῖος, ποία, ποῖον, what, which, what kind of (interrogative pronoun)
ποιῶ (-έω), I do, make (cf. 26.4)
πόλις, -εως, city (cf. 14.4)
πολύς (gen. πολλοῦ), πολλή, πολύ, much, many; πολλά, many things; often πολύ as adv., often (cf. 7.4)
πονηρός, -ά, -όν, evil, bad, sinful
πορεύομαι, I go, proceed; travel

πόσος, -η, -ον, how much, how many; πόσῳ μᾶλλον, how much more?
πότερον, whether (adv.)
ποῦ, interrogative adv. where? at what place?
πούς, ποδός (m.), foot
πράσσω, I do, practice
πρίν (and πρὶν ἤ), before (conj.)
πρό (w. gen.), before (time or place)
πρόβατον, lamb, sheep
πρός (w. acc.), toward (prep.)
προσέρχομαι, I come or go to, approach
προσεύχομαι, I pray
προσκυνῶ (-έω), I worship, kneel
προσκυνητής, worshiper, one who worships
πρόσωπον, face, presence, appearance
πρότερον, previously, earlier
προφήτης, -ου, a prophet, one who has a close relation to the "breath of the Lord" (*ruach Adonai*)
πρῶτος, -η, -ον, first, foremost
πῦρ, πυρός (nt.), fire
πῶς, interrog. particle how? in what way?

Ρ

ῥαββί, rabbi, teacher, master (honorary title of address), my lord
ῥῆμα, -ατος, what is said, a word, a saying

Σ

σάββατον, the Sabbath, the seventh day of the week
Σαλείμ, also Σαλίμ Salem (John 3.23)
Σαμάρεια, Samaria (region or city)
Σαμαρίτης, -ου, Samaritan
Σαμαρίτις, -ιδος (f.) a Samaritan (woman)
σάρξ, σαρκός (f.), flesh, physical body, human nature (cf. 14.2)
σεαυτοῦ, -ῆς, yourself (cf. 26.26)
σημεῖον, a sign or distinguishing mark, a portent
Σίμων, Simon
σκηνοπηγία, the Feast of Tabernacles (celebrating God's provision during the wilderness wanderings)
σκληρός, -ά, -όν, hard, difficult
σκοτία (nt.), darkness
σκότος, -ους (nt.), darkness, evil
σός, σή, σόν, your, yours (sg.)
σπείρω, I sow (seed)
σπέρμα, -ατος, seed; pl. children, descendants
στάδιοι, -ων, stades, furlongs (about 607 feet)
στοά, shaded porch or portico
σύ, you (sg.) (cf. 8.2)
σύν, (with, dat.) with, in company w., together w.
συνάγω, I gather together, assemble
συναγωγή, synagogue
Συχάρ, Sychar
σφραγίζω, I mark w. a seal or stamp; I set my seal upon, I mark to indicate ownership
σῴζω, I save, rescue, deliver (cf. 25.41)
σῶμα, -ατος, body, physical body
σωτήρ, -ῆρος, deliverer, savior (cf. 14.3)
σωτηρία, deliverance, salvation, rescue

Τ

τέ, and; τέ … δέ …, both … and … (usually follows the word it coordinates)
τέκνον, child
τελειῶ (-όω), I make perfect, make complete, fulfill, make mature
τέρας, -ατος, an object of wonder, omen, portent
τεσσεράκοντα, forty
τέσσαρες, τέσσαρα, four (cf. 15.9)
τηρῶ (-έω), I keep, observe, obey
Τιβεριάς, -άδος (f.), (city of) Tiberias, Sea of Tiberias (Sea of Galilee)
τίθημι, I put, set, lay down, give up (cf. 25.44, 26.8, 10–12)
τιμή, honor, respect; value
τιμῶ (-άω), I honor, reverence; set a price on
τίς, τί, who? which? what? why? (cf. 15.6)
τις, τι, anyone, anything, someone, something, some, any, a certain, a/an (cf. 15.5)

τοιοῦτος, -αύτη, -οῦτον, of such a kind, such as this
τόπος, a place, location
τοσοῦτος, -αύτη, -οῦτον, so much, so many, so great, so large
τότε, then, at that time
τράπεζα, table, bank
τρεῖς, τρία, three (cf. 15.9)
τρίτος, -η, -ον, third
τροφή, food
τρώγω, I eat, chew
τυφλός, -ή, -όν, blind

Υ
ὑγιής, -ές, whole, sound, healthy, cured
ὕδωρ, -ατος (nt.), water
υἱός, son, descendant
ὑμεῖς, you (pl.) (cf. 8.2)
ὑμέτερος, -α, -ον, your (2nd pl. possessive adj.)
ὑπάγω, I go away, depart
ὑπάρχω, be at one's disposal, exist
ὑπέρ (1) (w. gen.) for, in behalf of; about, concerning; (2) (w. acc.) over and above, beyond
ὑπό, ὑπ', ὑφ' (1) (w. gen.) by; (2) (w. acc.) under, below
ὑψῶ (-όω), I exalt (sby), lift up

Φ
φαίνω, I shine, give light
φανερῶ (-όω), I make known, show, manifest, reveal
Φαρισαῖος, Pharisee
φέρω, I bring, carry (cf. App. 1.47)
φημί, ἔφη, I say, mean, imply (cf. 21.2, App. 1.31, 26.9)
φιλῶ (-έω), I love, have deep feeling for
Φίλιππος, Philip
φίλος, a friend
φοβοῦμαι (-έομαι), I fear, am afraid of
φόβος, fear, terror
φυλακή, prison, jail
φωνῶ (-έω), I call, call to, call out
φωνή, sound, voice, utterance
φῶς, φωτός (nt.), light (cf. 14.2)
φωτίζω, I give light to, shine on

Χ
χαίρω, I rejoice, am glad
χαρά, joy, happiness
χαρίζομαι, grant, freely give, deal graciously w., pardon
χάρις, -ιτος, ἡ, gratuitous service (free from contractual obligations or counter-service), beneficient disposition, goodwill toward someone, sign of favor grace, benefaction (cf. 14.3)
χείρ, χειρός, ἡ, hand
χολῶ (-άω), I am angry
χορτάζω, I feed, satisfy
χόρτος, grass
χρεία, need, necessity
χριστός, Χριστός, messiah, Christ
χρόνος, time (chronological), period of time
χωλός, -ή, όν, lame, unable to walk
χώρα, country, countryside, field of crops
χωρίς, (w. gen.) without, apart from

Ψ
ψεύστης, -ου, a liar
ψυχή, self, life, person, one's innermost being, that which gives life

Ω
ὧδε, here, in this place
ὥρα, moment, an hour of the day, short indefinite period of time
ὡς, as, like, about (w. numbers/time), when (w. time)
ὥσπερ, just as, even as, like
ὥστε, so that, w. the result that
ὠφελῶ (-έω), I gain, profit, achieve (sthg); help, benefit